Beside Me Still

The author, 26 October 1940

❧ *Beside Me Still* ☙

A Memoir of Love and Loss in World War II

Elizabeth R. P. Shaw

NAVAL INSTITUTE PRESS
Annapolis, Maryland

Naval Institute Press

291 Wood Road

Annapolis, MD 21402

Library of Congress Cataloging-in-Publication Data

Shaw, Elizabeth R. P., 1919–

    Beside me still : a memoir of love and loss in World War II/

  Elizabeth R. P. Shaw.

    p. cm.

    ISBN 1-55750-986-7 (alk. paper)

    1. Shaw, Elizabeth R. P., 1919– 2. World War, 1939–1945—

  Personal narratives, American. 3. Navy spouses—United States—

  Biography. 4. Perkins, VanOstrand. 5. Shaw, James Clair. I. Title.

    D811.5.S464 A3 2002

    940.54'8173—dc21   2001044773

Printed in the United States of America on acid-free paper ∞

09 08 07 06 05 04 03 02 9 8 7 6 5 4 3 2

First printing

This book I dedicate to Van, Jane, and Jim, the stars of my life

Contents

Acknowledgments

Without the aid and encouragement of my daughter Pamela this book would never have appeared in print. All of my family have been supportive of my effort.

I wish to thank Evelyn Cherpak, Archivist of the Naval War College Museum and Archives, who helped me numerous times with facts that eluded me and with copies of many of our personal papers already housed in the archives.

For portions of the book on the USS *Atlanta,* I had help from Lt. Ed Carboy, Cdr. Leighton Spadone, Cdr. Charles Dodd, and James C. Shaw. For sections on the *Birmingham,* I had to depend mainly on letters and independent research, though Robert Swinny sent me his treasured ship's history and gave me his version of what happened. Cdr. John Reed's description of Van Perkins as a fellow officer on the *Birmingham* was invaluable. I relied on many sources for information on the *Bunker Hill.* Jim Shaw's junior officer, Joe Cahill, told me much of Jim. Twenty-six hours of videotape made of Jim at our house in New Hampshire has been an incomparable source.

Also, I wish to thank Capt. William J. Lederer, U.S. Navy (ret.), for his help and encouragement, as well as Michael Marine and Robert Pierce, who gave me useful information of a technical nature.

The professional criticism of Prof. Robert Ginna and Robert Graff has been invaluable. As for the late Adm. Kemp Tolley, his verification of my facts and his critique of my manuscript were most helpful. That I had never met Admiral Tolley makes his support and penned friendship doubly appreciated.

My dear assistant, Melinda Sweeney Smith, has been with me throughout. She has sorted and copied all the letters, helped with all phases of the research, given me her young perspective, and sustained me when the highly emotional nature of writing this book threatened to undo me.

My helpful editors are too numerous for me to mention them all, but my special thanks to Alice Ward and Tracy Hanson are certainly warranted.

Finally, I thank my animals for keeping vigil in the lonely hours of the night while I wrote this book.

Beside Me Still

❧ 1 ❧

Presents to Nane

DECEMBER 1938—AUGUST 1940

Whatever caused fate to turn my pleasant life chaotic is a mystery that cannot be solved. It was my plan to become a fine portrait sculptor, marry a nice young man, and take up residence near a cosmopolitan center where I could build a reputation in my chosen field. My plan was coming true.

In the fall of 1938, everything changed when Ens. VanOstrand Perkins showed up at the door of my parents' home in Greenwich, Connecticut. He had spent the previous two years aboard the USS *Raleigh* stationed in the Mediterranean, where the Navy was involved in escorting refugees from civil war–torn Spain to safety in France.

My father, Col. J. W. Riley, had gone to West Point, retiring in 1919 after World War I. Honor, duty, and country were all-important to him. From our childhood, keeping secrets was drummed into our heads. We understood this to be the military code. Both my sister Nane and I spent many weekends at West Point. Nane's fiancé graduated from the academy in 1935. We knew little or nothing of the navy; in fact, I didn't think "military" meant Navy. The Navy was our football rival—that's what I knew about the Navy. Both Nane and I had been trained to be good service wives, entertaining, running a household on our own, being well-informed and traveling when necessary. Nane put all of this to good use in 1936 when her best beau, 2d Lt. Joseph C. Anderson, received orders to join a regiment stationed in Manila, the Philippine Islands. Mother managed to put together a beautiful wedding in one month's time, and away to the Orient my dear sister sped. She put our training to good use within a week of her marriage.

In the two years since Van's graduation from the Naval Academy, things at home had changed a good bit. His glamorous USNA girl was engaged to someone else, having not pined away for Van any more than he had pined away for her. Most of his friends of old no longer lived in Greenwich. Strangest of all was the blacktop that had been spread over the dirt road that wound within twelve feet of his charming old home, "Craggy." It had changed the whole aspect. If that was progress, it did not thrill Van.

Two nights before he had to return to duty, his mother said, "Van, Nane Riley has married an Army officer. They are stationed in the Philippines at Fort Santiago in Manila, I believe. It would be nice if you called Mrs. Riley and asked her if you could take Christmas presents out to Nane." That sounded reasonable to Van, so he phoned our house and made arrangements to call the next evening about eight o'clock.

Van had gone off to the Naval Academy at age seventeen, more than six years earlier, when I was a scrawny tomboy who hated wearing dresses, preferred arm wrestling boys to playing dolls with girls, and loved to sail and swim, particularly in races, as I found it exciting. As to the splendid training to be a good service wife, well, that was not going to be much use to me, for I was going to be a sculptor despite my father's disapproval. "Young ladies don't do a man's work; it is not appropriate or proper" was his dictum. Also, I had recently become engaged to a nice young fellow, Dick Warren, who had graduated from college that spring and had a job in Muskegon, Michigan; hence, I was not dating. I was wondering what a naval officer would be like. They were mysterious beings to me.

Mum snapped me out of my reverie. "Betty Riley, will you kindly hurry up with those packages! Here, I've written all the tags. Oh, I must say you've wrapped them prettily."

"I can finish up here, tag the presents and put them in the bag," I said. "You go on downstairs and see if you can pry Dad away from the radio to eat his dinner before Van arrives."

Answering the doorbell, I was taken aback by Van's height. I was almost five feet eight inches tall; with two-and-a-half-inch heels I was five feet ten. Here was a man who had to look down at me. What a nice sensation that was.

"So this is little Betty Riley," he laughed, his blue eyes twinkling in amusement.

"I have grown a bit since I was four, haven't I?" As he took off his hat, it struck me how handsome he was.

Mother and Dad greeted Van and told him several tales about life in the Philippines from 1912 to 1914, when they were stationed at Fort Stotsenberg, northwest of Manila. Dad even sang an edited version of "The Monkeys Have No Tails in Zamboango," leaving out the two racy verses because young ladies should not hear such vulgar words.

"Having lifted my voice in song for you, I will now take my leave, as I brought work home from the office," he said. "Betts, you could offer Van a drink."

Mother left, too, saying goodnight to Van and leaving him with messages for Nane about how she longed to visit her. "Tell Van the other two verses, Betts; Dad doesn't know I taught you the words—he'd scalp me," she whispered as she kissed me goodnight and followed Dad upstairs. Van stayed on, talking about his Spanish Civil War experiences and about how he thought of me as little Betty Riley, Nane's little sister, but now found a grown-up young lady in no way resembling a little girl.

The mantel clock bonged eleven times. Van sprang up startled—so did I— and in seconds we were in each other's arms, not exactly sure how we got there. I was shaken and a bit confused by this. It was a strange feeling, and I was not sure what was happening. Finally, Van left at four o'clock in the morning, carrying the Christmas packages for Nane and leaving me thoroughly befuddled, as I was tentatively engaged to the nice young man named Dick and shortly due to visit him in Michigan. Van had made me wonder whether I was really in love with Dick, as Dick had never aroused that kind of emotion in me.

The next day I told Mum all about how grand I thought Van was—how he was exciting to talk to and fun to be with. Laughing, Mother said, "Betts, you are a fickle young lady! What about Dick?"

"Oh, I don't know, Mum, he is a dear young lad, I do love him, but I'm not sure I'm *in* love with him. It is really confusing. Van seems far more mature, which I suppose pleases me, plus he has that intangible thing service people have which I've admired in all Dad's friends. Darn it, Mum, you know what I mean—I guess he'll never let a person down."

"Well, young lady, what are you going to do about Dick?"

"Of course I'm going to Michigan. I may never see Van again, but this encounter with him has left me with a question in my mind about my feelings for Dick. It is imperative to go out to see him. Please don't tell Dad; he will think me, as usual, improper. I hate it when he gets so disapproving. This is for me to work out."

No sooner had my visit to Michigan begun than Mother telephoned to tell me to get the appropriate shots and meet her in Chicago. We were going to Manila for Christmas with Nane and her Army husband Joe! Van would probably be there, and that might clear up my turmoil about Dick. That was a pretty exciting prospect, though a twenty-four-hour association was in no way a commitment of any sort from either of us.

We took the train across Canada to Vancouver, arriving at the pier at midnight. The dock shed was dimly lit, even a bit spooky. There were no passengers about, and only the passengers' gangplank was brightly illuminated. The ship was due to sail at midnight, so we were hustled to our cabin just as the winches started pulling in the hawsers and detaching the gangplank. There was one long, low blast of the ship's whistle as we inched away from the dock and glided into the stream. We began to pitch a bit as we picked up speed. It hit me suddenly that we were heading for the Orient. How amazing! It had happened so unexpectedly that only the ship's motion finally brought home to me the wonderment that what had been a girlish dream of one day going to China was actually coming true.

Salt air smells different when you are actually at sea, so it was not just the musty, unoccupied smell of a closed-up cabin that began to clear when Mum opened the port. Soon the oily, brackish stench of the harbor was replaced by the invigorating tang of the open sea. I climbed into my bunk and was soon cradled to sleep. Any thoughts of Dick were banished from my mind. Other than China, all I could think of was maybe I would see Van again.

Stuff Like That

My experiences in Japan centered around eating my first raw fish at a lunch given for us by a gentleman who boasted the longest mustache in the world, "twelve inches on either side," he claimed. After lunch we were shown our first non-flower garden: sand, stones, a little temple, and a small pool, here and there an odd-shaped plant. The effect was reverently calm. I found myself bemused by this utterly foreign concept. England, Europe, South America, all the places we had visited previously, none had seemed so at variance with our own traditions.

Then came an unscheduled stop. Thank goodness, we only stayed overnight in Nagasaki. Sleep was impossible. All night long, winches whirred and clanked as we unloaded scrap iron for a warship being built across the harbor. Mysteriously, the ship was shrouded in canvas curtains, but you could see its pagoda-like superstructure plainly.

Our first port of call in China was Shanghai, which was thrilling to me; I loved the smell of joss sticks and sandalwood that permeated the bazaar area. The varied faces of the sea of people were an artist's dream. This artist was in her element. Shanghai, the "Pearl of the Orient," was at the mouth of the great

Yangtze River. The port of the city stretched up its tributary, the Hwang Pu. One area, called the International Settlement, was comparatively modern. The native part was a river of humanity—the noise, the dirt, the human smell, and always the people flowing back and forth, with a depth about them that was more felt than seen. I wanted desperately to know them well but knew it would take a lifetime to understand their ways.

We had been met by American friends of my father, who shepherded us around the city then drove us through the Japanese barrier into the war-torn countryside where their house was located. At the barrier, Dad's friend, Ed, reached back and snapped on the dome light while the Japanese guards went over our papers, jabbering away with an occasional "Ah so," poking their faces into ours, comparing our passport pictures to the real-life objects in front of them. Finally they waved us on. I reached back and turned off the dome light.

"My God, turn that back on; they'll shoot us if they can't see we're white!" Ed shouted.

Once in the house, there was one imperative objective: a fresh-water bath! With only salt water to bathe in for three weeks aboard ship, Mum and I both itched. Just as I settled into a lovely, warm, salt-removing tub, there commenced a hellish noise in the garden—bang, bang, bang, bam, and more banging. I ducked down. The tub seemed a good safe place to be.

War. It was unreal. I knew the Sino-Japanese War was going on, but it had sounded foolish and far away, and I had read enough Chinese history to think the saying "The Chinese simply absorb anyone who tries to invade them" was true. Well, who was absorbing whom outside my bathtub was beyond me. Certainly this was a shooting war. The shots faded away to the north. I could hear everyone about to go down to dinner. Scurrying into my clothes, I attempted a calm entrance to the living room.

"Did that racket shake you up a bit, young lady?" Ed asked.

"Oh good heavens no," I replied, attempting to be nonchalant.

"Doesn't it bother you to have fighting right in your yard?"

"We have to put up with it. It happens quite often, sort of a running battle, running here, running there, lots of shooting, not much accomplished. They take a bit tonight, they'll lose a bit tomorrow night. It would be a silly war if it wasn't so serious."

Next, Hong Kong—not quite British, not quite Chinese, thoroughly Victorian yet teeming with Chinese, and always the elusive whiffs of sandalwood from burning joss sticks that delighted my senses.

And now Manila. We nosed into the long, narrow harbor entrance with mountains rising over the misty shore, the ship barely moving as we passed Corregidor, the Army fortress that looked more like a battleship than an island, though Mum said it looked more like a beached whale. It seemed an interminable time before we were finally waving and shouting at Nane and Joe. It was 15 December, ten days to Christmas, seventeen days until the New Year, 1939.

Nane and Joe had quarters in Fort Santiago, an old Spanish fort built in the sixteenth century, surrounded by a now-dry moat turned into a golf course. Entry was through an ornate sally port. The walls of stone were topped by a guard walk with sentry boxes at strategic points. On top of the original stone barracks the Army had built wooden quarters for the officers. There Mother and I settled in with Nane and Joe.

Van had delivered the Christmas packages to Nane two days earlier, on 13 December, and she said he was both incredulous and excited when she told him we were aboard a ship due to land the very next day. He came by to see us the evening of our arrival and took me to the Army-Navy Club, where we talked and danced. I was excited about being with Van. It could have been that this invitation was just a casual gesture, but it seemed a bit more than that to me, for the way he held me when we were dancing was not exactly casual. This was our very first time dancing together, yet it was as though we had danced a thousand times before.

When we got back to Fort Santiago my family was asleep. We went for a stroll on the battlements, and, once the sentry passed by, Van kissed me tenderly as he might a little girl. I leaned back and looked at him, trying to understand what he meant by the gentle kiss. Neither one of us knew we were falling in love. We looked tentatively at each other, as best we could by the light of the moon. I was entranced with this lovely, tall man looking down at me—that much I knew. All of a sudden it dawned on me that he was a bit afraid of where we might be headed. I knew I must not change this mood or I could spoil something wonderful, so I just stood there until he took my hand, and, tucking it through his arm, walked me along in silence. I knew I had never felt so content with any other man, and I wanted this to go on.

We returned to the quarters. Van poured me a glass of milk, and just as he handed me the glass, a huge tropical cockroach flew at me. I struck out at it, dashing the milk over both of us, and threw myself at Van. This time he put his arms around me, laughing at my fright, and kissed me roundly; you would think I had never been kissed before. I went all dizzy inside. When he left to go back to his ship he asked me for a date.

Shortly after that, Van wrote his family:

Betty Riley is having a wonderful time and she is so attractive, she has set everyone on their ear. I am with her almost every night I'm ashore either in the capacity as an escort or as a member of the party. She knows all the boys and girls and is a regular member of all gatherings. Friday night I had dinner with her and another lad after a session of bowling but at eleven I folded and returned to the ship.

Last night we were all out on a big party, there were seven or eight of us which lasted until the wee hours and then tonight I have a date with her myself, then we go to sea at 0800 Monday and work like mad all week, come in next Thursday or Friday all set for another weekend.

Van came for Christmas Day. "It is hard to believe that today is Christmas," he wrote his family. "It has been hot all day, everyone wearing white suits and instead of having eggnog or Tom and Jerry's I have been drinking mint juleps. . . . I went over to Nane Anderson's this morning about eleven thirty. . . . We had a perfectly wonderful dinner, turkey and all the trimmings. After dinner we sat around perspiring, it was that hot, and people dropped in. About six we all went down to the club where it is cooler and stayed there for a while."

When Van took off Christmas night, he said the ship was going into dry dock at the Navy yard in Olongapo for the week and asked me to go out with him the night he came back—to which I happily agreed. The next day I sent Van a letter via an officer going to Olongapo:

All this business about how hard Navy life is on a young wife doesn't cut much ice with me—granted I grew up, to age ten, in what I guess you call the lap of luxury—so did you for that matter, only you were sixteen when the crash hit and you were aware of the war while I wasn't born until 1919, just before Dad left the Army. Well anyway, Mum didn't lose money in the crash so we didn't go broke. Life changed a lot but not compared to a friend of mine whose dad committed suicide and her mother opened a dress shop that I went to work in when I was sixteen—stuff like that which I think made me grow up early.

Any way you look at it, Mum always said the best service wives seemed to come from service families—I'm not sure about that but I know that a lot of my training comes from Mum's experiences as an Army wife living all over the world and having to entertain a lot. Well, I certainly am being very forward with you but by now you must know I'm no clinging vine—if that's what you want you better forget about me right now.

Hopefully you won't have the duty Thursday night so I won't have to wait twenty-four hours after you get in before I get to see you. Friday, the big table gang are planning to go to Jai Aali (how do you spell that?). Presently I plan to go with them, but that's subject to change, if a certain gentleman I know wishes it otherwise.

As it turned out, the ship was late leaving the Navy yard so it was New Year's Eve before Van came ashore.

Twenty Pesos Later

Between Christmas and New Year's I had a whirl of dates with young bachelors from both the Army and Navy. My days were spent sketching Filipino faces and flowers; oddly, the indigenous flowers had no scent, with the exception of ginger blossoms, which had a heady, exotic, almost sensual message. After siesta I went bowling, swimming, or playing tennis with the wives of Van's Navy friends, four of whom became my friends for years to come and had a profound influence on me, the "Army Brat": Tek Lyster, Mariah Novitski, Betty Miller, and Marge Wilson, whose husband, Don, was Van's shipmate.

Van wrote his family on 30 December:

> Today we returned from Olongapo where we have been for the last few days in dry dock. Olongapo is a small place about eighty miles from here at the base of Subic Bay. It is a lovely spot in a landlocked bay surrounded by the greenest mountains you ever saw. The country is really wild. Fifteen minutes from the Naval station, so they say, you are in an impenetrable jungle in which you find all kinds of wild life, both animal and human. . . . The small town of Olongapo is just a squalid native village with three or four dirt streets and one paved main street lined with Filipino and Chinese shops and families living on the porches up over the stores. The Naval station is about a half a mile from town, which is more or less controlled by the Navy I suppose. The station used to be an old Spanish fort and Naval base and when we took it over we established a Navy yard there. It is well sheltered and suited for a Naval base for it is in a protected harbor. . . .
>
> I have the duty today so I don't go ashore until tomorrow at which point I can celebrate New Year's Eve. I am taking Betty Riley out but I asked her before I realized what night it was. Had I realized Saturday night was New Year's Eve I wouldn't have asked her or anyone else. I think with everyone out trying to have a good time and it costing a fortune to do anything the best thing to do is to avoid the merrymaking and have a quiet evening with a good book.

Van came in from his ship on New Year's Eve, arriving to pick me up at Fort Santiago about 6:30. I had dressed in my most spectacular evening dress, white organza with a black lace apron, black velvet sash, and black velvet band in my hair. I knew I looked fetching, but I was unprepared for Van's reaction. He just stared at me, his blue eyes sparkling, holding a corsage box at his side. I thought he must think me overdressed, or that he did not like black and white, or that possibly he thought my beautiful sister's dress was more to his liking.

I squared my shoulders and gave a bit of a shrug, at which Van broke his silence, handing me the box and saying, "Lord Almighty, Betts, that's the most beautiful dress I've ever seen, I hope the flowers don't spoil it, you look gorgeous."

"You look gorgeous yourself, Van," I replied. Then he took a wristlet of white butterfly orchids from the box, the perfect complement to my dress.

I had never seen his evening dress uniform before and found it spectacular. (Later I was told the young officers referred inelegantly to these as "bum freezers.") Joe hustled all of us, including Mother, off to the club, where we had a table for five. Van and I started table hopping, holding hands, telling several people we were engaged.

The following night we went for a walk along the sea wall, finally coming to a spot where we could get over the wall and climb down to sit on what looked like a secluded rock by the water's edge. The full moon was beginning to set, sending shimmering paths toward us over Manila Bay. Eight of the thirteen World War I destroyers that comprised the Asiatic Fleet were silhouetted in the bay, their lights twinkling in the distance.

Finally Van broke his silence. "Betts, do you like Fergie a lot, or what's going on anyway?" I had been on a date with another young officer named Fergie.

"He's a nice young man and a good dancer, but he doesn't talk about anything profound, just trivia. Why?" Obviously my answer startled him, for he shook his head almost in disbelief.

"Well, my dear girl, and that's what you are, a mere girl, I think it might be—oh, nuts—it's that I think, maybe, well, the truth of the matter is . . ." Silence, while I sat there smiling, not about to help him. An eternity passed while Van continued, with his elbows on his knees, gazing at the moon across the rippling bay. Then he put his head down, took a deep breath, and muttered, "Betty—Betts—Bettsy, oh Lord, I love you, dammit, and you probably love that guy, Dick." Quickly, before he could change his mind, I leaned forward and whispered, "I love you, Van" and kissed him on the cheek. As I did so, he straightened up and enveloped me in his arms, kissing me thoroughly.

"I don't believe this," he said. "What kind of crazy miracle brought us halfway round the world from home to fall in love? Oh, Lord, thank you!"

Suddenly, up behind us popped a Philippine constabulary officer. "Ha! I have arres' you for indecency, come with me to police station!" he ordered.

I jumped out of Van's arms, and he vaulted back over the wall, saying as he went, "That's not what I had in mind, Lord!"

Twenty pesos later, Van had mollified the man. No doubt his considerable height helped the rather shorter constable back down. In any event our love affair started on a hilarious note. Certainly the whole romantic spell was broken, and Van took me back to Fort Santiago to tell the family of our "arres' for indecency."

A couple of weeks later, as I was waiting for Van, expecting to go out with him, I received a message from him that about floored me: "Jan 15th. We leave in a hurry for Hong Kong this afternoon."

The ship returned as quickly as it had taken off, however, owing to some sort of snafu with another ship. It was gone from Manila only twenty-four hours, thank heavens. I certainly learned how suddenly, and with what little warning to the ladies ashore, the Navy could dispatch a ship. It was an easy lesson, as the ship was brought back so quickly. I was beginning to discover what Navy life would be like.

All of January and February 1939, Van never failed to have a new idea for a date. Once it was the cockfights. I hated the fights but loved the people and the spectacle. Another time it was the Jai Alai, a balcony restaurant, where we had dinner in utmost luxury while watching that incredibly fast game. We took a couple of sightseeing trips, made doubly interesting as Van read up on them before we set forth and told me fascinating bits of history or geology or whatever applied.

One day he announced we were going to the local carnival; he said we must leave our rings behind at Nane and Joe's quarters. "Good heavens, why?" I asked. "It's easier to steal them when we are not wearing them."

Van answered, "We are going to the 'Finest Fortune-Teller in the Orient' and find out what the future holds for us. Our rings would give us away immediately."

Off we went, wandering among the concessions for a bit, finally finding the "Finest Fortune-Teller in the Orient" sitting cross-legged in a dingy tent. Taking Van's hands first, he said, "You are a leader of men, and the women— ha—they adore you. I think you are a man of the sea. Perhaps a naval officer? You are a loyal friend, you will be a devoted and faithful husband. I recommend you!"

"Now comes the lady." He scrutinized my hands. "You are an artist, a maker of statues. You, too, are loyal to your friends, and, like this man, you have many. You are not so old as he but you have wisdom beyond your years." Then taking both our right hands, he looked earnestly at first one then the other, back and forth for what seemed ages. Finally he shook his head, made a decision, and said, "You will be married to each other. You will be sublimely happy but only for a short time. I cannot tell you more." We left holding hands, a little afraid because he had been so right about us that perhaps his prediction was also true, though we could not fathom his meaning for sure.

We spent every brief moment together no matter how impractical. When Van had the duty I would go out to the ship for the evening with him, despite Mother's declaration that it was not proper to go out there "alone with all those men." We would have dinner in the wardroom. Van would put his elbows on his knees, fold his hands into a church steeple and tell me about his tours of duty in Europe, the Spanish Civil War, and the Southern Islands of the Philippines. I could listen to him for hours, and I would get tickled when he would wag his finger-steeple for emphasis. His blue eyes danced with excitement when he talked of China, which lured him as it did me.

We had so much that needed sorting out. We talked about maybe getting married. Van was an ensign, and he thought his pay was too low to support a family. He also thought the "China Station" a poor place to bring a young wife, and I was undeniably young. I was worried about our age difference for fear I might be an embarrassment to Van with his older friends, who might chide him about robbing the cradle. Then there was the whole Perkins family: his mother, his father, and his younger brother, Woodie, who was three years my senior and whom I had dated. I did not want them to have any reservations about me. Last, in utmost cowardice, I broke my engagement to Dick by letter. I should have done it in person, though surely, I thought, the infrequency and increasingly impersonal tone of my letters had alerted him.

Van and I had a brief talk with Mother. Van told her he would be getting his promotion within the year, which would give him sufficient finances to support a wife. Mum said she thought we should be separated for a while to determine if this was genuine love or just the tropics. She said she would bring me back in six months if we were both sure of our feelings.

The Royal Navy Never

Van left for Hong Kong at the end of February. Two nights before he left he gave a formal dinner at the Army-Navy Club. It was a *despedita* (farewell party) for me. He had asked our close friends from the club and of course Nane, Joe, and Mum. It was a perfect party—the food, the wine, the flowers—and he had done it all by himself. I was so overcome I just sat next to him holding his hand and looking at him. For me not to talk was so unusual that everyone there now knew something was up for sure—no kidding this time. When the music started, Van asked me to dance. "Up on your toes, darling," he said. Even on my toes I could not do more than dance with my forehead against his chin, mashing my nose against his neck. This night he held me so tightly I could hardly breathe. No matter, I loved to dance with him, and it would be a long time before we could dance again.

The next night we sneaked off by ourselves to a funny little place we both had a fondness for called Tom's Dirty Kitchen, where they had private dining rooms, one of which Van had reserved for us. The violinist came in and played "All the Things You Are," my favorite song. When he left, Van held me in his arms and kissed my tears away. As he had to go out to his ship at midnight, we said our real goodbye there in that funny little room at the restaurant. Then Van took me back to Fort Santiago. While the taxi waited I clung to him until finally he took my arms from around his neck, bent down, and kissed me one last time, saying, "I love you, I do, I do. Go home my darling little girl, think hard and so will I. Now I must go, so long dear heart! One more time—I love you." Off he went through the gates of the fort, and I fled upstairs to the quarters in tears.

Both of us knew what my background was. Although I had not had many problems during the Depression, it had affected me, as I was unable to follow my desire to go to college. It had heightened my already keen sense of compassion, but real suffering had not as yet touched me personally. I was not a spoiled brat, but you certainly could not call me deprived. That worried Van at first; he knew I would have to face hardships and be alone a lot. He wanted to be sure I could cope with such vicissitudes. We had decided Mother was right. We needed to be separated for six months to be sure this was genuine.

Van left on 24 February 1939. My family was to leave on 12 March for a two-and-a-half-month trip around the rest of the world. The excitement of seeing places like French Indochina, which included North and South Vietnam and Angkor Wat, the ancient deserted city in Cambodia that was just then being dug out of the jungle; Burma; Siam; the Taj Mahal; the Amber Palace in Jaipur; and the Vale of Kashmir in India was a thrilling prospect that temporarily took the edge off Van's departure.

We were all involved in packing up Nane and Joe's quarters, as they were being transferred stateside, and all four of us would be traveling together. What to pack to take with us? What to send home via transport? Joe's campaign hat, pressed between two pieces of plywood, one with a hole in it where the peak stuck up (the idea being to keep the brim rigid), went with us for some unknown reason. Equally odd were two badminton rackets. Mother and I were supposed to pack our belongings into one large suitcase and one overnight bag apiece. Impossible for Mother—she had to have in addition her shoe bag, hat bag, medicine case, and knitting bag. All this hubbub sandwiched in between *despeditas* our friends gave us kept me hopping, but it did not stop me thinking about Van constantly. I wrote Van in early March:

> One last jump into the land of the unknown. What would you do if I were here when you returned in September? With a bit of persuasion do you think you could stand the idea? The more I sit here by myself the more convinced I become on the subject and the more I want to come back out. Every time I've written you I've made some allusion to the above and every time have been scared of the ensuing consequences. This time I'm not—not one bit afraid of what you think or what you will tell me in your next letter. Who knows how I'll feel when I get home but certainly I feel pretty strongly now, that I know my own mind. As a matter of fact I don't know why I go home at all.

The twelfth of March 1939 was the last day of my stay in wonderful Manila. We boarded the Dutch ship *Ruis,* which had come down from Hong Kong and was already fairly full of passengers. Crowds of friends were there to see us off, so a bit of time passed before the steward, who had his hands full, delivered me a letter from Van, which I tore open and read hastily.

I kissed everyone in the cabin excitedly and burst into tears as the gong sounded and an ominous voice intoned, "All visitors ashore—last call—all ashore who are going ashore." The ship nosed out into the harbor and when I could no longer wave goodbye to my friends and as night descended, I went to my cabin and read my letter over again:

> I owe Lt. Alexander A. Cavendish, Royal Navy, a debt of gratitude and many, many thanks. The mail service may fail but the Royal Navy never! Your letter was delivered this morning about twenty minutes after the "Daring" arrived.
>
> Betts you don't know how much I wanted to hear from you and how glad I was. For the last two weeks I have been going around and around wondering just what the correct answer should be.
>
> Frankly, Bettsy dear, I can't get you off my mind, you have definitely gotten yourself a permanent place in me. But the soulless heathen that I am tempered with too much reserve and common sense for my own good, somehow prevents me from asking you to stay out here with me. You know Betts I don't think this part of the world is such a good place for a new young Navy wife. The Army is different because they don't go to sea in March and come back in June, you know how it is. But darling don't ever change your mind about me because the day is not too far off when you will be coming back to me, or I will come to you, or we will meet halfway.

I hate to do it and don't want to do it Bettsy but I must let you go home this time and when you are in the States look wisely and well but don't change your mind. Because I love you!

And write too, please Betts, everything that is on your mind and in your heart.

This letter from Van needed a positive answer, so I took pen in hand and wrote that same evening:

There's a lump in my throat big enough to choke me to death. We're just sailing past Corregidor. It has gotten dark all too quickly. I have watched Manila fade into the horizon with a greater sense of loss than I ever experienced before in all my life. My two consolations are your letters, dearest, and the fact that I shall come back in a while if you'll let me. As we pulled away from the dock I felt it was you I was saying goodbye to, not thousands of natives, palm trees and blue water, not our friends nor the ships in the harbor but you and you alone. I wonder if you felt as I do, experienced the same sensations when you left, though I imagine you were far too busy and well used to steaming out to sea to feel this way. Other people didn't know why I was crying but you and I do. It is such a very big ocean to put between us and somehow you seemed so near while I was still in Manila. Now—two hours from the time we sailed—I feel lost—oh gee Van, I love you. . . .

Early this morning I woke up and was conscious of discreet knocking, got up and struggled over to the door; to my delight it was a package from you which on opening turned out to be champagne. I carefully clambered back into my bed and curled up with my champagne hugged tightly and dreamed for a while. You are the most thoughtful person I have ever known in all my life and the sweetest. . . . I am hoarding the champagne until my birthday and then I'm going to drink it all to you!

You said in your letter that you thought the China Station was no place to bring a young new Navy wife, I beg to disagree. At least from my point of view you are wrong, but then I love the Orient what I've seen of it. Going out Mondays and coming back Thursdays, to my way of thinking, would give me time to do as much sculpting as I want, to write as much as I feel like and accomplish all the things that I'd never do if you were around. I've had two weeks taste of what it's like, for after you left I didn't feel like going out more than a couple of times so I worked during the day and went over to see Marge Wilson or Mary Novitski or Tek Lyster in the evenings. Got more done than I've accomplished in all the time I've been out here and didn't find it one bit unpleasant. I think that after living alone for almost twenty years that getting used to married life would be quite a problem. Learning to share your room with a man when you've never shared your room with anyone. Taking it in small doses would be far easier on a girl. . . . Having you away three months at a time is a little tough but if a girl has any strength of character at all she can make a go of it.

I'd like to know more of your ideas and ideals. I think from knowing you as I do that you don't take marriage lightly—I don't!—to me it is the most serious thing in life, not to be entered into with the attitude that if this one doesn't work we can try something else. I wouldn't expect you to be the kind to whip around having affairs, nor would I want you to be the kind of person who just stayed on board ship because your wife wasn't in port. I'd hate it if when you get mad you just freeze up and won't say what's wrong or hold a grudge. You've never even been annoyed with me or around me. You're going to have to write me all about that sort of thing.

Later I found that Van had sent three baskets of flowers. One for the Andersons, one for Mother, and the prettiest one for me. All delivered to the Andersons' stateroom by mistake. Nane and Joe were wowed by such attentions but finally figured it out. They were the first of many flowers Van sent me wherever we stopped, often with the help of the Royal Navy, who were charmed to play Cupid for Van. Our two navies were working the China coast patrol together, going from treaty port to treaty port. Van would take his card with his message on it, along with the appropriate money, to a friend on board one of His Majesty's ships about to return to Singapore, their home port (as the Philippines was ours), who would see to it that the flowers and the card were delivered to our next port of call, which he had on our itinerary.

Such names those ships had! HMS *Dainty,* HMS *Daring,* HMS *Dauntless,* and HMS *Delight*—the lads on those ships were all darlings to me, for they helped mightily with our romance. Even this service was erratic, however, and from the sequence of letters it quickly became clear that our letters would cross and often I would have an answer to a question before Van had received my question or I would have no answer at all. As I sailed west and Van sailed east, our letters became more and more out of sync.

The destroyer squadrons patrolled the China Sea, keeping the sea lanes open for commerce and protecting their nationals ashore. The great Yangtze River, winding its way hundreds of miles into inland China, was patrolled by little U.S. riverboats that ensured the welfare of our cargo and oil vessels, which went upriver as far as Chungking. The flagship of the Asiatic Fleet commander (Admiral Yarnell and then Admiral Hart) was the old cruiser USS *Houston,* which in 1938–39 stayed in Shanghai, up a tributary of the Yangtze, the Hwang Pu River, at the International Settlement waterfront. Then there was the British Crown Colony of Hong Kong and the Portuguese settlement of Macao, both under the rule of those two countries, not under China or Japan.

I Want to Shout Stop

I was jittery waiting to hear the answer to my query about what Van would do if I were in Manila when he came down from China. Until he answered this, it was hard to enjoy my trip, which had been touted as "the opportunity of a lifetime." There was the matter, too, of Van being involved in the Japanese bombing of Swatow, one of the treaty ports. I had been unconcerned when the Japanese and Chinese banged away at each other when we had stayed with Ed outside Shanghai, but now I had become fearful because Van wrote he was involved in one brief Japanese bombing incident when he went ashore on business. Strangely, it is true that when one's self is involved in a dangerous situation it does not seem so important. Let it be someone you love, and it becomes a mountainous event. Not until the bombing of Swatow happened did it dawn on me that Van could be seriously involved in a war between China and Japan.

At long last the answer to my query arrived. Glancing over the first part of his letter, I found the paragraph I wanted to read:

> Eons ago, just before you left Manila you wanted to know what I would do if you returned to Manila in September, the answer is easy. I would marry you of course. . . .
>
> Don and I have been exchanging ideas and trying to pin down this intangible quality, love—he says that I am a fool for letting you go home and I know it, but Bettsy I want you to be as sure of yourself and of me, when you are in familiar surroundings, as you are now. . . .
>
> Bettsy, I love you so, I want to shout "STOP" at every mile that comes between us. A kingdom to be able to have you here in my arms now. . . .
>
> Darling I want to keep right on writing because it somehow bridges the gulf and brings you closer and that makes me realize how much I am missing you.
>
> Love, with all my heart,
> Pei Ching (my chop) ["Perkins" translated into Chinese]

As my trip around the world progressed I became surer and surer of my ability to be a good Navy wife—to make Van happy and be very happy myself. Every place we went there were young English officers, all of whom were delighted to chase a single, blonde girl in a world of Oriental ladies but who all convinced me further that Van was the only man for me. I described their silly antics for Van. He was as amused by this sort of report from me as I was about his escapades in China. Van not only wrote me about the ship rolling and making him seasick (which amazed me because I did not get seasick even in vile weather) but also told me all about his duties on board. He was the communications officer, the intelligence officer, the weatherman, and the mess treasurer—a job he loved, for he enjoyed cooking and good food. He stood watches and fired gunnery practices (at which he excelled), earning himself a letter of commendation for the latter. He took his turn at torpedo runs and loved high-speed runs best of all. He made Navy life sound to be the most wonderful thing a man could do. Whatever Van did it was always "the most fun you can imagine."

In May 1939, we sailed from India for Africa. My stateroom was filled with flowers. We headed for Masawa, as it was then called, in Italian Somaliland (Ethiopia). When we arrived there, the news from Hitler was now bombastic and most upsetting. If we stayed on our Italian ship, the *Conte Verdi,* we would sail with 750 Italian troops through the Suez Canal to Italy, as Mussolini was recalling men from wherever they were stationed to swell his home army, now that he had joined Hitler in what was soon to become the Axis. We could leave the ship and take our chance on traveling south to Capetown, going home by the southern route to avoid Europe, or go through the Suez Canal to Venice. Various cables between Mum and Dad in New York finalized our decision to stay with the *Conte Verdi.* "Don't tarry in Europe. Go directly to London" was Dad's advice.

The trip through the Suez Canal was scary. All those Italian troops in the hold and swords rattling in Germany. We went ashore at Port Said, the dirtiest, most malevolent place we had hit in our travels, and there I picked up a strep infection that laid me low for the rest of the trip. A few days in Venice, then through the Simplon Tunnel, not even stopping in France. At long last we arrived in England, where Dad met us carrying a "wonder drug" to cure my ailment: sulphanilamide, which was not readily available to civilians.

We both began to worry about how Van's parents would take the news that their eldest son had decided to marry the youngest Riley daughter, and who would tell them. I need not have worried, for Van had prepared the way, writing them in April 1939:

> You may have suspected this bit of news and it's not for publication yet. So while you may feel like bursting just keep it to yourself. I sent Betty R. home—or rather did nothing to prevent her from leaving. But notwithstanding that just served to crystallize something which had been growing for four months, so after much thinking, until I nearly went crazy, I have asked Betts to marry me. We give it the acid test by returning her to the States and then in the fall sometime when the *Whipple* stops chasing about and comes back to Manila, Betts and I hope she can come out here again. Both of us have done a lot of heavy thinking and I am sure of what I am getting into and want to.
>
> The only thing I want you to do now is see that Bettsy gets one of those good photographs of me when she arrives home. That is important! . . .

I guess you want to know more about Betts and me—you know Bettsy's family and all that as well as I do. Perhaps you think she is too young—but no—she may be young in years, however none of the girls or young wives here can come near Betts in common sense, etc., etc. and I would never have asked her if she wasn't just the girl I wanted for my wife.

Not until we were leaving London did I get the letter Van wrote to me the same day he wrote his mother. He thought it would reach me as we sailed up the Suez Canal, but mail from Manila to Port Said took much longer than a clipper letter to the States. In fact, I was lucky that the steamship company had the good sense to send it via air to London instead of Venice, or it might have followed just behind me all the way home. Van had never formally asked me to marry him. Just that phrase, "I'd marry you, of course," was all I had to go on. It was a relief to get the letter he wrote despite the brevity of the message it contained:

> Here we've been three days in Manila and still I look about the club and the table by the pool expecting to find you. It is just natural that you should be here someplace and I can't get used to and don't like not seeing you. I was afraid it would be like this. There is too much in Manila to remind me of Bettsy. Everything about the club, the rocks where we were arrested, and every place I go we've been there together. . . .
>
> At one point you mentioned that perhaps I'd be surprised or maybe everyone had forgotten you, us. But no, I am neither surprised nor have we been forgotten. Quite the contrary Bettsy. They all want to know where you are and what I've heard from you. No end of people have described your departure—you have loads of friends here. Everybody speaks to me of you.
>
> We had quite a trip down from Hong Kong. The ship didn't stay there as long as we expected to. We left with the Barker on the third and immediately ran into rough weather so that for the entire trip, everything in our rooms, the silver in the wardroom, everything was skidding around on the deck. Nothing would stay put and it was so rough you just had to hang on to something the whole time. On the second day we were more or less used to it . . . but they couldn't cook. So we fared on some awful Bologna sandwiches and tea. A couple of more days like that and I'd be tempted to turn in my suit and join the Forest Rangers. . . .
>
> Bluntly and frankly I know there is a question which we have both hinted at but never in so many words have mentioned it and the question is, "I wonder if this is a case of old friends from home in a foreign land, the romance of the tropics—something very nice which will blow over in time?" I think you know exactly what I mean Betts. It is ever so much deeper and lasting than that. I know Bettsy we are right. I'm sure, I know what I want.

Bettsy, have you any preferences in jewelry, stones or what have you. I am going shopping in Shanghai when we get up there and thought that if you had any particular likes or dislikes I could do something about them—you could pick up a cheap ring which fits the third finger of your left hand and send it to me so I will know the proper size. I can't think of any other way of going about it. . . .

P.S. Have told my family.

This certainly left no doubt in my mind that one Ensign Perkins—soon to be lieutenant (jg) if he passed his promotion exams—in the Orient had totally committed himself to marrying me, even to getting me an engagement ring. At least I presumed he was not planning to get me a "friendship" ring to put on the third finger of my left hand.

Throughout our trip we had collected bits and pieces—a Balinese head, tweed suits in Kashmir, saris, Venetian glass—all in well-wrapped packages or in raffia or string bags. Dad, the porter, and the doorman at the hotel in London were appalled at the now-enormous pile of luggage. Somehow they rustled up a lorry and two taxis, and we left the hotel for the Liverpool train station in a caravan worthy of any potentate. I'm sure the doorman and the porter were much relieved to see us depart. Their embarrassment was evident while they attempted to load the motley collection of bags, boxes, and bundles. The final insult to their dignity was Joe's campaign hat and the badminton rackets, which they gingerly moved from the sidewalk to the lorry.

We traveled bag and baggage north to Liverpool to catch a British liner for home. The ship was darkened, black curtains over all the ports and windows, and we participated in a lot of boat drills, which everyone scrupulously attended. We donned our preservers and lined up by our assigned lifeboats, which were uncovered, swung out, checked, and returned, twice a day. No fooling, we were seriously practicing to be sunk by a U-boat, even though England had not yet declared war on Germany. Nor had France been invaded, or we would not have come through the Simplon Tunnel and crossed French territory.

My first order of business on arriving home was to see Dick and return his engagement ring. He was a bright young man and had pretty much surmised from the infrequency and tone of my letters that I was not pining away for him. Nevertheless, he took leave from his job in Michigan and was there in Greenwich when I arrived. All my innate compassion went out to him, for he was torn apart when I told him about Van. Having to hurt him distressed me, but at the same time I knew for sure that I was truly and utterly in love with Van as I never had been with Dick.

There was a great deal of commotion going on in the house, as a large party to welcome Nane and Joe home was being prepared. Once Dick had gone, I went upstairs to dress. Van's family were coming to the party, and I had no idea how they would greet me. Perhaps they would reject me, or worse still, perhaps they had not yet received Van's letter. That would be the ultimate horror, for how could I keep such a secret?

Finally, Van's parents came through the door. I tensed up, waiting to see what they would do. Briefly they welcomed Nane and Joe home and greeted Mother and Dad. Then they turned in my direction, and Aunt Kate smiled with such warmth that I knew she had found out about Van and I. I described the party to Van:

> You know I said that I'd never marry you if your family didn't approve but I've no doubts about how they feel towards me for they certainly made it clear in every way. First of all, Tuesday night when we had the party for Nane, they arrived and I dashed over to see them not knowing how I was going to be greeted and knowing that was going to be my indication of how they felt. Well, Aunt Kate kissed me and I almost burst into tears and then so did Uncle Allan and I had a hard time controlling the old flood gates. Later on Aunt Kate and I came up to my room and we talked at pretty great length about us. . . . This afternoon I went over to Bedford and spent a wonderful time just talking over ideas. . . .
>
> This evening was just like I'd always been part of the family, or at least that's the way I felt. Even Randy spent the evening with his head parked on my knee. If you had been there, it would have been perfect. Everything is just right though. My family loves you and I think it works the other way around. That may sound conceited but really they didn't give me much room for doubting how they felt.
>
> On our way out last Fall, I would have been the most surprised girl in the world if I had known that you would fall in love with me. Why I had to travel halfway around the world to fall in love with someone from here is quite a mystery to me. . . . With all my heart, I love you darling.
>
> Your Bettsy
>
> P. S. Have been wearing this ring for the last couple of days and it has left a nice green circle on my finger—"Good goods" what? Cheap it surely is. Hope it's what you wanted.

When I had been home long enough to calm down from all the excitement of going to Van's home, "Craggy," and becoming part of his family circle, I realized that if I was to think and talk intelligently about China and Japan I must learn all I could about modern oriental political history, so I sought out my beloved history teacher, Miss E. Audrey Rich. She had taught me all about the dynasties of China, their art, their political structure (which centered around the family), and, most important, Chinese philosophy and the country's quiet custom of absorbing its enemies. This was all in antiquity; now I wanted to know more about modern China, Japan, and the Europeans in the Orient.

Miss Rich outlined Japan's more recent history—her crowded homeland, her lack of natural resources, and her new contacts with the Western world. She told me about Japan's seizure of antiquated Korea in 1895 and her taking of Manchuria, on the northeastern reaches of China, in 1927. By 1935 Japan had established its Army headquarters in Peking, where it set up a provincial government with the deposed emperor of China as a puppet ruler. The Japanese attempted to subdue the warlords and unite the land, but they were thwarted in their efforts by very active guerrilla bands that they were unable to contain.

England, France, Germany, and the United States signed treaties, which Japan honored, to control the seaports along the Chinese coast known as the treaty ports: Amoy, Tsingtao, Tientsin, Chefoo, Chingwantao, to name a few that our ships regularly visited. In addition, there was the International Settlement of Shanghai, the roadway to inland China and the provincial capital of Chungking, as well as British-governed Hong Kong and the Portuguese colony of Macao across the bay. The French had control of Indochina. This information, together with Van's description of China and Miss Rich's atlas, gave me a real handle on that part of the world.

The United States' interests were in trade, oil, rubber, arms, and religion. Our Navy and the British Navy kept the sea lanes open for commerce. When the Spanish-American War freed the Philippines of the Spanish yoke, we occupied the islands, all seven thousand–plus of them, eventually making them a commonwealth under an American high commissioner. We based our Asiatic Squadron there, from whence we patrolled the northern Christian islands, dominated by Manila, and the southern Islamic islands, where the island of Mindanao held the provincial capital. In the summer months the little squadron of destroyers patrolled the treaty ports up and down the lengthy China coast.

Too Damned Hot

In May 1939, I had a letter from Van, a portion of which amused me:

> I was sitting off by myself on the porch of the Army Navy Club, studying for my promotion exams, when Jim Shaw happened by; he stopped and asked me when I am getting married. I told him "as soon as I can get Betts out here again. Maybe

before Christmas; I'm going to have to ace these exams if I hope to support her."

Jim laughed. "I don't see how you manage to study with this crowd around."

I told him "It's too damned hot in the ship to study, it's too damned noisy here to study, so let's go sit in the bar and to hell with exams for tonight."

Van called in June from Manila to tell me he had passed his exams promoting him to lieutenant junior grade (which I quickly learned to write Lt. [j.g.]). He mentioned that Jim Shaw had done the same.

"Which one is Jim Shaw?" I asked. "I think I met him. Did I?"

"Remember the shy fellow you met just before I left for Hong Kong? He's a classmate of mine. Look him up in my *Lucky Bag*. It's in my closet. That will tell you some about him and has his picture. Don't let's waste money talking about him on the overseas telephone."

Doing as Van suggested, I found the following statistics in the Naval Academy yearbook about Jim Shaw, who was to become Van's best friend. He had been appointed from Minnesota and served as football manager. He was on the reception committee and in the Radio Club, he was a two-striper, and he was on the editorial staff of the Naval Academy *Log*. Under his picture, which looked vaguely familiar, was the following description of James Clair Shaw written by his roommate: "Jim demonstrated his ability before he left the Minnesota Reserve for Maryland; he startled the Examining Board by obtaining a perfect mark on the English Exam. The ease he has with such subjects has enabled him to repeat this extraordinary feat often. Bred in the wintry north, Clair has missed his ice skating and skiing but at times Maryland Aprils and Novembers satisfy him. . . . Practically every hop finds Jim on hand dragging a beautiful damsel; it's a different one each time. An all around good fellow with a fine sense of humor is Minnesota's Shakespeare, Jim.

As Van mentioned him more and more often, I began to find out more about Jim Shaw. He was a shy, reserved officer on the USS *Stewart* on the China Station. His mother had died suddenly, and Jim had left behind in Honolulu a younger sister whom he wanted to get to Manila, if she could get a job, so he did not have to support her. Her name was Betty Lou, or Bou, as Jim called her. One of his dear friends wrote me a letter containing a poem from the *Log* that belied the picture I had of him:

We know a man from Minnesotaw
Who goes by the name of James Clair Shaw
When he eats oysters he eats them raw
Lady Killer, Lady Killer, Lady Killer Shaw

Incidentally, I looked up Van's class picture in his Naval Academy yearbook at the same time. His lower lip was twice its natural size and you could see his chin was shiny with drool. His mother told me the dentist had pulled his wisdom teeth that morning using massive amounts of novocaine and exerting great pressure on his lip. Though he asked to be excused from the picture, his request was denied. No wonder Van had told his mother to "give her one of those good pictures of me—that's important!"

Pretty Crazy in China

By the summer of 1939, Europe was boiling over, and the effect of it on Hitler's ally Japan was galvanizing. The Japanese started off by harassing the French and English up and down the China coast wherever those countries had treaty ports, making life very unpleasant for their citizens. Van wrote at length about the situation, assuring me that the Americans were not involved.

Every morning I read the shipping news in the *Herald Tribune*. All the ships' movements, including those of the thirteen World War I destroyers on the China Station, were reported. All one needed to know was the name and number of the ship and one could find out exactly where it was.

Van and I had no reason to believe Mum did not intend to stick to her original statement that she would bring me out in six months if we were both sure of our feelings for each other. We set about making plans to get married when Van came down from China in the fall. Six months from Van's departure in late February meant September 1939. Not much time, as it was now June and we must work out our plans. It took weeks to exchange ideas by mail.

For me, it meant putting together a trousseau of linens, clothes proper for the tropics, sufficient shoes to last me two years, and bathing suits before they were all sold. Mother and I clashed right away. She ordered me monogrammed sheets for single beds. "Mum," I said, "we're going to sleep in a double bed, not twin beds."

"No you're not," she told me. "It's not healthy to sleep in a double bed. You don't get a good night's sleep; you disturb each other. You can ask any doctor who'll tell you so."

"Oh Mum, that's old-fashioned baloney. Van and I are going to have an extra long double bed, we've already decided that."

"Well young lady, you can just get your own sheets for that bed." I did just that.

Van looked into the kinds of apartments available in Manila and also at the Episcopal cathedral, to see what it was like. I was particularly anxious about marriage preparations and wrote him in late June 1939,

What kind of wedding are we going to have? I always thought I'd be married in a real white wedding dress with bridesmaids and you'd have ushers and we'd be married in a real service. Will that be what we have if I have to come out by myself? Of course in the past I imagined it would be in Christ Church and we'd have a reception here at home—Now I don't know.

Dad is being difficult right now, but once you write him I think he'll change his mind. He's so old fashioned, almost Victorian in his views. In fact he seems to think he owns me and that I am to accept his every dictum and he presently says it isn't proper for a girl to be married away from home. I'm so tired of what's PROPER!!!

My answer from Van came quickly this time, for he was temporarily in Manila:

Of course you will have a full scale wedding. Not as big as if we were in Greenwich but between our Navy friends and your family's Army friends, I'd guess we'd have about one hundred. I'd always planned on that and that's why I went to see the Cathedral. It's the Episcopal church out here and only a bit bigger than Christ Church. There is a little chapel too but it is probably too small. We can talk about that when we know, but mainly I want you to have the prettiest wedding your heart desires, and mine, too. We are only going to do this once and it should be something to cherish always. . . .

I have sent your ring by way of one of the Officers returning home. Please cable me when you get it. How I wish I could be there to put it on your finger, my darling. We'll just have to do that when we get together.

Van wrote a community letter, sending copies to his mother and father and my parents, also enclosing it in my letter. He summed up the situation in China in July 1939:

The day before yesterday I returned from five days in Peking. . . . [It,] of course, is controlled by the Japanese and has been since 1937 and the place is overrun with Japanese soldiers, as Peking is apparently the military headquarters for North China. . . .

We couldn't get out to the Great Wall because that was too far from the City and it is not supposed to be safe because the [Chinese] guerrillas are still operating around there.

About what is going on out here now between the Japanese and the British, . . . they certainly are doing their darndest to whip up anti-British feeling among the Chinese. The Limeys are catching it in the neck too, from the Japanese on all sides. One of the humorous results is the sudden fondness and cooperation (in small things only I guess) the Americans get from the Japanese. It of course is just to make the British feel more discriminated against. I think possibly the

British are on a toboggan, as far as China is concerned because she naturally is in no position to use a military show here to win her point and at the same time keep Europe in a state of flux. The French aren't going to help and we won't help. What is needed is a fleet equal to Japan's steaming around the China Seas but nobody is in the position to send that many ships out here.

If the British are turned out of Tientsin I think it will only be a matter of time before the third powers will be ousted from all the foreign concessions including Shanghai. And that will include France and the U.S.

The guerrillas are whittling away at the Japanese Army to a fair thee well, and the Japanese are wearing themselves out trying to subdue and control all this land. That is probably one reason why they would like to have an interested third party and arouse the Chinese against someone else. I suppose too Japan might have something cooked up with her European friends in case England did become occupied out here.

I don't know what the great American press is saying about us. It probably has the whole Asiatic Fleet steaming madly around guarding Americans, rescuing missionaries and what not. Such is not the case. Months ago the ports we were to visit this summer were decided upon and as yet no one has deviated from the schedule. And because one lone destroyer happens to be in a port or on its way to one where something is happening we have, "Admiral Yarnell [then in command of the China Station] ordering American warships to guard American interests." We probably will be ashore drinking beer with the British or in swimming. So don't let the press kid you.

I haven't seen much of Chingwantao as yet. The reason we came here is because the Marines have a summer camp and a rifle range so we sent all of the men ashore and put them through a course on the range because sailors, although they never get any practice except maybe once a year, must know how to use a rifle too. Did you know the Navy is organized to furnish and can equip infantry, and machine gun and artillery companies? They probably aren't as well trained by a long shot as the Army or Marines.

To be good in any profession but the Navy, must be a snap because you can specialize but in the Navy you must know about everything from gunnery and navigation to accounting and law.

Same Disease, Same Cure

By July I had gone through one fuss after another with my family. The strain was beginning to take its toll. With my engagement ring on its way, however, my spirits rose, and I went in search of an engagement present, finding just the thing at Mr. Tiffany's emporium: a folding picture frame made like a traveling clock, sterling silver and measuring two and a half by three and a half inches.

I had "V O P, July 17, 1939 E H R" engraved on the back. All in all I thought I had done well. Van could keep it on his desk or fold it up and slip it in his pocket when he traveled. I was pleased with having chosen 17 July as the date to put on it, that being the day I expected my engagement ring to reach me; in my mind that was the day we would be inextricably bound to each other. I went home and ate the first good meal I had had in quite a while and then settled down to wait for my ring to arrive. Did I say settle down? Better put, I settled up in the clouds. I wrote Van two days later:

> Last night I woke three or four times because I'd dreamt the post office had called me and told me they had something of utmost importance for me. This morning at seven I had the same dream again, so I got up and dashed downtown. . . .
>
> The mail box had a lone slip of paper in it which said to go to the registry window, which I did rather gingerly for I was deathly afraid of being disappointed, but indeed it was a small brown package and it was from you! . . . I held it all the way home and took it up to my room—I had to unwrap it slowly because it was done up so well and then I did get it open and there was your card. I sort of cried over that because it was so much what I wanted you to say—so very simple and lovely. Then I sat there and held that blue velvet box in my hands and just thought that inside it was the symbol of what my life has come to mean. When I finally opened it and saw my ring which is our ring, my dearest, to describe my mingled feelings of pride and joy are impossible. I never before in my life felt that way. I hope I never will again and know I never can. Aside from what it stands for it is so exactly what I wanted and it is perfect for my hand. In every way it is perfection. This morning only missed perfection by the fact that you weren't here with me or I with you. I should like to have had you put my ring on my finger for me, I would far rather have you see what I'm trying to say in mere words and I would like to have kissed my blessed Van so that he would know to what depths my feelings for him go.

The card was eloquently simple:

> *With this ring eternal happiness*
> *All my love my dearest*
> *Van*

My ring was an elegant, round, blue-white diamond set to look square. On each side were three smaller diamonds stepped down, two together, then one, no fancy etching to detract from the stone. I could not take my eyes off it and waved my hand to watch it sparkle. Even more special was knowing that Van had designed my ring himself.

No sooner had I received my ring than I was called in to talk to Mother and Dad. Dad started right off telling me that I must wait for a year to go to Van. In fact, he argued, Van should come to the States.

Turning to Mum, I said, "You promised us I could go back in six months. Why would you go back on your word?"

"When Van and I had a brief conversation in Manila about marriage he said he thought probably it would be good to wait a year until he makes lieutenant junior grade, and besides, both your father and I think you had better think long and hard about the Navy."

I was so upset I fairly shouted, "What in heaven's name do you think I've been doing since December 1938? And here it is almost August 1939. Damn it! He made lieutenant junior grade in June! You've let me get my trousseau, you've both been pleased about Van, you've let us think we could be married in October and *now!* You got married when you wanted to and went carting off to the Philippines in the Army. You let Nane marry Joe when she wanted to and go tearing off to Manila. Why, tell me, do you want to punish Van and me for wanting to get married *in* Manila?"

Mother's face went from reasonable to fierce. Dad glared at me and pulled his favorite stunt. "You will do as you are told, young lady, because I say so! That ends this discussion!"

Biting my lip to keep from crying I turned and marched out of the room directly to the telephone, thinking to call Van until I realized he was in China and, by phone at least, incommunicado. *A year.* Dear Lord, what did they mean? From February when Van left, or March when I left? Did they realize Van was twenty-six years old and I was twenty? Did they realize how unfair they were being to Van? Did they doubt we loved each other? Well, this coming March I would be twenty-one and then they could not stop me. My poor Van—and for that matter, my poor self.

I jumped in my car and sped up to Craggy and the comfort of my darling mother-in-law to be. She would know what to do, I hoped; but Aunt Kate was not there, so I sat on the porch and wrote my Van:

> It looks like we've come to a blank wall. You can't possibly get back here and my family won't let me go out there at present. I'll keep hammering away at them and see if I can't get them to look at it from my point of view. They would have not one objection if you were in the States, in fact they'd be more than pleased. I refuse to give up hope though things look black as night just at present.
>
> There's nothing that can make me give up the fight either. I've made up my mind I'm going to marry you at the earliest possible moment and that's what I'm going to do. . . .

If I can only manage to continue to hold my temper maybe I can swing this alright. Not meaning to cry over spilt milk but why couldn't I have fallen in love with you here at home and married you before you went out there.

I had asked Van what his real opinion was of the Japanese. I didn't mean what he was writing to Mum and Dad; obviously he was trying to prove to them that I would be safe. He wrote me candidly at the end of July:

We sit here on the end of a limb that the politicians are sawing off. The Japanese with no natural resources for modern war, steel, iron and oil primarily, are being slowly pushed into a corner by the sanctions our politicians are wanting to place against them. It is obvious they must go after the Dutch oil fields and we with our squadron of World War One destroyers, the Dutch in Java and the British in Singapore, must stop the Japanese Navy our scrap iron has built. They must have oil and we will throttle them. It is not a case of can we avoid war, but just where and when will it start. If we keep our head we could avoid it, as I told the family. This shouldn't change our plans though Bunny, for we'd know ahead of time.

You are too precious to me to put in harms way.

Dad had been so disgusted with Neville Chamberlain and his attempts to appease Hitler that dinnertime had become an unpleasant tirade on the subject. As Germany invaded one country after another, Dad would expound anew in strident terms. Obviously he was talking in like ways on the commuter train to New York because I was frequently accosted with remarks such as "Your Dad is a real warmonger" or "Of course your whole family are military and love to fight, that's why your Dad wants to go to war."

This was tough to take. The men in my family hated war more than any civilian because they knew what war really meant. Their reasons for becoming military and naval men were idealistic; they wished to keep their homeland safe from aggression, and they wanted to lead an adventurous life not tied to a desk. I had a hard time explaining this during the day to people who could not understand, and listening to Dad at night riled me further.

On 1 September 1939, Germany moved into Poland, convincing England and France that appeasement was not going to work. After two days of agonizing confusion, on 3 September, they declared war on Germany.

I became increasingly nervous as I could see Dad hatching another objection to my going back to Manila. Van, however, wrote his family with his assessment of what was happening in China. His letters helped me to understand what I would undergo later:

For us things are very serene, so tranquil in fact that our stay is becoming damned boring. The British destroyer and French gunboat that were here left of course and withdrew their Consulate guard, forty-two men. All the British and French people and their consular representatives are staying and there is no reason in the world why they should leave. We are all so far removed from the outside world that none of the residents ashore are particularly disturbed. I can't think of a better place than the Orient to be in if there is trouble in Europe and you wish to be removed from it. As a matter of fact the Japanese are showing indications of becoming more reasonable all the time and the foreigners may reach an understanding with them yet. The Chinese are still running them ragged in spite of the men and supplies they continue to pour into the interior.

The Japanese and the Russians are the big question mark for us. You can't tell how they'll turn. If they stay on opposite sides of the fence as they are at present, everything should be rosy. If they decide to become friends conditions might change. The one interesting thing about the Orient is that nothing is ever done the way it would be in the Western World nor do things turn out according to the Occidental rules. There is much beating around the mulberry bush to make face and to save face. Face is a funny thing but it is everything to the people, white or yellow or brown in the East. Right now no one can hazard a guess as to what might happen, although my guess is that they will continue their more or less present natural state, with the Japanese little by little backing down as far as the Europeans are concerned. . . . The Americans in their highly altruistic manner are missing a wonderful bet. Anybody but an American would not fail to take advantage of it. This superior move, which I don't share alone, will make all the righteous churchgoers' hair curl and consists first of reestablishing the good relations between Japan and the U.S. which would be very easy as the Japanese have a healthy regard for our nation and are trying now not to tread on our toes. Japan is an excellent market for us. I saw more American things in the stores in Japan than I did of any other nation. Next on this master scheme, we would allow the Japanese to do as they please with trade. All the time I have been in Manila the only merchant ships which enter the harbor flying the American flag are the Dollar liners [American freighters] but there are never less than three or four Britishers, a couple of Norwegians or Germans, Dutch ships and Japanese. Every nation but America has freighters running in and out of Manila all the time. We should start a drive in South America and clean out the British, German and Japanese trade and get all those markets, or at least the lion's share. And God help us if we don't take advantage of the breaks now and build up our Merchant Marine to something to be proud of . . . ending all this stupid bickering between the ship owners and operators. We can step in now and easily take everybody's ocean going trade throughout the world and pocket it for ourselves. . . .

In three or four days we are going to be in Hong Kong, and such civilization as a British colony can offer, and perhaps there we will find some dope on what we are expected to do. Speaking of what we are expected to do brings to mind the message the Navy dept. sent out to the entire Navy. It said in substance that Great Britain and France had declared war on Germany and that "you would govern yourself accordingly" which meant nothing in particular although the captain suggested perhaps it meant we should go ashore and get drunk.

You may think me crazy and Col. and Mrs. Riley will, to suggest Betty come out now but I don't think I am for many reasons and please back me up if you can. . . .

As Americans we are the one nationality that the Japanese do not wish to offend. Now with a new cabinet in Japan the whole attitude of the Japanese seems to have become more reasonable, so I simply can't see why this China affair should worry anyone unless they read too many American newspapers. It does cause inconvenience, yes, but hardly anything more than that. Now for the affair in Europe. We are as far removed as can be from that and it will have no effect on the people in the East. If in the highly improbable future Japan and Russia kick up something that involves us, Kismet. The American government scares easily and one of their first moves would be to round up all the dependents of Americans in the Orient and ship them to some place of safety. The Navy would sense any trouble long before it would happen and have all the wives evacuated so there would be no danger of being caught someplace. I am telling you this in case you might wonder what would happen if trouble did arise.

. . . Last but not least and very important. I feel that putting off our marriage and waiting until "times are better or more favorable" is foolish. Something will always keep turning up which will be grounds for an excuse if you have that point of view. It will be a war, a revolution, the stock market will go down, they will suddenly retire two hundred Naval Officers, it will be a cloudy day or something. Both Betty and I will be one hundred and two and a half years old if we have to wait for wars to stop, dictators to die. and good will to reign among men. . . .

I will add one thing which turned up after I made up my mind that Betty should come out, hell or high water, and that is our overhaul has been postponed for a month so it now covers the last of October and all of November. My drive now is to arrange it so that Betty comes out then. I will have to work fast but you watch me.

It seemed that my pounding on the family was getting somewhere, and they had been very taken with Van's latest letter from Manila on the second of November 1939:

Conditions in the Orient, as a whole, have shown continual improvement from late July and I have every reason to expect that they will continue to do so. The first definite step to improved relations between the Japanese and the foreigners came with the fall of the Military cabinet and the establishment of the more conservative cabinet in which Admiral Nomura is Foreign Minister. Following in the footsteps of the formation of the new cabinet came a change of face on the part of the Japanese Naval and military leaders in China. Their attitude became more reasonable. . . . Next, and in rapid succession, came the abandonment of Japan by her Axis friends, a slap from Russia and the war in Europe. This left the Japanese breathless with surprise and not knowing quite which way to turn. It was quite apparent that the Japanese public and military did not, and do not, want to become mixed up with the European powers in their war. I believe the Nippon government realize they have their hands full with the Chinese and even now have stopped trying to advance and would be quite content to make an "honorable" peace to retain what they now hold.

Had they been more set on driving the Europeans out of China I think they would have taken action against the International Settlements by now. Instead places like Swatow and Amoy, which were hot spots in July and August, have cooled practically to normalcy and local differences settled. I believe I am correct when I say that most of the differences concerning the municipal government of the International Settlement in Shanghai are settled also. Conditions there certainly can't be too bad for I understand Admiral Hart [who was now in command, having relieved Admiral Yarnell] is coming to Manila this month with the Augusta. Last winter the Admiral remained in Shanghai.

It is quite evident to me that the Japanese are greatly concerned over their commerce, their supply of scrap iron, fuel oil and other raw materials. . . . The United States has threatened to revoke the 1911 trade agreement. If that occurs Japan loses another customer for her exports and a source of scrap, oil, and imports. The Japanese are trying desperately to get a new trade treaty and I would not be the least bit surprised to see one. America incidentally is most foolish to deprive herself of the Japanese markets, but whereas we can stand the loss the Japanese can't. On the whole the Japanese want to continue friendly relations with the Americans. . . .

[Van was talking about the sanctions we were thinking of placing on Japan, which cut off oil not only to its Army and Navy but to the homeland as well, making it imperative that the Japanese take the Dutch East Indies. For this reason, the U.S. Navy war plan was based on that assumption.]

In spite of Germany trying to throw the blame on England, and the Allies . . . trying to get us to join them, I can't see how, if the people of the United States keep their heads, we can get actively mixed up in it.

The European trouble will stay where it is and conditions here are better than they have been for the last year and a half and will continue to improve. . . .

But considering that there might be trouble here in the Orient, or elsewhere, don't you think we, in the Navy, would get the first hint of it long before anything broke? . . . You read of unrest in Shanghai, shooting of pro-Chinese by the pro-Japanese and vice versa. Yet in spite of accounts of gangster killings in New York, of the national guard called out to quell labor troubles in Detroit with machine guns and tear gas and of the CIO refusing to let ships leave San Francisco those cities are not considered unsafe to live in.

When I ask to marry Betty and take responsibility for her and her well being on my own shoulders I do so knowing full well what it means to us both. . . . If I thought that there would be risks, dangers or undue inconveniences for either of us I would be the first to tell you.

Van had told me he was going to apply for flight training or submarines so he could get home to marry me in the "proper" fashion, as Dad said he should. I wrote Van saying I did not want him to do any such thing as it could only bring us unhappiness later if he changed to a service he did not really want just for the sake of marrying a few months earlier. Van wrote me from Manila on 9 November 1939:

You are right of course darling about my not wanting to change my present duties and the possible ill effect such a change might cause. For both our sake Betts I won't think about it any more. I wouldn't make any voluntary changes anytime without talking it over with you beforehand anyway. So while I will do anything to hasten our wedding I will at least let you know what I'm planning, aviation and submarines are out!

Why you were ever afraid dear of sending me your poems I can't imagine. They are wonderful. I love them and think you have put into those few lines words and sentiment which pages of ordinary writing could not express. Darling you have marvelous talent. I am dying to see some of your heads [sculpted portraits]. You know sweet, you are the gold mine I said you were and I am oh so lucky to be getting the most marvelous wife in the world. Just thinking about us being together makes me so happy. Hurry, hurry, hurry! . . .

I will check on the name of the local Episcopal Church and let you know in case you want to use that on the invitations. . . . We could probably set the date perfectly safely a month ahead by cable then have the invitations air mailed to me and I could mail them to the individuals out here all within a month and while you are on your way out. Anyway there is no use crossing that bridge yet. The only date I am worried about is the day you arrive. After that dates will mean nothing.

I am quite sure you will have to have your passport made out for Elizabeth Riley. When you arrive we take it with the necessary evidence, ie. the marriage license, to the Consul and have it amended to read as it should.

. . . According to Don we just have to appear on the scene together. I have to have the Captain's permission to get married but I hardly think he will have any objections. . . .

How is the neuralgia, better I hope? I can understand how it would be caused by nervousness and I hope Doc Amos knows that there is only one cure. When an old steady person like myself can become nervous as a cat and upset for as long as I have been there is something serious. We are both in the same state I guess Betts darling. Same disease, same cause and same cure for us.

My darling I am yours through eternity.

I'll Jump the Traces

All summer and fall of 1939 I had attempted to be calm, quietly reasoning with Mother and Dad. This, however, seemed to be futile. They would not give me a plausible answer as to why I could not go to Van. Mother allowed me to continue to make plans, but Dad flatly refused to discuss the matter. Christmas was fast approaching, and there was no way the family would budge over the holidays.

If I was to talk to Van on "his Christmas day" I would have to make a radio telephone date well in advance to be completed Christmas Eve our time. When the appointed hour came, the family was decorating the tree and imbibing champagne. The first report from the overseas operator was "we have lost contact temporarily with Manila." The next report was "Lieutenant Perkins is not available, we will try again." This went on all evening—and so did the champagne. By midnight the call had not come through. Finally, Harold, one of our group, grabbed the phone when it rang, shouting, "Operator, operator give me Vanilla!" Amazingly, the call went through, and I got to talk to Van on his Christmas late afternoon and my Christmas very early in the morning. Harold forever after took credit for getting the call through. Unfortunately, I had no wonderful news to give Van as a present. Christmas for both of us was mostly a dull ache, but thereafter, every time we ate ice cream, we would say, "Operator, give me *Vanilla*" and giggle over Harold's success.

As a Christmas surprise present, sister Nane told the family she and Joe were to have a baby in late July. Right after New Year's I told the family I wanted to get to Manila in time to marry Van in March or April so that I could go with him to China. I came up against a stone wall and began to suspect Dad was using the baby as an excuse to not leave the country. Finally, I confronted him.

In no uncertain terms he told me that his firstborn grandchild was, at present, the most important thing on his agenda. I was so mad that I simply exploded in a most unseemly fashion. "What in the damn hell do you think I am anyway—a piece of dirt to trample on?"

"You will not speak to me in any such disrespectful manner, nor will you use such words as damn and hell," he commanded.

I turned on my heel and went directly to the phone to tell Van I was going to come out on my own. He agreed with me, so we made plans over the phone.

After our conversation, Van wrote his family:

First of all you may know all about the long wire I sent but if you don't I will tell you. In brief Betty called me up to find out my reaction to the idea that she just up and leave. It seems she had a row with the family over coming out. They apparently are strongly against it but will give neither of us any reason whatsoever why. I wrote them a letter which they received prior to the row and undoubtedly helped bring it on because in the letter I put it right up to them and said we expected to be married in February. . . .

Well I was not surprised that Betts suggested she jump the traces. I have had more than one friend out here wonder that she hadn't done so before, and I know that she is impulsive and equally that she has a mind of her own and won't be bossed about. For that reason I have attempted not to bring up such a subject before although I had planned to suggest it myself if I got no reply from this last letter. It is simply a matter of saying, "We are going to be married, do you want to come and help make everything nice or not." So when Betts so definitely came out in the open with it I was ready and knew I would support her no matter what she did and told her so. . . . Now I think I will play my way. If there was anything to be reasonable about I would be "reasonable" but I have nothing to go on, unfortunately and it makes me sad and helpless, Betty has to bear the brunt of it all. . . .

Now last January I knew I was in love with Betty but was afraid to admit it to myself for various reasons. For equally various reasons I wanted her to go home before I said anything. In March I was sure of myself and all but tried to stop her from returning to the States. . . . I didn't mind waiting all summer and a couple of months extra because I felt we did owe it to the families to show that Betty and I were serious, that we did have definite plans and ideas and that our love was more than infatuation which time and distance (plus tests) would cure. Betty & I are handicapped by the fact that she was involved with a lad before they came to Manila. . . .

I feel this way too. Betty and I are already married, in every way except legally and physically, and that this question of whether Betty comes out or not is no longer one of parental approval. It has assumed the proportion of someone trying to run my life, my married life, and I won't tolerate it. I will not have anyone telling me how I should live and what I can and can't do. . . . That brings up one other point. What legal hold in the State of Conn. do parents have. None I know if you are over twenty-one but what is the legal age of responsibility for a girl?

I don't want Betty to walk out because it isn't fair to us or to you and can't help but leave a bad taste in your mouths. . . . I can think of no worse condition than not to have the wholehearted support of both families when we wed. But neither can Betty and I continue to go on like this, nor will we. . . . Be good to Betts for she is having a rotten time.

I told Mother what I intended to do and that Van was behind me because he felt we had both been reasonable for far too long and that there was no reason why Nane's baby should hold us up.

"Nane's baby?" she said. "That has nothing to do with this. Your father and I are involved in a lawsuit and we must stay here for our court appearance. However, I promise you we will take you out in September."

"Oh Mum, that's terrible. Why didn't you tell me about the lawsuit? I thought that foolishness was settled long ago. Dad said it was because of the baby coming next July, and I thought that was utterly ridiculous. I so wanted to go to China with Van this summer and you could have taken me and been back in plenty of time."

"We thought it was settled," Mother replied, "but it has been reopened. Your father wanted to keep this whole thing to himself, and only your threat to leave has made me tell you. Of course, if this can be settled before Van leaves for China we'll take you out, but I doubt it can be. You know how slow lawyers are. I hope we'll leave by September and get you there no later than early October."

I called Van to tell him this, and I told him I felt badly for Mother and Dad and did not see how I could leave them after Mother's promise. He, poor darling, was the one who must take the brunt of it all now. This was surely the heartbreaker of the whole long series of delays, for I did not know how to fight something that seriously threatened my family.

Extra Special

With Mother and Dad's promise to take me to Van, leaving in September, they also said they would formally announce our engagement on 8 June, at a party for our friends and family in Greenwich. I called Van immediately in Manila to tell him the wonderful news.

Good to their word, they announced our engagement. I wore Van's favorite dress, the one that had stopped him in his tracks that New Year's Eve in Manila when we first "joked" about being engaged. I wrote Van that night about the party, and then told him the latest "scuttlebutt" from Washington: "Have just heard Japan is afraid Germany will take the Dutch East Indies and she doesn't want that one bit, thank the Lord. I now feel that Japan may change her policy towards us in the hope that we may try to help protect the East Indies. That would be alright by me, I just want to stay out of this mess as long as possible, and Japan has been worrying me for a long time now."

It was ages before Van heard about the details of the party, for now that he was up in China, mail took several weeks to reach him. His letter about it was nonetheless enthusiastic:

> Give Joe my compliments for I have never seen so many photographs that I wanted to have. Bettsy they are wonderful and look divine. All this talk of yours about not being pretty—my goodness such nonsense, you always were, since I've noticed, and always will be. Quit hiding your light, I love your eyes, your smile and everything about you. My beautiful one, you are going to make everybody sit up and take notice in Manila. I couldn't be happier or more pleased with myself.
>
> I loved seeing the pictures of the family; there were some grand ones of Mother and Dad. No one has changed, even all our old friends seem the same.
>
> I received a sweet letter from Aunt Gene [Van's term for my mother] and she said how happy she was that our announcement was made public. . . .
>
> I have just written my family a great long letter and asked them to come out with you all. I think it would be grand if they did. Our wedding isn't going to be an ordinary one I know. It will be something extra special for you and me because of all that we have gone through. A wedding for people who just decide to have one can't possibly mean all that ours is going to mean. I couldn't explain to you what it means to me Betts, it is far too deep for that, but in years to come I can show you. . . . As I have said before, I will only be happy and carefree when we walk out of the church together this fall. That day, my love, will be my real birthday!
>
> Betts old girl keep working on those nerves. I know what it is like, even I who thinks he is old calm, cool and collected and easy going in the flesh, gets terribly upset at times. My trouble is nerves too, caused by worrying whether or not these wars will upset our plans. I honestly am not afraid that we will get mixed up or that conditions will be unsafe for you. I am worried if I can convince others of that at times.

At last we had reservations to sail in early September on the SS *Coolidge*. It was definite. No more delay. By the time we were finally together, we would have been separated for eighteen wasted months, but with an end in sight I became jubilant and wrote in August:

Thought this might amuse you. I ran across it when re-reading some of my poems; it's dated 1931 which means I was twelve.

> *When first I started in to flirt*
> > *I was in a dress with a long green skirt*
> *At least, that's when first I became aware*
> > *Of the strength and power of my stare*
> *At that time I'd just turned ten*
> > *A fierce age to go conquering men.*

Now I ask you if that isn't a masterpiece.

You say that you knew but wouldn't admit to yourself that you were in love with me New Years Eve. Well darling as long ago as last Oct. '38 when you came over to call on Mother you hit me where I didn't want to be hit. When I got to Manila I fought the only losing fight I've ever fought. I didn't want to fall in love with you and I blamed it on everything except you. The moon, the weather, just anything, but it didn't explain my waiting for you to come off the ship for hours on end. It didn't explain my wanting to be with you every minute. If I'd thought I had a chance I wouldn't have fought so hard. I thought you were being nice to me because I was from home and that was all. . . .

New Years Eve sticks out in my mind because I was so contented just wandering around with you. You don't know how I felt when I first had any idea you might be in love with me; Mariah Novitski told me and I didn't believe her, not long after that I knew from you, but my, we were noncommittal. All that business about "I think I'm in love with you" stuff—Gee darling, weren't we crazy to be so darn conservative. . . .

Doctor Amos is going to give me shots beginning next week. Vaccination, Typhoid and Cholera and my teeth are being fixed so when I get to you I shall be as sound as can be. . . .

By late August I was involved with wedding presents galore and so excited I was hopping up and down. I dashed off a letter to Van:

I have been packing all this week. Gosh, I never realized what it meant to move everything that is essential for living. Every few minutes I think of something else I have to get. My last few days at home ought to prove perfectly frantic what with people popping in and out, generally getting in the way, four of us trying to pack for the Philippines, Nane and the baby trying to pack to go down to Columbia [South Carolina] and brother Jimmy packing to go to college. It will be a madhouse to say the least. That brings me to another piece of good news.

Lord, the crazy things people say on occasions. I've heard rumors that Germany is going to war with South America. That Japan started to attack Hawaii and that's why the fleet made such a hurried return there.

Dearest, I have figured out that day after tomorrow and a month from that date I will sail from San Francisco. Two months from day after tomorrow we will be married. . . . If anything happens this time, well darling, I will just go on waiting and hoping but, dearest, I want you and reality more than anything in the world.

My remarks about Germany and Japan would have been startling to Van if he had not known Dad's classmates at West Point were in command of several branches of the Army. Frequently I heard their opinions at the dinner table, for Dad kept in touch with most of them by letter and often they came to visit at our house. Germany did use South American ports for two of their battleships, one of which we blockaded and sunk when she tried to run the blockade. As it turned out, both rumors were valid.

Beginning to Hum

Once again it happened. This time the delay was not the family, not the baby's arrival, but, of all things, a strike that disrupted the steamship line schedule on 20 August. It was unbearable, and I cried bitterly when Dad showed me the letter. It took all my strength to write Van and sound cheerful. Dad's assurance that we would take any means of transportation, Dutch or American, getting us to Manila by mid-October helped dry my tears.

I would find a way to get to Van if I had to build a ship of my own to make the trip. For now, I pulled myself up by the bootstraps and wrote,

This is the first time in ages that I've had to write you bad news. The *Coolidge* is sailing late—October 4 instead of September 20. It arrives in Manila Oct. 27th instead of the 13th. First thing tomorrow morning I'm going to call and find out if there is another ship sailing earlier. If so, we will take it and I will cable you about it so you can just ignore this letter.

. . . I cannot understand why everything has to happen to our plans or why we must be put off and put off, ad infinitum. . . .

Poor darling, you've taken an awful lot and you've been wonderful about it. I don't know how you've done it but I want you to know that I realize how terribly hard it is for you and I think you're splendid to take it as you have. . . . Whenever I get down in the mouth I go up to the house and sit in your room for a while and that calms me down, so this afternoon I went up and calmed down. So many miserable hours I've weathered in your room. I don't know how I started it but it always works. . . . Thank you for leaving your room behind dearest. . . .

Your letters are always a triple combine of interest, good sense and affection that is just perfect and they are so natural sounding that I feel as though you were talking to me. Now as the time draws near for us to stop writing each other I want to tell you how much each letter of yours has meant to me for I doubt that I will ever find the opportune moment to tell you again darling. They have been an inspiration to me. Every letter has made it possible to go on just a bit longer. It is my feeling that with each letter you've given a bit of yourself which I treasure beyond measure. If in the past I have provoked you or hurt you in any way you've never rebuked me which I thank you for, and if I have made your burden harder, as I know I have, you've taken it all and more besides and never made me feel I'd wronged you or let me know that it is harder for you. You've let me know you loved me in a thousand little ways and always remembered to reassure me in every letter. You've seemed to sense what I most wanted to hear and you've told me.

Monday we were able to make new reservations on the *President Pierce*. I sent Van a cable saying so. He would not have to worry about this setback, thank heavens.

The last letter I received before I left home assured me that I was on my way to a man whose love would be beyond anything any of my friends had. It was incredible that he could and would do a multitude of things usually left to the distaff side of a marriage. It was infinitely reassuring and endearing that he was not afraid to express his emotions. "My heart is beginning to hum," he wrote,

for there is something about being in the tropics and getting to Manila tomorrow morning that is making me feel very happy. Right now we are coasting along easily some twenty miles off the coast of Luzon. Earlier this morning we could see it sort of green and hazy in the distance. The water is deep dark blue again, so different than China's greenish gray and even the sky seems bluer and the clouds whiter. What a fool I am but I love the tropics and the Maker of the Universe did a more perfect job with colors in these southern latitudes than He did in the northern ones, and tomorrow morning we arrive in Manila!

I received your letter with the lists of people to whom we want to send invitations and I can get all that straightened out in no time at all. . . .

My first move was to find Betty Miller and find out if she and Sid had gotten the apartment, which of course they had. . . . The Millers get our vote of confidence for I couldn't have done better in choosing a place myself. The apartment is on the seventh floor. The living room is practically all windows which look out over the harbor. We are way above all the surrounding buildings so there is nothing to spoil the view, the breeze or the quiet. In the evenings we can enjoy

Manila's famous sunsets in our own peace and quiet. Betts, it is wonderful and I know we'll be crazy about it and very happy.

The apartment is as barren as Mother Hubbard's cupboard so during the next month I will scout around and buy, borrow, or steal the essential furniture we need. I thought we might as well buy a living room set of rattan consisting of something like a couch, chaise lounge, a couple of chairs and a table. The dining room table and chairs and the bed and a chest of drawers I will try to rent. Things like curtains, lamps, small tables and other odds and ends I will leave for you. I just want to get enough so the place will be livable when you get here. I will have beer and Coca Cola in the ice box too.

. . . Also in the course of the afternoon I saw Mr. David, he is the club's steward. As I walked into his office he greeted me with, "Well Mr. Perkins which is it, the 19th or 26th?" Here again I said I guessed it was the 26th and we decided there was plenty of time to make up our minds exactly what we wanted. He is going to have his man draw me some designs for a wedding cake.

I will radio you when I know whether I can meet you or not, God I hope I can. Also I understand they have gotten very particular about well wishers when ships arrive and depart so perhaps I couldn't get aboard and would have to wait on the dock. However, all that remains to be seen.

If I am out when you arrive Betts dear, go to the club and I will leave a note there for you with the keys to our domicile. Incidentally, the address of our apartment is—Apt. 7-A, Michael Apartments, 1188 A'Mabini. . . .

Darling, the time is getting short and soon you will be on your way. What tremendous happiness we have in store for each other and being together and married will be reward enough for all we have gone through.

Quarantine

SEPTEMBER 1940–SEPTEMBER 1941

I was about to leave Greenwich forevermore as Elizabeth H. Riley. My trousseau was packed, including my gorgeous wedding peignoir and night-gown, which was so sheer I had had a satin slip specially made so as not to shock myself! My wedding dress with its three yards of tulle train was packed in a giant box folded over blue tissue paper to keep it wrinkle-free and guard the "Rose Point" lace bodice. My Mary Queen of Scots lace cap and veil were packed in a separate box. Both boxes traveled in the upper berth all across the country. Changing trains and stations in Chicago was a trial to my family, as I insisted that the boxes and I must not be parted. By now my parents were indulging my whims and we took two taxis.

Our stay in San Francisco was fraught with tension and phone calls to Dad's Army officer friends with the latest communiqué on the conditions in the Orient. There was but a short time left until we boarded the SS *President Pierce,* and unless I was forcibly taken off the ship in Honolulu, I would be on the way to my Van.

I had just talked to Van; he was as gleeful as I but terrified that General Short, who was in command in Hawaii, would persuade Dad to go no fur-ther than Honolulu. I was even more worried about the admiral whom we were also to see. The Army was much more complacent than the Navy about their dependents in the Orient.

The year I was supposed to wait to marry, according to Dad, had stretched to more than a year and nine months. It was evident he was now doing all in his power to get me to Van, and I wanted to forgive him for causing us such pain. I wrote Van a letter on board ship summing up our stay in San Francisco:

> I write this now with the fervent prayer that it will reach you not long before I do. Knowing full well the grave possibility that the letter may go on but that I may be stopped. It is hard to write at all with that thought in my mind for I do not know whether to be gay or happy or to be sad and cry. The mere idea that I might have to turn back makes me—Oh, I don't know darling, it is too ghastly a thought to dwell on and I am too much upset to know how I feel except that my tummy keeps churning over. . . .
>
> Dad is of the opinion that we will proceed as per schedule and that he is not going to let anything but you and the law stop us. As he says if you ask the people their particular opinions you will get ten different answers, so he will do the thinking for this shebang unless helped by you or the State Department. . . .
>
> We have had no hysterical outbreaks or silly talk during all these past trying three weeks and when at last I broke down in San Francisco, Dad made me cry until I was tuckered out, then shoved me in bed and off to sleep, having first of all put in a call to you, so that I could get all straightened out in my mind. Not that he has treated the situation lightly, he hasn't, he's just been so calmly undramatic and sensible while the rest of the family have been having duck fits.

General Short conferred with Dad and proved to be amenable to our continuing on to Manila. Dad canceled his appointment with Admiral Kimmel. I guess he was fed up with advice; for Navy advice he would trust in Van. I sent Van a cable when we cleared Honolulu so he would not worry.

Finally we started up Manila Bay, and, oh my lord, we dropped anchor miles from the shore. There was an announcement over the loudspeaker: "Due to the outbreak of cholera on board, this ship is in quarantine." Dad, Mother, and brother Bill went to see the captain to remonstrate with him. We, of course, had had our cholera shots. I had spent the wee hours of the morning bathing, dressing in my outfit specially chosen of loose weave for coolness but oh-so-good-looking to please Van. Now all I could do was gaze at the distant shore knowing Van was there. Also awaiting us was a luncheon party. Then off to get our marriage license and a thousand other things, and here we sat at anchor—quarantined.

My eyes were straining, my throat aching, as I tried to stay in control. Then I noticed a tiny boat putting out from shore, probably the medical officer and port authority. At least there was something to watch. As it got nearer, I began to make out a white uniformed figure standing in the bow. Of all the dumb things, I ran to my stateroom and reapplied my lipstick, then went back on deck to the railing. Sure enough, the boat was now near enough to see Van. The ship's crew lowered a ladder, and before the boat made fast, Van took a flying leap. Seconds later, half laughing, half crying, I was in his arms and had bedecked his face with new lipstick! I hurried him off to my cabin, where we both talked at the same time, laughing, hugging, kissing.

All the months of waiting and longing for each other were swept away in a gloriously passionate moment as though we had never parted. When Dad knocked softly on the door, we made not a sound, so off he went. Neither of us talked of the war or of the waiting; we just marveled at our luck in being together at long last. Van looked pensive briefly, but that was all.

Finally, Dad knocked on the door again to tell us we were to go ashore in the cutter immediately. We quickly straightened ourselves out and dashed on deck to board the boat for a very choppy ride ashore. My boxes went with me, much to the chagrin of the boatswain, who had to find a tarp to cover them. As we came alongside the pier in Manila, I noticed my handsome skirt was getting in my way as Van handed me out of the boat.

We had to hurry now to make the luncheon party on time. I do not really remember much more than holding Van's hand and looking at him every time he squeezed my fingers. I think we must have been utterly foolish. One glass of champagne and we were both giggling like school kids!

As we got up to leave, I looked down, and to my horror my skirt, which was bias-cut linen, had stretched in the humidity and was now just above my ankles. Hitching it up, I fled to the ladies room. There the Filipino attendant took scissors to it, hacking off a good six inches. So much for loose-weave, breathable material in the humid tropics. With my dignity again intact, and my skirt in fringes, we proceeded to the town hall for our license and thence to a conference with the minister. Van had wanted me to have a diamond wedding ring; I had wanted a plain band. We had compromised and had both. The minister, High Episcopalian Father Grey, said he could not marry us with two rings.

Van gave my hand a tug and winked at me, and when we got outside he said, "We have an added errand, we need to find some very fine, near colorless silk thread. The dressmaker next to the hotel should have some."

"Now Van, what are you cooking up?" I asked.

"Simple darling. We just tie the two rings together, and when Father Grey says 'with this ring I thee wed,' I say, 'with these rings I thee wed' and the deed is done. Father Grey will have blessed both rings without knowing it. Now isn't that simple?"

It worked. Father Grey was aware of it, but other than a slight start, he never made it an issue.

Earlier in the year, Van's good friend Jim Shaw had been married in the same church where we were to be wed, the Episcopal Church of St. Mary and St. John. The society pages of the Manila paper covering his wedding had been sent to me so that I would have some idea of where Van and I were to be married.

Jim had not come to the Philippines with the intention of getting married. His sister Betty Lou had at last got her passage in March 1940 on the SS *President Pierce,* arriving in Manila in April. Jim left for a cruise in his ship to the southern Philippine Islands. Betty Lou started going to the Army-Navy Club, where she joined a group of young people at the table by the pool, one being Jane Holt, daughter of Col. and Mrs. Rufus Holt. He was an army doctor stationed at Sternberg Army Hospital in Manila. The girls took to each other immediately, and Betty Lou could hardly wait to introduce Jane to Jim on his return.

Early in May the *Stewart* put in to Manila Bay. When Jim came ashore, Betty Lou, with Jane, was there to meet him. Jim took one look at "tall, beautiful, black-haired, dark-eyed, beautifully dressed, obviously intelligent" Jane, and there was his dream of a wife he had written about in his journal back in Honolulu days. He fell madly in love at first sight of her. Lord, he was leaving the end of June for China to be gone for the summer. He would have to work fast if he was to marry this lovely girl. Fortunately, Jane fell in love with him just as quickly.

When Jim and Jane announced to Jane's family that they wanted to be married, the Holts were understandably taken aback. Jane, now twenty-five, had turned down many a fine fellow, and here she was wanting to marry a man she hardly knew and "kite off" to war-torn China with him. They were perturbed that "young Shaw" was in the Navy, that Jane would be left alone a lot of the time; mostly, they knew very little about either Betty Lou or Jim's background, so they set out to check up on them. Both Jim and Betty Lou underwent thorough scrutiny—family history, academic accomplishments, and financial status. They passed all tests with flying colors, and Jane and Jim's engagement was announced on 8 June 1940.

Shortly thereafter, at the boat landing, Van sought Jim out and said, "Congratulations Jim, you and I have something very much in common."

"Oh so? You haven't fallen for my girl, have you?"

"No Jim, I haven't, but my girl Betts and I announced our engagement on June eighth also. Only you, lucky duck, have your girl here. Mine is still in Connecticut and can't get out in time to go to China. When are you getting married?"

"You poor guy, you sure have waited a long time, but congratulations on your announcement. Jane and I are getting married on the twenty-second, so she and my sister can go to China. Also, it's her mother's birthday, so I guess I'm sort of a birthday present or something."

"That's neat; I envy you more than you know. This past year and a half has been hell for Betts and me, but her family promises she can come out in September."

"You going to be around for my wedding?" Jim asked.

"I'm afraid not. We're due to head for China before that, but thanks for thinking of me. Anyway, I think I'd be green with envy. Well, there's my boat. Catch you in China. Maybe you'll be in when I get married."

As he stepped into his boat, Van shouted back, "Hey, we're both marrying Army brats!!"

We'll Take Our Chances

The Navy did not even take twelve hours to make itself evident. Van had to leave the very first night for Olongapo to join his ship and bring her around to Manila. He had done a superb job of arranging the essentials of our wedding: reserved the church and the Army-Navy Club for our reception, sent out invitations, rented an apartment and furniture. He had even ordered our wedding cake from a picture. It looked to be a reasonable size but in actuality was embarrassingly large.

With Van gone for a night and a day, Mother and I went into action, buying flowers for the bride, bridesmaids, church, and club. We ordered food for the reception and unpacked and stowed essentials for the apartment. We bought victuals to stock our kitchen. Lastly, we sent the family's driver out to get a big black spider in a bamboo cage and a gecko lizard to keep the mosquitoes down in the bathroom—normal procedure in Manila. I was ready to drop but still had to attend the fitting of my two bridesmaids' dresses, which had been made in New York to exact measurements taken four months previously. By a miracle they fit beautifully; only one hem needed to be shortened.

Dad had gone over to call on his old quarters-mate at Fort Leavenworth, Gen. Douglas MacArthur, who, having retired from the U.S. Army, was now in command of the Philippine Army and living in much splendor in the penthouse of the Manila Hotel. Dad wanted to find out the general's opinion of the war situation between China and Japan, and our chances of becoming embroiled. I do not think the general told Dad anything he did not already know, but he did say that, as he was no longer working for the U.S. Army, he would have to stay at his post. To send his wife, Jean, home would only serve to panic the Filipinos; he and the high commissioner had no choice but to stay on. He had confidence in Adm. Thomas Hart and felt that any decision he made concerning the wives of the Navy would be conservative, certainly not a capricious decision. This was so close to Van's assessment in his letter to Dad that Van's stock went way up.

The general said he wanted to meet the bride and see Mother to explain to both of us that Jean would come to the wedding but he would not. Anywhere he went a crowd of Filipinos followed him, and his presence would overshadow the festivities. I think Mother and Dad were disappointed, but I could not have cared less. There was only one man I wanted to be sure would be at the wedding, and his name was Van, not Douglas.

What a fuss it was, getting the general in the back door and up the service elevator to our suite of rooms. I had arrived seconds earlier and discovered a giant cockroach crawling on my wedding dress hanging in the closet. I had called the management to come clear the rooms of the pests. Here came the general and Jean, and hard on their heels, four Filipino houseboys armed with brooms and "flit guns" to do battle with the bugs. There was much shouting and banging going on in the next room as we tried to be graciously unconcerned and hospitable to our famous guests. At the height of the commotion in walked Van. I flew across the room, tripped on something, and literally fell into Van's arms.

My father had a pet saying: "Don't ever apologize, it's a sign of weakness." Heeding his own advice, he kept right on chatting, as though everyone lived in a kettle-drum atmosphere. Van played out the scene to perfection, righted me, said he was glad to meet the MacArthurs, and then, holding on to me, told us he had just heard the order sending all Navy wives home.

Somehow I lived through the next few minutes as the general and his lady took their leave by telling myself over and over, "You're a Navy wife, act like one!"

"These last two years we've considered ourselves married, if not legally and physically, certainly in the eyes of God. That's what you said Van, right?"

"That's what I said Betts, and that's what we both meant, dear heart," Van answered.

"Well then, we call off the wedding, I stay here, and now we are together. We are married in the eyes of God and that leaves only the legal part not yet attended to. Then the Navy can't send me home until we can go home together."

Van was shaking as he answered. "My own darling girl, I can't let us do that. The ships will be out all the time on patrol, you would be here alone. I would be frantic all the time wondering if the Army wives had been ordered out and you were utterly alone. We might snatch a couple of days here and there when we were in port, but even that would be iffy, as probably they will double up the watches of the junior officers. I couldn't do my job worried about you all the time. I just can't take the chance with the person who means more than anything in the world to me. Do you understand it's because I love you that you must go home?" He took me by the shoulders and looked down at me, saying, "Do you understand?"

To this day I can feel the anger receding and compassion for Van taking its place. Here was a young, vital man who had put his life on the back burner for two whole years to wait for me to be his wife, and he was going to lose me again in order to defend a bunch of islands against a vicious enemy whom he had observed firsthand in China. He was going to need his wits about him and he wanted me safe in the States. So I smiled, though a bit wanly.

At that, Van's face lit up as he put his arms around me and kissed me right in front of my startled family. "Mom Riley and Colonel, you may not know it, but you have raised another Queen Elizabeth," he said over my head. Stupidly, that made me cry.

Bill Parham, who had arrived in Manila shortly before with his submarine, was to be Van's best man. Late in the afternoon, he and his wife gave a cocktail party for us that was attended by all our friends and classmates who were in Manila. It turned out to be a blast of a party, and afterward the family repaired to the Army-Navy Club for a bite to eat. Mother and Dad tried to persuade Van and me that I should accompany them home on the *Taft,* sailing shortly after our marriage. Van firmly said that he and I needed time to talk alone and that we would go to our apartment after dinner by ourselves.

Ridiculously, Dad admonished us. "That would not be proper," he said. "You are not yet married!" All my pent-up resentment overflowed, and I rounded on him. "What you have deemed proper all these past two years has cost us precious time together! I thought that was all over. Now you are going to let us alone to make our own decisions. We are going to our apartment by ourselves and that's that!"

Once alone, Van started reiterating all his fears about the Japanese: their brutality to the Chinese, their need for raw materials, their obvious course of action to ensure their needs, and their imperialistic sense of destiny. He held me close in his arms while he spoke, and I felt him shudder when he talked of his fear for any Americans caught by the Japanese in what he now thought to be inevitable war. In particular, he mentioned his fears for me and how he could not abide the thought of my being caught and imprisoned.

"Nevertheless, I think you should not go home with your family Betts. We are about to become our own independent unit and I think we should act accordingly," Van said with conviction. "We'll take our chances on Navy orders, OK?"

"You bet it's OK. I want to stay as long as I can."

We returned to the hotel to find Mother and Dad waiting up for us as though we were a couple of teenage kids staying out past curfew. This time Van spoke firmly. "I'm going to Betts's room with her. We have little enough time together, and I am going to stay with her until the last boat goes back to the ship." He was not rude, just positive.

All the Victorian starch went out of Dad. "Young man, well spoken!" he replied. "I guess I have already gained a son, so Mother and I bid you good-night."

The next morning was a blur. My bridesmaids gave a luncheon for us, but I do not even remember who was there. All the talk was about the evacuation. Who would go on the transport *Chaumont?* Would Tek Lyster, one of my bridesmaids, be able to go on the clipper? If so, would I take her dog, as Ted could not keep him on board his ship? There was an awful excitement about breaking up housekeeping and leaving husbands to face God knew what. To me, it was bewildering and frightening. In a few hours, I too would have a husband that I must leave. There was only one thing to do if I was to enjoy our wedding day: put it out of my mind.

One in a Million Matches

On 26 October 1940, our wedding hour approached. Mother helped me into my dress, struggling to fasten all the little buttons down the back. Then she kissed me, saying, "Bettsy, you have been a good daughter. Now be a good and happy wife. We all love you both."

"Mum, I have something I want you to do," I said. "I brought dear old Rabbit with me for good luck. I have always carried him to exams and other important events ever since I was a little girl. I'm about to become a wife and it's time Rabbit should go home with you, for I'll have a real live Rabbit now." Giving silly Rabbit, my stuffed toy, a kiss, I handed it to Mum. She took it, understanding that it was my final gesture of love and trust in her before becoming independent of my family.

The moment had come to start down the aisle. My father took my arm, saying, "We'll have no 'quaking Aspen' bride quivering down the aisle," and he started to sing, "Here comes the bride, fair, fat, and wide" as the organ boomed out the wedding march. We proceeded down the white carpet flanked by potted palms toward the candle-lit altar. There, by the chancel, stood my groom, "skinny as a broom" all right, but gorgeous in his dress whites and beaming at me. Far from quaking, I tugged at Dad to get him to hurry the military slow march he seemed to think the occasion called for.

After the ceremony, Van and I came down the chancel steps as the organ again boomed out over the cathedral. I stopped to kiss Mother and Dad. I was aware of our ushers sheathing their swords behind us with a sharp clank of metal striking metal. We almost ran down the aisle and out to the car.

We had such a good time at our reception that Bill Parham came to Van and urged, "You two have to leave. There are people here who need to go home but can't until you depart." We left for our apartment, which was full of flowers from family and friends. A stack of cables from home awaited us, along with a cold supper and a bottle of champagne cooling in a bucket. A table lighted with candles was all newly laid, though there was no one in the apartment. (I made sure by looking in the kitchen.)

We helped each other out of our wedding finery. My dress had forty-eight tiny buttons down the back and Van had a time getting them undone. "These damn things, I mean darn things, I can't get the damn strings, I mean the darn strings to go over the buttons."

At last I could get out of my wedding dress and into my beautiful nightgown and peignoir. I floated out of the bedroom to find my husband arrayed in his new white silk pajamas with blue piping and small monogram on the pocket. The food was forgotten; Van simply picked me up and carried me to the window that overlooked the harbor shimmering in the moonlight. My heart sang in utter contentment.

Later, we sat down on the couch, and Van, picking up a cable to read, threw it aside, saying, "Let's read these in the morning. I didn't get much, if any, sleep last night, did you?"

"Lord no, I tossed around thinking about leaving you out here with these howling maniacs."

"You know, we'll spoil our short time together if we keep thinking about that. Besides, I'm due back in April or at the latest May, and that's not near as long as we've already endured. Six months will go by in a hurry, Wee Rabbit."

"Well then, there is the fact the tropics don't agree with you and you're much too thin and I should be here to cook you good meals."

"You should be here for a lot of reasons, and you shouldn't be here for other reasons. Right now we're going to go back to bed and have the first good sleep we've had in two years."

That was not quite to be, for about two in the morning the phone rang. I answered and heard a Filipino voice ask, "Aloe, Whoopee Café?"

"Wrong number," I said and hung up.

Five minutes later the phone rang again, and the same voice said, "Aloe, Whoopee Café?"

"This is not the Whoopee Café."

"Aloe, aloe, you send me two—" I hung up disgusted.

A slight pause and the phone rang again. This time Van answered curtly and decisively, "We're having a whoopee time all right, but this is *not the Whoopee Café!*"

Our assailant finally got the point, and we had no more phone calls. The next morning, out of curiosity, we looked up the number of the Whoopee Café and found that ours was only one number off.

Van wrote his family, telling his version of the wedding and married life:

I said we are going to make quite a pair I think. One of those "One in a million" matches. I've enclosed a couple of clippings of the wedding which can tell you more about what actually happened and how things looked than I can.

I don't believe I noticed anything in particular except Bettsy all the time we were in church. The whole thing went off as smoothly as clock work, and except for the Colonel getting trapped in the train as he and Bettsy started down the aisle, it couldn't have been more perfect. I think that I was as cool and steady as a cucumber and Bill Parham didn't have to prime me to get me in shape. I found out later that Bill felt if anyone needed a drink it was he. . . .

I thought Bettsy was beautiful and loads of people said they had never seen a prettier bride. The reception was a success too and everybody and their brother was there. In fact, we had so much fun we wanted to stay and enjoy the party. We probably did stay too long as it was and when we left it was amid a shower of rice. . . .

The first night we stayed at the apartment with the idea that perhaps on Sunday or Monday we would go away. Well things being as they are and the apartment is so nice we have just decided to stay here. It is so much easier and more fun to just relax and do nothing in Manila than go tearing about the country side. . . .

Both of us slipped into this married life business so easily and naturally that we had rather be around here acting like we are than going off.

The only thing that amazed me was that from the second I saw Betts on the S.S. Pierce everything seemed all right, natural and as it should be. I'll bet there isn't one couple in a thousand that just click the way we do.

The idea behind the evacuation of Navy people is that the Admiral feels, and rightly so, if there is to be any trouble and the ships are operating, his officers and men would worry about their families. This way, with no families, we can put our whole efforts on our job. The evacuation of Hong Kong last summer was more or less the same idea. Of course it is a political move too, like taking out a knife and sharpening it for it shows that we mean business and are not bluffing anymore. . . . But as for actual danger I don't think it exists now. The situation seems much less tense than it was two or three weeks ago. . . .

Betts' things are marvelous and even out here the presents haven't stopped coming because our friends in the Islands are sending odds and ends. The most complimentary gift we received was from my radio men on the ship. It isn't often that enlisted men give officers presents and I've never heard of an officer getting a wedding present from his men. For me it was about the highest compliment I could receive. . . . Then another unexpected gift came from six of my classmates on the USS *Augusta*. . . .

Betts is tremendously popular you know and of course everyone remembers her and has known all about our plans so she is hardly a stranger in Manila or Navy circles.

Your letter addressed to Lt. and Mrs. VOP came in this mornings mail and it is the first we have received like that.

A Fire in a Feather Factory

Van's ship had gone back to Olongapo for further work in the Navy yard. When Van's leave was up, we were driven to Olongapo so he could rejoin the *Whipple*. We drove through the squalid barrios and gorgeous countryside and were deposited at our cottage, designated "guest house," just outside the Navy yard. The car had to return to Manila, as no cars were allowed in Olongapo.

Our cottage was really one room built on stilts at the edge of the beach. The interior was divided by beaverboard walls reaching to about my shoulders and Van's chest above and Van's knees and my midthigh below. We had running water, cold that is, in the half bath and kitchen. The kitchen had a three-burner kerosene stove. A tin oven on the floor could be used by lifting it and putting it on two of the three burners. Cooking this way required more organization than I was used to. The sink had a rubber stopper. Water fell freely through a six-inch hole in the floor without aid of a pipe. There were no screens on the large windows. One lone bare light hung from the ceiling in the living-room end. We soon found this to be a sound arrangement, for as soon as it got dark, the glaring light attracted an array of flying insects the likes of which I had never seen before. Turn out the light and the bugs flew out, so we sat in the dark, which suited us just fine.

Immediately after we arrived, Van had to report to his ship. Off he went, with a wave in the general direction of town. "Grab the bike the Navy's given us, ride to the market and get dinner. I'll be back about 6:30."

My shopping tour was unique. I wobbled on the unfamiliar bike down the one main street of the little village. The native market was an open air affair where I picked up some vegetables and sweet potatoes and asked for a chicken.

"You pick him out, I chop," said my helper.

I picked "him" out. After the chopping, "his" legs were tied together with raffia and "he" was slung over my handlebars along with the vegetables in a little string and newspaper package. I pedaled back to the cottage to try to make a gourmet meal out of my gleanings. Three hours later Van arrived to be greeted by a smell reminiscent of a fire in a feather factory, a wife with a scorched hand, and a bird in the oven, burnt on the outside and raw on the inside. Singed wet feathers were everywhere. We went to the Officers' Club for dinner.

A few days later, Van's ship left for the southern Philippine Islands. Marge Wilson, the wife of Van's shipmate, and I were driven back to Manila in deep despair. It was more than possible that I would be handed an envelope by a sailor who would come to the door with my orders to sail in twenty-four hours. No one knew for certain what would happen to the wives, or if we would see our husbands again.

On 19 November 1940, Van wrote from the southern islands:

Bettsy sweetheart, I miss you so, just this thought of not seeing you for a week makes me miss you. I suppose I will have to get used to the idea but I never want to have you away from me for long. This morning it wasn't so bad being away but now it is dinner time and by rights I should be home. Furthermore, it's our second week anniversary and we should celebrate. These past two weeks have been the most perfect ones in my life and I've never been happier. I so love being married to you, Betts, and I wonder how I ever managed to get along all these years without you. Darling, I love you so desperately. . . .

A dispatch came in this afternoon which doesn't make me any too happy for, as I interpret it, it means that some of you wives might possibly be sent back on the *Taft* or the *City of Norfolk*. I trust, however, that the families of the Officers and men who are in the Southern Islands will be sent on the *Washington*. If anyone goes on the *Taft* or *City of N.* it should be those who are in Manila now.

If they try to do anything like that to you, use what charm and tricks you have to have it changed. Perhaps a person could be found who would rather take the *Taft* and get the trip to China and Japan. My fingers are crossed, however, and I hope my uneasiness is just something I am imagining.

At last I knew I was to leave on the SS *Washington,* sailing on the twenty-fifth of November. Van would get into port the week before I had to leave. My attempts to see Admiral Hart and ask him for a delay until after Christmas never even got past the front office. I knew Van would ask no favors. I thought maybe I could sneak in to see the admiral without Van's knowledge; that would not have hurt his reputation. At least Van would be home before I had to leave.

A quick knock on the door and there he was. In a second, I was in his arms. It was unbelievable that we would be separated again with an ocean and a continent between us. The prospect was so overwhelming we put it out of our minds.

We went to the movies, seating ourselves in the balcony, pretending to be old hands at marriage. Shortly, Admiral and Mrs. Hart took the two seats right in front of us. Admiral Hart sat ramrod straight in his high, white, starched collar. Fascinated, I watched a small cockroach move from his shoulder and traverse the pristine collar.

Here's my chance, I thought. I'll just flick the odious creature off and then quickly say, "Admiral Hart, please let me stay through Christmas."

As I started to raise my hand, Van caught it and whispered, "I wouldn't do that, Bunny, if I were you." A sign of things to come, for, ocean or no ocean, it became increasingly evident that we read each other's minds.

I might have had a chance to speak to Admiral Hart at the end of the movie, but half way through, the balcony began to sway. The screen went dark, and in orderly fashion we headed for the exits. Earthquakes were a rare sensation to me, but the audience and Van knew what to do as they were a common occurrence in Manila. I decided fate was now guiding me and I had better just accept the inevitable and enjoy our time together.

The *Washington* was to sail in the late afternoon. That gave us a whole day to act normally and be happy. I did fairly well, but every so often I would fling myself at Van, choking down a sob. We made little ceremonies of stripping our bed and washing our dishes. We drank some of the champagne. We talked of what I needed to do to change our finances back to the States and how Van would send me an allotment. As the moment approached to leave our lovely apartment, I sneaked into our bedroom and changed his white cap cover for the last time.

When I brought him his cap, now pristine white and neatly starched, he put it on the back of his head, picked me up and carried me to the window as he had the night we were married. We clung to each other, and though I tried not to, I finally cried, as did Van, in a man's way. He shuddered as tears ran down his cheeks.

"It's all right, little darling, it's all right, we'll be together soon, and nothing can be worse than what we've already been through. You know I'll love you always." Brushing tears out of his eyes, he gave me one last kiss, saying, "It's time to go, so this then is our good-bye. When we get to the dock we'll just pretend I've got 'the duty.' Do you think we can pull that off?"

I assured Van I would do my best not to disgrace him. Picking up my purse, I marched to the door, but Van had one more tear-jerker for me. He had managed to get me a last corsage, which he retrieved from the icebox and pinned on my shoulder. I fished in my purse and handed him a very small stuffed rabbit I was going to give him on the dock. I kissed it first to bring him luck.

From then on it was all a blur of noise—the elevator grinding, traffic snarling and honking, people shouting goodbyes on the dock. The *Washington*'s whistle blared a last call. One heartrending hug and I stumbled up the gangway and ran to the boat deck to get a last glimpse of Van, with Tiger, Tek's dog, under one arm. It was agonizing to watch the water widening between the dock and the ship. I could stand it no longer and blew a final kiss to my wonderful new husband. With my last ounce of courage, I turned my back.

Now What?

Van wrote me just after I sailed from Manila, addressing the letter to Mrs. VanOstrand Perkins:

My darling wife,

Much as I hate to have to write you letters I certainly have been asking and hoping for the day when I could start my letters to you this way. Since we've been married everything is so much more worthwhile and you have made me so terribly, terribly happy. My sweet, it can't mean anymore to you than it does to me. No one could love a person more desperately than I love you. You are my very heart and soul, Betts.

I certainly hated to move out of the apartment and give up housekeeping. . . . Darling, you are an excellent housekeeper and marvelous hostess and a perfect wife. . . .

God will be generous to us and bring us together soon and we most certainly have a lot more living to do. I agree Betts, that this wonderful month together is but a sample of the full and happy life we have in store.

How was your trip? I am very anxious to hear what it was like on the ship. How the passengers got on with each other, how you made out with the Stewards, what sort of service you got and everything else. There were no more wild newspaper accounts but I hear gossip that the Captain was not satisfied with the crew and where there was so much smoke, as in the contradictory newspaper accounts, there must have been a little fire. . . .

Goodnight my Betts, I wish you were here with me. I just received your "Thanksgiving" cable a few minutes ago. Thank you for it and I am glad to hear that everything is going alright. . . .

I really don't know what time of day I miss you most Betts. I am so always aware you are not here. Afternoons are lonely, suppertime is no fun, evenings and bed times are worse but I think it's worse when I wake up and realize where I am and that I can't roll over and kiss you a sleepy good morning. I'd like to be able to reach out, touch you and say "Betts."

Right after the movies tonight I was sitting here in the ward room drinking a Coca Cola and your radio[gram] came wondering what I was doing. I will whisk you back an answer tomorrow saying that I am doing nothing but thinking of you and trying to make the days pass quickly.

After I sent you a wire tonight Ned Dougherty came along feeling no pain and thought we had better send you another one which we did. I love to send you messages, it's fun and I know you get them while the thought is still "Hot" and I can visualize what you are doing. . . .

I am so happy that we have each other at last and I am only disappointed in that I didn't choose a profession which would permit me to be with you constantly. . . .

Your devoted husband, Van.

I had promised Van I would tell him what the trip on the *Washington* was really like, but it was too gruesome. The *Washington* was an Atlantic Ocean luxury liner that had been commandeered along with its German crew to come out to Manila and evacuate Navy families. We were terribly overcrowded. Even the most sophisticated among us found the heartache and lack of privacy difficult to overcome. I had a hard time even finding a place to write. Finally, I retired to the pantry at two in the morning to write to Van. As I wrote, a thoroughly soused bimbo came in and started telling me all about the officers who had made passes at her. If all these "damn snotty officers' wives" only knew how many of their husbands had had a whirl in the hay with her, she said, they would not be so high hat to her. I quickly put my hand with my miniature of Van's class ring (which he had given me just as an additional present, not as an engagement ring) behind my back, and she was none the wiser about my status as an officer's wife.

The captain, in his attempt to make a speed run, headed us straight into a typhoon. The result was disastrous: major injuries as well as seasickness. I did not bother to mention this to Van, who, as weatherman on the *Whipple,* would know about the storm anyway. I told him about all the seasick ladies, the lack of food and milk for the babies, and how I managed to fair well enough in a really nasty situation. During the height of the storm I went to the dining saloon for breakfast. I found myself the lone occupant of my half of the area. In all there were three of us in the saloon cared for by a few stewards. My steward pulled up the sideboard on my table and then startled me by pouring water on the tablecloth. The reason became clear when a plate, glass, and a couple of utensils were put on the sodden cloth where they moved not even a fraction of an inch. My juice and coffee were oddly served, in tall glasses, half-filled so they would not slop over the rim. Keeping my chair upright was accomplished with the help of a young, surefooted steward wearing a starched white coat and tennis sneakers.

I tried to minimize the frightful distress all the women on board felt, some hopelessly crying in a corner, some raucously drunk, others just staring into space. The decks were closed off because of the storm. Unattended kids were racing and screaming in the corridors, their mothers too seasick to control them. When the ship ran out of baby food, the distress became acute and there was a mini-revolt in the lounge. Many of the women on board were far from prepared to be ripped away from their husbands and thrown helter-skelter into a mix of wives, of both officers and enlisted, some of whom became abusive, using incredibly crude language to let us all know what bums we were. Poor souls, they were not only scared of the future but half-seasick. They became totally so when we ran into the typhoon.

My cabin, designed for two, held three adults and one baby in a crib that rolled around on its casters. No use telling Van that his arrangements for me to have a bunk backfired because my roommates were so violently seasick. I traded my bunk for Judy's army cot, which collapsed every time we hit a big wave. Consequently, I carried Judy's baby from his crib, and he and I spent the nights in the bathtub. Poor baby, he existed on tomato juice and water for three days.

When the storm abated there was little celebration. Most of us were not, after all, heading for a joyous reunion but a bleak, uncertain future. The captain had cards stating that we had endured 128-mile-per-hour winds printed and distributed among the passengers. Those little cards obtained miraculous results: there was no more foul language and even the drunks got sober. Everyone seemed to straighten up and get a bit proud of themselves.

On 16 December 1940, I wrote to Van:

Here I am at home, darling, and writing to you at Grandmother VanOstrand's desk in the guest room which is now our room officially as we'd be a bit cramped in your room. Aunt Kate has it all fixed up so nicely, lovely bright yellow chintz curtains at the windows and three wonderful Currier and Ives prints hanging over the desk of "The Sailor's Adieu" and "The Sailor's Return." They are a present to us along with the one Aunt Kate gave us before which was "The Sailor's Bride."

Darling, everyone keeps telling me these long winded sob stories about their best beaux being drafted [the United States had initiated the first peacetime draft], how they can only get twenty-four hour leaves and how they are all being sent all over the country starting January 3rd. So many of them are reserve officers and are being called, others are taking this "Ninety day wonder" course of the Navy's. . . . There are going to be an awful lot of raw officers floating around in the Navy because of all this. I should imagine they would be far more hindrance then help as far as work is concerned though as far as we're concerned it's fine because at least they are men who can relieve you, and plenty of them, just providing they get them out there in time.

The most amazing thing to me is the difference in the issues between the two coasts. Here, European issues hit the headlines, oriental issues the subtitles. On the West Coast the reverse is true. Mostly everyone is pepped up over the manner in which the Italians are being beaten to a pulp in Greece and Africa. . . .

What a gorgeous day today has been. Cold as they come. Bright sunlight and a nice stiff breeze. After luncheon we went skating for a short bit but finally gave that up because it was so darn cold. Then I went down to the post office and guess what? A wonderful letter from you, my second addressed to Mrs. VanOstrand Perkins. But my first addressed "My darling wife."

Sweetheart, I was sorry to hear that you had gone back to the apartment after I left. I don't see how you could stand it and I hate the picture that comes to mind of you having to go back there by yourself. I can't explain how I feel about that apartment of ours. . . .

Funny thing happened the day before yesterday. I started in to put through a call to you for Christmas Day when the phone rang so I answered and it was the overseas operator from S.F. calling to tell me you were calling me. So we have started our mental telepathy to work again.

Van had told me to play dumb about the Navy in general and the war in particular. He thought it inappropriate for a Navy wife to expound on matters military. I was used to keeping such things to myself; I had heard them all my life.

On hearing that I was to be evacuated, Van and I had decided not to use the birth-control device I had managed to get by going across the border from Connecticut's strict anti–birth control laws into New York's more sensible atmosphere. We thought that as anything could happen, having a baby right away would be a good idea and we would let fate decide.

By the time I left Manila, we thought it more than possible I was pregnant as six weeks or more had passed. But it was not to be. Eight and a half weeks into this "probable" pregnancy I was rudely disabused of that possibility, and though we were a bit disappointed, I consoled myself by saying it was a good sign that Van would come home. Van was not overly perturbed either, though he did think that a puppy would be a comfort and asked his mother to buy me one for Christmas. I promptly named the charming little Welsh terrier A. Mabini, after the avenue we lived on in Manila. I had also set about looking for and buying a car, a green Chevrolet convertible.

Maybe Tomorrow

Van had said our separation would only be for five months, as he was due home the end of April. April came at last. Van would be home any minute now, I thought. Such was not the case. May, no relief. June, still no orders.

On 16 June 1941, I wrote Van a long letter of distress over the way the government and the press were handling the war:

> How I wish you were here to do so many things with me. Lord how I miss you dearest, sometimes, as at this moment I wonder how I can stand it without you another minute. Still life does go on and I do stand it, that's all though. This is not much of a life for either of us, is it? Now it will be awful for you with all that constant rain; rain is so depressing.
>
> Darling, they've started to play "All The Things You Are" again all the time, and every time I hear it I just get all choked up. So many things come to mind when I hear it, so much of our life together seems to be sad, yet it isn't, it's the happiest part of my life. I guess that is what bittersweet means, for when my thoughts are darkest, one glance at your picture and I am again my happy self. . . .
>
> You said in your letter to Uncle Allan [Van's father, whom I'd not yet begun to call Pop] that if shooting began you'd maybe be out there indefinitely, all of which looks like you will be just that, for this *Robin Moore* incident is about all that was needed to start everything rolling. Every one around here feels we ought to just skip it more or less and do what we feel like doing under cover but all these letters passing back and forth between Washington and Berlin being made public doesn't help the cause one bit.

The government was trying to counteract the strong isolationist sentiment in the country. World War I was still fresh in people's minds, and the loss of more young American lives in defense of another country was abhorrent to most of the populace. The president, however, was now determined to go to the aid of England and France, so although we had lost destroyers without comment, he tried using the sinking of the civilian ship *Robin Moore* by a German submarine to arouse indignation:

> I think it is amazing that this democracy of ours can be denied the right to know the whole truth, but half truths told them put in such a way as to sway them to one man's point of view, like putty in an artist's fingers—
>
> . . . I know for a fact this isn't the first ship that has gone down, but the others were hushed up, and now when "he" needs an incident to arouse public feeling, the sinking of the poor little *Robin Moore* is used as a prime example! . . . The *Robin Moore* wasn't much of a ship, it's a freighter about half the size of the *Pierce,* if that big. All those *Robin* ships are small, there really isn't much lost by its sinking.
>
> What I'm really mad about is the method in which all this information is suddenly given to the press when it's been held up so long. . . . Gosh, all you have to do is go to Washington for a very little while and listen to some people tell their own experiences, or sit right here in Greenwich and listen to some of the known facts that have been withheld, not only about what's gone on at sea but right here in these United States; strikes, sabotage and espionage. My lord how can a man be expected to endanger his life when he doesn't know the facts and doesn't trust his leader. . . . The old American way was the whole truth and that worked. No truth at all is the new German way and that works. Good God, are they so naive as to think the country wants to go to war before they've even cleaned up their own back yard. Oh yes we're being fed atrocity stories only this time the last war is too close to forget the falsehoods they're starting again. . . .
>
> The way I found out what Lindbergh had said was through Punk Purdon who went to hear him speak at Madison Square. You can read the whole newspaper through and nowhere do you find an isolationist statement that isn't colored with some derogatory remark by the press. "Mr. Wagner in his *blustering* speech to the Senate" and such equally unfair statements are in every paper. I've heard so many men whose opinions I highly value express opposite opinions to the press that I am beginning to feel that Mr. R., the radio and the press are sending us to war. Oh I don't fool myself that we're not at war now, but the shooting will start shortly I'm sure. Lord help us when it does. Maybe I'm almost glad you'll be out there but that's one too many to ask of me. I love you so terribly much that everything I think is colored by my feeling for you and so I still say hurry back my darling.

Thankfully, Van telephoned at just the right time, for it had been a particularly lonely week for me, made worse by the death of my beloved puppy A. Mabini. After our conversation, I continued writing:

Dearest you won't ever know how much it meant to me to have you call this evening. I was out of sorts on so many counts that are all mixed up together. I'm missing you extra hard this week because Mother's roses are scenting the air, the weather has been so lovely, and there are so many grand things we could be doing together, and when our Bean pod was killed I thought I would die. Honestly darling, you see all the affection I shower on you and would have had for our bambino if he'd materialized, I gave to Bini #1. I just couldn't stand that she was killed. Poor puppy, what a one she was, so much personality and such a good friend. She had a hell of a good time living and when she was killed she was having a gorgeous time. Thank the Lord she was killed outright. . . . I went over to the Chisholmes and bought Bini the second, who is Bini #1's half brother.

What do you think of Russia and Germany fighting? I think it is the greatest surprise of the war. I used to say wouldn't it be marvelous if they fought thinking that it was an utter impossibility but it seems nothing is impossible in this war. Gosh I feel sorry for Japan for it certainly puts her on the spot, though the consensus of opinion here is that the Germans will make short work of the Russians and strengthen the axis powers considerably. Still I am inclined to doubt that for if she wins she has only one more liability on her hands. The Russians and Germans are as diabolically opposed as day and night, and to take a vast poor country will be one more burden. I am amazed that Germany is so foolhardy but perhaps she is desperate for lack of food and raw materials. I am utterly unable to grasp the meaning of what is going on and what the likely outcome will be is certainly beyond me. What Japan will do is what interests me at the minute but I am unable to find any solid opinion on the matter.

The Army-Navy Club rooms were full of enforced bachelors, so Van, needing surcease from the Navy, stayed at the Manila Hotel for the weekend, and from there he had called me. The morale of the overdue officers was dipping lower and lower, and Van was doing his level best not to allow himself to become bitter, as he thought that would serve no useful purpose.

In his letter of 25 June, he spoke of his frustration. He then gave me an assessment of Navy philosophy and a thorough picture of conditions in the Pacific from his vantage on the spot:

What most people resent is that we are all hanging on a limb with nothing more definite than rumors to go on. The Admiral should state something definite or announce what steps are being taken to get us back or what he plans to do.

The Navy is a loyal outfit but we have a saying that loyalty works both ways, *up and down.* That is, juniors are loyal to seniors but seniors must be equally loyal to juniors and I believe most of us feel we aren't getting a break by being kept in the dark. . . .

The best supposition advanced so far is that we actually are waiting for these reserve Ensigns to become qualified officers and then will be relieved by them. That little process is supposed to take six months. If that is the case my time will be up around August. . . .

In fact the great Russo-German surprise has practically made things stagnant. As the newspapers here said, the Japs are thunderstruck. What a surprise for them! I can't see any move for them which they can use to profit. For a couple of weeks they will pull in their horns and make up their mind. One good move for the Nips would be to become the "preservers of peace in the Pacific." It would be sort of face saving for them and at the same time not make conditions out here worse.

The Great Russian Democracy—what a laugh! It sure is a fine bunch of playmates we find ourselves with. However, I do believe the American government is smart enough to give Russia such aid as she needs as long as it benefits our purpose—and the Soviets are smart enough to realize that we will give it for just that long. . . .

I believe we, as a nation, are doing something never before attempted. It is a unique situation in international conduct but the U.S. alone is in a position to do it. Primarily we intend to see Nazism destroyed even if we have to do it ourselves, but Britain is doing a fair job alone and seems to be holding their own and even gaining a little now so it serves no useful purpose for us to have men in the field. The U.S. is secure from attack by any major force as things are going now. But because of our avowed wish to see Nazism destroyed we cannot expect to remain untouched. We have said we'd get supplies to Great Britain and we intend to, and by a show of force if necessary, but here again we can't expect to be immune from attack. Naturally any of our Naval ships fired upon will shoot back but I don't think the Navy will precipitate action by us as say, escorting a convoy to the very gates of England.

If England comes to the point where she is about to collapse and the Germans start getting completely out of hand, we will undoubtedly have to go whole hog—send an expeditionary force to push the Germans back to Germany. . . .

Betts I thank my lucky stars time and time again that we found each other and are married. There just isn't anyone else in the world that could make me happy and has all the things that you have, all the qualities and graces that I love. It is so convincing that we are meant only for each other. I have the sweetest and best wife in the world. . . . I want to be a husband again and live in the clouds with you once more. . . .

I see I have an argument with some people, whoever they are, that think husbands away from wives are apt to be untrue or play around or what have you. It is a fallacy to even give such a thing a thought if the marriage is a happy one in the first place, and in the second place it's been my observation that Navy people are a different breed of cat. I've seen a lot of married Naval officers away from a lot of wives, afar and in many places, but the amount of running around is negligible compared to the number of husbands. Another interesting tidbit on the marital condition in the Navy is that its divorce rate per capita is the lowest of any group. Both conditions I presume results because when the Navy is home it is very, very happy—and when it's away it wishes it was back home again. . . . I can't imagine a sadder arrangement than being married but not wholly, completely and head over heels in love. . . .

Oh, lest you think they are opening our mail and censoring it they aren't. We just have a moral or honor system type of censorship backed up by the fact if we let our pen slip badly and it was discovered somehow it might not be so good for us. Likewise your mail comes untouched. I understand however some units of the Navy have clamped down an iron bound censorship.

Morale dipped even lower as senior officers due home were relieved. Enlisted men were sent home on time, but junior officers were left on station as more and more reserve officers were assigned to the destroyers. The ships were constantly operating in the southern Philippine Islands area, most of which was devoid of anything worth going ashore for. In July 1941, now more than three months overdue, Van discovered one place he liked: the island of Leyte, which I had not heard of before. Neither Dad nor Joe, my brother-in-law, had any knowledge of this island either. I did find it on my big chart, but my geography book had nothing to say about it. Years passed before it was again mentioned.

Dad's former classmates who were heads of departments in the Army knew full well what was going on in the so-called Atlantic Neutrality Patrol, though there was hardly a word about it in the newspapers. Dad told me what he had heard but warned me not to divulge my source or he would hear no more. I wrote Van from Washington, where I was visiting the Novitskis that July:

Washington is a mad house. No two people have the same opinion as to what's going on. Some say war tomorrow, others that we're at war, others that we won't ever be at war. Everyone is mad at Lindbergh because they consider him a traitor as he's pro-German. . . .

Several people down there were of the opinion you might be stopped in Honolulu for station. The more I think about it the better I like the idea for if you get the East Coast you get convoy duty and as things are now set up, the ships are to convoy but they are not to fire a single shot. Well that leaves you completely at the mercy of German raiders and I don't think that's funny. If I were a man I guess I'd want to fight, I don't know but I sure wouldn't want to go be a target for a little German gunnery practice.

I've always thought men like to fight but François [Novitski, Mariah's husband] says that isn't so, that they're more afraid of what other men will think and of what women will think. How silly. I'll bet there are very few women alive who will willingly let their men go to war and hardly a man alive who doesn't envy the man who doesn't have to go.

When I returned to Greenwich, there was a letter awaiting me that Van had written on 23 July 1941:

About the only thing that is definite is that, barring a miscarry of plans, my relief is practically here. Now to get him on the ship and get me off before anything happens. The date of his arrival or my departure is still unknown and of course I don't have any orders or anything yet and won't get them until the last minute. However I figure I should be relieved in two or three weeks unless the Nippers become ambitious, thus ruining all the plans that now exist. If conditions were a little more settled I could be more definite and probably hazard a good guess as to dates and so forth. So my lovely, perhaps the next word I have for you will be that which I've been wanting to say and you've been wanting to hear for all these lonely months. Let's hope so.

Leaving here will be sort of a frying-pan-to-the-fire move I presume but it will be worth it a hundred times over because I will be getting back to you and that is the only thing which I am interested in doing. We have so much living to do darling. It is going to be so wonderful being where I belong, at your side. All these months I've thought of nothing except how deliciously happy we were during that short while and how even more glorious it would be when I got back to you. . . .

The worst mistake ever made in the whole personnel situation was not to send us back on time. It isn't so much the length of time people have to stay, it's the idea that one can't count on going home when he is supposed to that upsets everyone. I will be sort of mad all my life about this deal I'm afraid.

My own morale was at a low ebb. The last thing I wanted to do was add to Van's distress by writing him about it.

Our experiences were very similar to those of Jim and Jane Shaw's. We had announced our engagements the same day. We had been married in the same church by the same minister. Jane and I had worn the same Mary Queen of Scots caps (mine was lace and Jane's was satin) from which our veils fell. Even the potted palms that lined the aisle were the identical ones at both ceremonies. Jane and I were both Army brats; Jim and Van were both class of 1936 at

Annapolis. We were all separated that same year. Jim and Van were both held over in Manila getting their late relief orders in the same crazy way to sail on the *Coolidge* back to the States together. Our lives were soon to enmesh inextricably, for Jim and Van were to become shipmates.

A Little Heaven

"Beper. Arriving Sept. 5th or 6th. Kilud Voper." That was the incredible cable that had me beside myself with excitement. ("Beper" meant "Bettsy Perkins," "Kilud" was the five-letter code word that meant "Kiss, I love you, darling," and "Voper" meant "VanOstrand Perkins.")

On getting the cable from Van, I called friends in Washington to find out what his orders would be. He was to go to a new type of ship being built in Kearny, New Jersey, later to be outfitted at the Brooklyn Navy Yard—the USS *Atlanta*. No word on what his job would be, but obviously that meant finding a place to live halfway between the two facilities.

For the first time I took matters in my own hands. Easy access to both places was of utmost importance. Looking at a map of Greater New York, it became apparent that Greenwich Village was ideal. I called a real estate agent and the next morning tore into New York to look at several apartments near the Seventh Avenue subway (a quick shot to the Brooklyn Navy Yard) and two blocks from the Hudson station (the fastest way to Kearny at the time). I was unable to rent the apartment I found, as married women could not rent in their own name. Fortunately, the manager took a shine to me. She let me put down a deposit and promised to hold the very one I liked until Van could get home and sign the rental agreement.

The afternoon I arranged for the apartment at 95 Christopher Street, I whizzed over to Macy's and bought two lamps, a wing chair, a couch, and a lounge chair for Van. I had already purchased a bed, which was at Mother's. I ordered curtains for the living room to go with the rug Van had bought in China and went home exhausted, though thoroughly pleased with my day's accomplishments.

The next day I discussed with Mum and Mom Perkins having a wedding reception for our Greenwich friends when Van came home. Somehow I packed my things, including evening gowns, should we stay in San Francisco for a few days. I went to see Doc Amos, who gave me a bottle of Alurate, a mild liquid sedative, to calm me for the next two weeks, and I boarded the train for Portland, Oregon, to visit my bridesmaid, Tekla.

Arriving in San Francisco on August twenty-fifth, I went to the Fairmont Hotel, where, with the help of our friends the Rosses, a most gorgeous suite of rooms awaited me, complete with a balcony overlooking San Francisco Bay.

My letter to Van had described all I had done in New York and what his orders were to be and asked him to address mail to me at the Rosses' chicken ranch in Napa. His letter of the twenty-third, written from Honolulu, was waiting for me at the hotel. He was just bubbling over:

We arrived here a couple of hours ago, at the crack of dawn, and your wonderful letter was waiting for me. Everything you wrote sounds wonderful too. As a matter of fact I am so excited I am in a complete dither. As I feel this way now here in Honolulu just thinking about you I will be in fine shape the morning we arrive in San Fran.

The news about the *Atlanta* sounds too good. I guess we will get our break at last. From all you write I think the apartment in New York is the best bet. I don't think much of the one year lease in spite of the A & N clause [the Army-Navy clause that nullified a lease in the case of orders elsewhere] but I suppose—and remember—that practically everything in the States is rented that way and I'd certainly rather rent an apt. in N.Y. for a year than something in N.J. for a year which we know we wouldn't want. . . .

We had a day and two nights in Hong Kong and the same in Shanghai. I didn't enjoy either stop as much as I might have because I was so impatient to be on my way. . . .

We leave here at midnight or shortly there after and expect to arrive before noon on the twenty-eighth. Perhaps we will be in by eight or nine. See if you can get a pass from the Pres. Line Office to get aboard. I don't know how strict they are but I hate to delay our meeting one minute.

Bumping into a friend from the Manila days who was also in San Francisco to meet her husband, I suggested we join forces, sharing my room and access to information. I called Dad's friend, who was in command at the Presidio, to find out if the *Coolidge* was on time and to get passes for us to board the ship. The general could only tell us one thing—the ship had left Honolulu. To calm ourselves, we had a sip of the Alurate, Doc A's mild sedative.

Then we started our vigil on the balcony of my suite. Every time we saw a ship's lights moving in the harbor, we would call the duty officer at the Presidio to check on the *Coolidge*. Then we would have another little sip of the Alurate. Finally, at about six in the morning we were told by the general's aide that the ship would dock at eight. We dashed to dress, grabbed a bit of breakfast, took a sip of Alurate, and hailed a taxi. By seven we were standing at the barrier. No ship yet, so we had another little sip of Alurate.

Then a great low blast of the ship's whistle as she nosed around the corner of the dock shed. We had another little sip of Alurate. We had to stay behind the barrier while the lines were secured, but finally the guard said we could go out on the dock. Lord, we could see our lads now, leaning over the rail waving and shouting. We had a little sip of Alurate. Out came the gangway, and I dashed on board into the arms of my darling husband and promptly collapsed. Too much Alurate! I do not know how my friend fared; she had ceased to be of concern to me.

I will never forget those two hours, nor will I forget the utter joy it was to see Van, to touch him, to hug him. Van, whom I had been married to for three weeks and then once again separated from for more than three-quarters of a year. It was perhaps not too amazing that my knees shook with excitement, but to have me all but pass out must have been most bewildering to my new husband, who knew nothing about Alurate! Van plied me with coffee and revived me enough to disembark.

By the time we got back to the hotel, the staff had not only changed the bed and tidied up but also left a great bowl of gardenias on the coffee table, a bucket of ice with a champagne bottleneck protruding from it, and two champagne glasses on a silver tray. The porter deposited Van's luggage in our bedroom, Van tipped him, and as the door closed, Van turned and took me in his arms. As he bent to kiss me I was seized by a sneezing fit. Gardenias. It was the heady concentration of their glorious perfume, and all I could do was point to them and gasp, "Gar-ketchoo-dean-kerchoo-yahs-kerchoo." Van removed the bowl to the balcony.

Poor darling, first his wife almost passes out, no kiss. Then she has a sneezing fit, no kiss. We had a glass of champagne and at *long last* he was able to kiss his bride, who returned his kiss tenfold.

Van still had to report in to the Twelfth Naval District, pick up his orders, and sign leave papers. We were to stay in San Francisco for a few days. We went tea dancing, which was the popular thing to do at cocktail time before going to dinner. Van had arranged with Jim Shaw that we join forces with him and his sister Betty Lou. Jane, in Alabama, had decided not to meet the ship. Jim envied Van's having his wife right there on the dock when the ship pulled in. But never mind, he was home, and it would not be long before he and beautiful Jane were together again, and he thought how lucky he was to have come out of the Orient before the pot boiled over.

For the first time I was really conscious of meeting Jim. We must have met at the club in Manila. I had found out a lot about him from our many mutual friends but had barely remembered him. Van introduced me to this seemingly glum fellow, saying, "Betts, I think you know my good friend and classmate." In an aside to me he added, "He has a wonderful sense of humor."

If Jim had a sense of humor, he certainly kept it hidden that evening. Van and I held hands and laughed and danced. As was then considered only polite, Van danced with Betty Lou and I danced with Jim. I hardly said more than "Thank you" to him.

"You're welcome, thank you," he replied.

"You're more than welcome."

Hardly my idea of a great sense of humor.

That ended our conversation, and I went back to chattering about the airplane trip back home, the wedding reception awaiting us, and where we were going to live. All this punctuated with "Isn't that nifty, sweetheart?" and "What an absolutely divine time we'll have." Both "nifty" and "divine" were the latest East Coast "in" thing to say. I'm sure I sounded and acted utterly juvenile.

"We have reservations at Omar Khayyam's for dinner at 7:45," Van told Jim. "Betts says it's the most wonderful, exotic place to eat in San Francisco. Would you and Betty Lou care to join us?" Jim's reply was brief and to the point: "After three weeks on the *Coolidge* with nothing to do but eat, I just want to go walk on terra firma with my sister. See you on the *Atlanta,* friend!"

That was the first I knew that both Jim and Van were going to the same ship. I had been jabbering so much I had not even been mannerly enough to ask about Jim's plans or orders. As for Betty Lou, I was not my customary polite self. I was so excited and wrapped up in all my wonderful plans that other than the barest expressions of courtesy I do not think I addressed a single word to her. It took her a long time to decide I was an all-right sort, for which I don't blame her. I was unconscionably neglectful of her. I was, in fact, insufferable.

Omar Khayyam's was superb. George Mardikian, the owner, primed by the Rosses, gave us a dinner fit for royalty. Once again gardenias had to be removed, this time from the middle of the table. The waiter reappeared with a bud vase of white butterfly orchids. No wonder the restaurant was so famous. We hit all the high and low spots San Francisco had to offer, and we talked three years' worth. We would just look at each other and then we would laugh for pure joy. We were going to the East Coast. Van had escaped from the building tensions of the Far East, and the future was going to be wonderful. I could hardly wait to take up housekeeping.

The "sleeper" plane back home was twelve hours of misery. We slept in narrow berths separated from each other. We landed four times, and as the cabin was not pressurized, we woke on each landing with wild earaches. The cure was to hold your nose and blow with all your might to equalize the pressure in your ears. We slept fitfully and arrived in New York exhausted, to the distress of the entire family, who had come to meet us. As an added surprise they had brought along Bini and our little green convertible, which Van had never seen.

Van had not driven in three years, and we did a bit of interesting weaving around before he got the hang of the new car. By the time we got home we were sailing along in great shape. A good thing, too, for though we had landed at eleven in the morning West Coast time, it was midafternoon East Coast time, and there were already people calling to see Van and welcome us home. It was past midnight before we climbed into the big sleigh bed in Van's old room, kissed each other goodnight, and conked out cold.

We were awakened early next morning with a cheery "Get up, young Perkins. Tonight is your wedding reception and you have lots to do."

Van answered sleepily, "Like what? I can't think of anything more important than sleep."

"You need to get your white uniform unpacked and pressed," his mother replied. "You need to get Betts flowers. I thought you'd like to get them yourself this time rather than for me to get them for you. You should apply for a license to drive as your international license will expire shortly. And you need a hair cut. My, that does sound motherly, doesn't it? I hope you don't mind, Betts dear, but I'll have to get used to the fact there's another woman in Van's life." We all had a good laugh over that one. But she was right.

The family's wedding reception was being held at six that evening, and we were to dress in our wedding finery. Van's white uniform was somewhere in his bags, packed a month earlier. Our best bet was to get it to the Chinese laundry downtown for a rush job—not all that easy, as whites had to be heavily starched. Then to the flower shop, where we decided to have a wristlet made of butterfly orchids and stephanotis. This was a better idea than to carry the family psalter, which would be a nuisance. While we were about it, Van picked out corsages for both mothers and boutonnieres for both fathers. In fact, we went wild in the flower shop.

On arriving at my family's house we were presented with a giant anchor of red, white, and blue carnations, the top even taller than Van. Stretched across this floral offering was a banner that read, in large gold letters, "SUCCESS!" A tribute from sister Nane and her husband Joe, it was the centerpiece of our second wedding reception and, after three years of separation (bar three weeks), a most appropriate sentiment.

What a grand affair the reception was. The furniture in the big hall was pushed out of the way and the rugs removed. A small orchestra played softly while we greeted more than a hundred people. Van looked spectacular in his "whites." Both of us were bemused by the enthusiastic reception we were getting. Then the orchestra livened up and everyone danced until dinner was announced.

There, in the middle of the table, was a gorgeous wedding cake, our second, made by Mother and Dad's Filipino butler and general factotum, Iraneo, who was also a fine pastry chef. He had fashioned a splendid rendition of the Army-Navy Club, where our Manila reception was held. It took a bit of courage for us to take Van's sword in hand and slice into that particular cake.

I have never forgotten Van's toast to me. "Betts and I were separated for two years before we could be married," he said. "I would have waited forever, if I'd had to, to marry my beautiful wife. Thank God we don't have to wait any more. Here then is my toast to my darling. May she always be as happy as she is tonight." I have no idea what I said in reply. Van just smiled and, leaning down, kissed me roundly, at which everyone clapped. My heart was in my eyes, and I had to swallow hard to keep from crying for joy.

Over the next two weeks, Van and I talked at length about the Japanese situation. He told me that our Navy would head to join up with the Dutch and British Far Eastern fleets if the Japanese attacked the Philippines, something he now thought was inevitable. He said he was thankful to get out before the ax fell and told me how hard it had been to leave his friends, some of whom he felt he might not see again. He was so glad he would face the Germans rather than the Japanese if he had to go to war, because you could anticipate the German mind, but the Japanese mind he thought incomprehensible.

We spent a good part of our leave romping in the woods with Bini Number Two or taking him to visit friends. Van soon had the pup beautifully trained and so devoted to his master that he would wriggle between us if Van came nearer to me than Bini thought seemly. Part of his training was learning to walk on a leash so we could take him to live in the city. Persuading him to "go" on cement was a challenge—only grass, hard to find in the city, would do.

What fun those carefree days were. Van said, "God will be good to us," and for those few weeks God gave us more than a little heaven.

Except Nurse a Baby

OCTOBER 1941—SEPTEMBER 1942

The *Atlanta* was being built in Kearny, New Jersey, at the federal shipbuilding yard when Van and Jim reported for duty. Immediately Jim was sent to Washington, D.C., to gunnery school, as he was to be in the Gunnery Department. Arriving in that fair city, Jim and Jane lucked into a nice little house for their six-week stay. Gunnery was Jim's greatest "in-Navy" interest, so he enjoyed the school very much. He enjoyed life with Jane even more. Eight months without her had distressed him mightily. Walking with her in Rock Creek Park or going dancing was bliss indeed. Their leave in Alabama and Minnesota had been relaxing, but with all the family gathered, they had not had much time to themselves. Now they had what seemed like a real honeymoon.

Van, who was to be in the Damage Control and First-Lieutenant Departments, was sent to fire-fighting school right there in Kearny. His training involved working his way down from the top of a high tower, an inferno of burning oil, using hoses with spray nozzles to put out the flames and learning to use breathing apparatus in the acrid black smoke. Evenings he would come home to the apartment in Greenwich Village and do his darndest to get the smoke smell out of his hair.

Fire-fighting school was only the beginning for Van. He needed to study blueprints of the ship in order to be totally familiar with its many compartments and machines. Eventually he was much more knowledgeable about plumbing than he had ever wanted to be. He spent a great deal of time studying the various machines in the tool shop, where everything for fixing and replacing broken parts could be fashioned. I was fascinated with what his job entailed. Certainly it did not resemble anything he had done aboard the *Whipple*. I asked him to tell me about all he would be doing.

"Well," he said, "a naval officer is supposed to be able to do anything 'except nurse a baby.' One of my professors at the Naval Academy told a group of us just that when we were griping about learning something we thought beneath our lofty positions as midshipmen. I guess my job is the literal translation of that dictum. When the ship is just operating, the job is housekeeping, plumbing, carpentry, tool-and-die making, supply stowing, fueling, etcetera. All supplies need to be evenly distributed to keep the ship in trim. The first lieutenant keeps the ship shipshape, and I'm the assistant first lieutenant. Probably the most important part of the job is to supervise the stowing of those supplies, ammunition, and fuel, often to be adjusted under way—a tricky job. Also, I've just found out I will have to work with the doctors on health maintenance and first aid matters."

"Well, then, what exactly is a damage control officer? Is that sort of a wartime job?"

"Sure, but it's really necessary anytime. Fires do break out on a ship, and I'd have to organize a fire-fighting party. A big wave could hit and damage the ship; my department would be responsible for fixing that. A ship could run aground, and we'd be the ones to help patch her and get her to a dry dock to fix her." He paused. "Do you want a Coke or something?" he asked me, which meant he wanted a beer. "Thanks, yes, Rabbit. What about wartime?" I felt it imperative to know what it would be like if war actually happened, something that now seemed inevitable. When he came back with the beer and Coke I pushed him to tell me more. "Let's see, in wartime we'd go on with the usual housekeeping routines but we'd drill a lot in techniques for being hit under fire. Obviously fire is a main hazard. It involves many kinds of damage, often to vital parts of the ship. Knowing how to cut away metal would be a technique that needs to be learned. Get the idea, darling?"

Out in Manila, Van had already told me a good bit about celestial navigation in the open ocean. He had shown me how to read and interpret weather maps, something he did every morning, just as others did the crossword puzzle in the daily paper. He had told me about being a communications officer and how he had received a Letter of Commendation for getting a perfect score on a gunnery practice.

"How are you going to use all the past experience you've had in your present job?" I asked.

"Being a qualified watch officer means I stand watches on the bridge, four hours on, eight hours off. When it's my watch, I handle the ship. Betts, you're a sailor, you know what air and water currents do to a sailboat. You know how to tell what direction you're sailing by the sun and the time of day. That's rudimentary navigation. Well, I need to know a lot more than that—things like how fast the ship can turn, how much inertia is involved in stopping her, all that sort of stuff. You also have to know how to give orders to the helm. You don't stand on a bridge with a 'how to' book in your hand. You just do it from what you've been trained to do throughout your career. That's totally separate from my daily job on the ship."

I began to understand that these young officers, one of whom was my husband, were indeed a remarkable cadre. Of course a captain gave the overall orders and was ultimately responsible for the performance of the ship, but it was the younger officers who were the unsung heroes, the ones who kept the ship safe through the night when the captain was sleeping or by day when he was working or eating. Each officer was responsible for the efficiency of the men under him, and for their well-being to boot. In fact, I could see that it was an awesome job. My heart swelled with pride that I was married to such a man, and I told him so.

"Don't be silly, Betts, that's just my job. I notice you don't use a cookbook to make delicious meals, and so far you haven't poisoned us. It's about the same. Come on, let's go have some fun. I'm tired of Navy talk. I'll tell you more another time. Let's go dancing, Wee Rabbit." That was my first lesson in damage control but not my last.

Meanwhile, Jim and Jane moved up from Washington to an apartment on Brooklyn Heights, a stone's throw from the Navy yard and not far from the Seventh Avenue subway, which had a stop near our door. That made it easy for Jim to get to Kearny. He would get off at the Sheridan Square stop and join Van, Pat McEntee, and Ted Lyster, who had apartments near us in the Village. All four of them would go via the Hudson tube to Kearny. That did not last long, as the ship was soon launched and towed around to the Brooklyn Navy Yard to be outfitted. Ted Lyster's ship, the *Juneau,* was not long in joining her sister ship, the *Atlanta.* The two cruisers were tied up alongside each other, so the morning routine was reversed. Pat, Ted, and Van would take the subway to Jim's stop, then all four would walk the short distance to the yard.

Navy life causes women to make friends in a hurry. In a community in which a woman's only contacts are the wives of shipmates who will soon go to sea, cementing a friendship whose physical closeness may last only a very short time becomes imperative. Jane and I hit it off immediately, for we had in common not only our two almost identical weddings in Manila but also many other coincidences, including the date our engagements were announced. And we were both Army brats. Then we found out that her parents, my parents, Jim's parents, and Van's parents were all married in 1912. That one made us laugh hilariously.

Neither her family nor mine was exactly enthusiastic about our marrying Navy husbands, as they knew we would lead lives much harder than those led by Army wives. We both, however, had an understanding of military integrity as averse to civilian attitudes, where a beautiful place to live and a nice income gave you status. Neither of us measured success in terms of money—honor, duty, country having been drummed into us since childhood. We both had been brought up to think we should care for the youngsters under our husband's command. That was part of our job.

Jane was as talented as I; poetry was her forte, but she also was an accomplished sewer. She amazed me when she made Betty Lou a wool overcoat and tweed suit. She thought my embroidery was something she would like to learn, so I taught her a few crewelwork stitches and the basics of smocking, and in return she showed me how to bind off button holes and insert zippers. We became good friends very quickly, for we could chatter about so much we had in common. That gave us an unusual kinship.

In no time, parties and dances commenced in earnest and our small group of Navy wives became good friends. Only six of the younger officers were married, so Jane Shaw, Betty McEntee, Helen Hall, Stephanie Wulff, Ellie Broughton, and myself were the nucleus of the young *Atlanta* crowd. Tek and Ted Lyster partied with us, because Tek was my dear friend and bridesmaid and Ted was one of Van's ushers, a friend and neighbor, and Jim's and Van's classmate. Lord, we did have fun that fall.

Jim was increasingly proud of Jane. She was reserved in a crowd but stood out wherever she went. It was obvious to him that his young friends liked and admired her. As for himself, he knew the *Atlanta* was the newest, fastest, handsomest ship in the U.S. Navy. Captain Jenkins, her commanding officer, was gracious, kind, and thoroughly capable, all the qualities of a fine leader, and her executive officer, Cdr. Dallas Emory, was an evenhanded, efficient man who took the brunt of unpopular decisions without flinching. Jim had himself a happy ship and was mightily pleased with life.

Van and Jim gravitated toward each other. The bond between all four of us grew stronger by the day. Many times just the four of us would go someplace. We liked the ballet and going to hear Eddy Duchin play the piano at the Waldorf; the Philharmonic and the Coffee House Theatre drew us. At the latter we watched movies from the "loveseat balcony" and drank "demitasse" in the lobby during intermission. Elegance, New York style, was our hallmark.

Weekends, if he was not on duty, Van and I would go to Greenwich or go skiing, a sport at which Van excelled and I was far from good (though Van said my determination to learn was "commendable," a nice way of saying I was hopeless). Skiing was the one activity in which Jim and Jane, the southerner, did not get involved, though they were game to try most anything else, including going to the Bronx Zoo and the top of the Empire State Building. Jim continued to act in a rather reserved manner around me, while Van kept right on telling me he considered Jim the funniest man he knew. Van himself had a droll sense of humor, so I respected his opinion and kept watching for evidence of Jim's super brand.

Six of us, the Shaws, the Lysters, Van, and I, decided to go to the Army-Navy game in Philadelphia, the first the lads had attended since graduation. It was Tek and Jane's first Army-Navy ever, and it was the first time I had ever sat on the Navy side. I yelled indiscriminately for both teams, much to Van's amusement and the disgust of the people around us.

One outraged gent leaned forward to say, "Can't you shut that woman up?"

"Did you ever try shutting up an Army brat?" Van answered.

Jane was much more sedate; her father was an Army doctor, so she did not have ties with West Point as I did. Jim, however, was the most vocal I had ever heard him. In fact, he was positively boisterous. He had been manager of the football team at Annapolis, and he took the game personally.

After the game, Van and I had to put in an appearance at Mother and Dad's annual après-game cocktail party held at the hotel where my family took a suite for the purpose. We asked the Shaws and Lysters to go with us, as we did not want to be odd men out at an Army party after Navy had lost the game. Thank heavens they accepted, as we took an awful ribbing from Dad's classmates. One obnoxious old fellow was going at me hammer and tongs about being a traitor by marrying into the Navy, until Jim Shaw's quick wit, at long last apparent to me, saved the situation. Only his eyes sparkling with humor gave him away; otherwise, his face was innocently deadpan as he addressed the general: "It doesn't make much difference what happened on the field today, but it is obvious that the better team won when it comes to the distaff side, don't you agree, General?"

The old boy gulped, hurrumphed, and replied, "I bid you goodnight, Mr. What's-Your-Name," which we guessed was supposed to squelch Jim but only served to make all six of us giggle. We soon took our departure, bound for a Navy party, but not before thanking Mum and Dad for inviting us. Dad, who loved to make speeches, called for quiet. "I wish to call to your attention," he said, "that I am the proud father-in-law of a fine 'Navy file,' who, with two of his stalwart classmates, Annapolis 1936, has braved the inner sanctum of the class of West Point 1906. We owe them a cheer for their brave action—as we speed them on their way!" As we scurried out to the elevator he shouted, "Better luck next year!"

Oh, My God

Friday afternoon, December fifth, Van came off the ship. I met him with the little convertible, top down, Bini standing with his head out the window. We were off to Greenwich to spend two nights in the big sleigh bed. Saturday night we would go to the first dance of the Christmas season, and then Sunday morning we would take a good long walk in the woods before a gathering of both families for luncheon at Craggy. We were not even going to have to help prepare lunch, as pretty Jeanie Mullin, who helped Mom occasionally, was going to cook and serve the whole shebang.

On Sunday, when Jeanie was ready to serve lunch, she came to the living room and in her own most formal manner announced, "Well folks, soup's on!" We trooped in to luncheon and were totally enjoying good food, good conversation, and a glowing fire in the ancient stone fireplace when Jeanie burst through the door, her face red with excitement, shouting, "They just bombed a precious stone! They just bombed a precious stone!"

"Who bombed what precious stone? What are you talking about? Calm down, Jeanie, you're not making sense," Mom said.

"I don't know who they are, but they bombed it and it's awful and . . ." She trailed off as we dashed for the radio in the living room.

"Repeat, Japan has just bombed Pearl Harbor. All officers and men will report to their ships and stations in uniform immediately." We stared at each other stupidly. "Oh my God, war," someone said. Again it came over the radio, the voice now reaching a higher, nearly hysterical pitch: "I repeat. The Japanese have attacked Pearl Harbor! There is terrible damage. All officers and men will report to their ships and stations immediately, in uniform. Repeat, in uniform!"

The last "in uniform" galvanized Van. He shot upstairs and delved into his closet for the only piece of uniform he had out in the country, his old midshipman dress hat (fortunately with blue cap cover as a white cap cover would have been discolored after so many years of storage). He yelled at me to pack our bags while he rounded up our dog, who was romping in the woods. In fifteen minutes we were in the car, our families standing stony-faced in the driveway.

We hit the Merritt Parkway going seventy-five miles an hour. As we passed the New York state border, a motorcycle cop came up behind us, siren screeching. We started to pull over, but he shot ahead of us and signaled for us to follow him. Then he thought better of it and, waving us to stop, came alongside and asked, "Where am I taking you?"

A sensible question. "I'm reporting to my ship," Van replied, "but this cap is the only piece of uniform I had in the country, so I must get to 95 Christopher Street, Greenwich Village, and then to the Navy yard in Brooklyn."

"Well you jus' folla me an' I'll get ya to your uniform and your ship too an' don't worry none about lights an' toll booths an' things like that, see, an' I'll take care of it. Come on!" Off we sped, siren blaring whenever an obstacle arose.

"Good Lord, Van darling," I said, "what are we doing careening along like this to report to a ship that's not going anywhere. Can't we slow down?"

"I wouldn't deprive this nice young man of the chance to do something for his country," he answered. "Besides, this is the first and presumably the last time in my life I can go thirty miles an hour over the speed limit, shoot the red lights and break every law in the books with the aid of 'the arm of the law.' I'm having a ball! Just hold on tight, and don't let Bini fall out."

We drew up in front of our apartment, gave Bini to the doorman, and went up in the painfully slow elevator. Van changed into his blues, dropping his "civvies" where he stood, while I looked for his black socks. They could not be found, so charcoal gray had to do. Good to his word, the cop had kept watch over the car, illegally parked, and again we took off, Bini quivering beside us.

Lower New York was almost empty. There was a strange hush about the place, and not just because it was Sunday. What sky we saw, among the skyscrapers, was murky gray. The few people who were about were walking heads down. The whole aspect was eerie. We had worried so long about war, and now that it was here, a sort of lassitude descended on us. Once Van reached over and squeezed my hand, and that little gesture was reassuring.

Van was deposited at the ship. Returning to Greenwich Village, I parked the car in the garage, took Bini to our apartment, and hunkered down with a book to await instructions. Realizing I was looking at the book upside down, I stirred myself, picked up Van's clothes, put them in the hamper, and headed for the kitchen to make supper. It seemed eons before I heard Van's familiar tap on the door, then his key turning in the lock. There he was. He had "reported in uniform" but been told there was no point in his sticking around as he was not on duty and the ship was not ready to go to sea anyway.

We ate a bit of supper and we held hands across the table. Just touching each other seemed the only real thing in a world gone awry for us once again. As in Manila, we decided to make our time together, however short it might be, happy, not dwelling on the future and what would or could happen. Just as we had done every night since living in the Village, we walked Bini out by the park in Sheridan Square. When we got back to the apartment, we talked about giving the party we had planned for the *Atlanta*'s skipper and his wife, Captain and Mrs. Jenkins.

Finally, when we climbed into bed, we clung to each other and talked about having a baby. Van asked, "Do you think you're strong enough to be able to take having a baby without me around? I think we can be pretty sure of the ship being away in Europe or even possibly the Pacific, so I won't be here to care for you."

"Van, there is nothing I want more than to have your child, more so now that you are going off to war. It seems imperative to me that we have a child, for should anything happen to you, I would have somebody to love that would be you and me together. Emotionally I'm strong enough to take anything so long as I know you love me."

Not until early next morning did we really know what this war was going to be like. We turned on the radio at breakfast and got the first reports of the extent and enormity of the damage at Pearl Harbor: our fleet devastated, our planes bombed and strafed on the ground. Besides that, Japan had also attacked Hong Kong, Guam, Wake, and the Philippines, where planes were destroyed on the ground, and the U.S. Army, woefully inadequate, would soon be backed onto Corregidor, the island fortress. It was worse than just Pearl Harbor. All our bases in the Pacific were gone, or about to collapse, with nothing to stop the Japanese forces save the little fleet in the Philippine Archipelago that now had to make a run for the Dutch Indies, an almost hopeless task. The seventh of December in Hawaii was the eighth of December across the International Dateline, where our other bases were located. Within twelve hours Japan had attacked us simultaneously with devastating effect all across the Pacific.

"Dear God," Van said. "Do you realize what that means on the China Station? Those pitiful little ships with no big fleet to back them up? Our friends still out there will not have much of a chance against those murdering bastards! I've got to get to the ship right now."

"What do you want me to do? Go ahead with the party for Captain Jenkins, go to Greenwich, or just wait for further developments?"

"That last, my girl, is what I want you to do. Listen to the president's emergency speech, write a list for the party, keep busy, and I'll call you as soon as I know something."

Off Van went, this time in proper uniform, which he was to wear in public for the rest of his war, the first of many changes to come.

Never before had I felt lonesome or afraid in our pretty little apartment, but as I listened, all by myself, while the president declared the United States of America at war with the Axis powers, the whole colorful apartment turned gray and empty.

"A day of infamy that will go down in history"—one word spun in my head. Infamy! Infamy! Infamy!

"Stop this," I chastised myself. "Write the list for the party, call Tekla or Helen. Clean the apartment. Just get going. Stop wallowing!" Keeping very busy would be my crutch from now on.

Immediately, watch standing was doubled up and the Brooklyn Navy Yard accelerated work on the ship, so much so that now when Van got home he would be exhausted. His particular job was perhaps even harder than jobs in some of the other departments, as he had so many different activities at this juncture. It seemed he was constantly plagued about the plumbing, and in particular the captain's "head." That is not the very best piece of plumbing to have nonfunctional when you are the junior officer in charge. Granted, the yard was still working on it, but it would be Van, the junior control and repair officer, who was notified and would have to light a fire under the yard supervisor. The pace picked up to such an extent that nerves were taut and tempers short. Fortunately, Captain Jenkins was a saint, and Van had a sunny nature, so they managed the plumbing fiascoes without too much commotion.

The day before our party for the Jenkinses, I went grocery shopping. Coming out of the shop, I ran right into Van, emerging from the Seventh Avenue subway station, resplendent in uniform. I started to hand him one of my bags but stopped, abashed, when he said, "Betts darling, I can't carry packages in uniform, you know. Sorry, Bunny, I feel awfully rude letting you carry that load and me empty-handed. Maybe you better walk way ahead of me, then it won't look so awful. What a silly rule! Supposedly, it looks unmilitary. Personally, I think it looks ungentlemanly. Trot along darling, I'll catch up with you at the apartment entrance." Young reserves saw no sense at all in this convention, and soon everywhere one looked men in uniform were unable to return a salute as their arms were full of packages.

The appointed hour for the party finally arrived. The apartment was festive, flowers in our only two vases and all the lights ablaze—as yet no blackout. Our buffet dinner was ready and waiting in the closet-sized kitchen. As our guests were arriving, one ensign came through the door carrying two dozen gladiola. I shoved the flowers into Van's arms and whispered, "Quick, stick these in water while I greet Captain and Mrs. Jenkins." In seconds he was back, mission accomplished.

By now we were a large crowd—twenty-six people. A very handsome group indeed, and none handsomer than Jim and willowy Jane in her black-and-white outfit. She was always beautifully dressed, and with her dark eyes, fair skin, and almost black hair, and being so tall, she was invariably magnetic.

During the after-dinner coffee, the captain asked where the bathroom was and excused himself. In seconds he was back. "There seems to be an obstruction in the facilities, Perkins. I'm not sure how you'll handle this one," he said.

"What's wrong, sir?"

"Well, there seems to be a large flower arrangement in that part of your bathroom most interesting to me at this moment."

When the laughter died down and the master plumber had removed the flowers to the bathtub, Captain Jenkins retired once again with a nod at Van. "You wish all your plumbing problems were that easy and smelled as fresh, don't you, young man?" he said.

That was our last party, and a smashing success it was, despite the flower incident, or perhaps because of it. The fact was, we had become more than a ship's company. We had become a family. The men liked one another, the wives were good friends, we all had great pride in the ship. Underlying the pride and the friendship was a strong interdependence. The wives knew they must put on a courageous front and that they would need one another's support in the months to come. The men, of course, were to be a close team. It gave them comfort that their wives had formed such bonds.

This was to be our own first Christmas together in our own home. We had spent it together four years ago, when I was visiting my sister Nane in Manila and we were on the edge of our love for each other. Two miserable Christmases had passed since then. On the last one we were married and apart, but now we were going to have our very own Christmas tree in our very own home. We went hog-wild. I bought Van a velvet smoking jacket and slippers on which I embroidered his initials in gold thread, outlined in red. They were elegant, outrageously extravagant, and totally silly, as he was about to go to war and could not use them in the ship except off duty in his own quarters. I bought him a new briar pipe, a handsome mahogany humidor, and enough of his favorite tobacco to fill it to the brim. Then I went to Tiffany's for a gold strap to match the wristwatch I had given him for a wedding present the year before. While there, I spied a very small gold rabbit tie tack and included that.

We both had stockings to be filled, and I had a ball finding silly things. For a topper, I went to the FAO Schwartz toy store and bought a small white rabbit with long ears as near as I could find to the one I had owned since I was a child, the one that caused all the rabbit business in our dealing with each other. It was a good-luck talisman to take to war.

As to Van, he went totally overboard. He bought me a silver fox jacket and a set of Revereware pots and pans. He went to Saks 5th Avenue, where the saleslady persuaded him I should have a black nightgown. She brought out one sheer one after another for his approval, and he kept rejecting them on the grounds that I was modest beyond belief. Finally, she found one that had lace on the top; the bottom was flowing, silky satin. Of course it was the most expensive one of the bunch, but he thought it perfect and so did I. He found a ridiculous pair of high-heeled mules in black satin, trimmed in marabou. I looked a perfect tart in the outfit, but we both loved the whole idea of my being so out of character. As though that was not enough, he then ordered a green orchid corsage for me to wear on Christmas Day in the country.

Van was on duty Christmas Eve, but some kind lad relieved him, and he arrived home at four in the morning, my first and best Christmas present. We had the most luxurious breakfast: cheese omelette "à la Mama Poulard"; homemade sage sausages; biscuits hot out of the oven, filled with marmalade; and, for an encore, grapefruit laced with honey and sherry, popped under the broiler, then served with a red cherry and a mint leaf in the center to give it a Christmas touch.

We opened our stockings and presents with Christmas carols playing on the Victrola and our very own tree twinkling with lights and topped by a tinsel angel I had made out of gold and silver paper. Once we were through with our own celebration, we headed for the country, I in the silver fox jacket with Bini tucked under my arm, Van smoking his new pipe. A Christmas never to forget!

We put war totally out of our minds for twenty-four glorious hours and did not even listen to the news. Van sang carols all the way to Greenwich. He loved to sing, and he had a marvelous time that Christmas at the top of his lungs.

The *Atlanta*'s commissioning was accompanied by speculation as to what the city of Atlanta would give the ship as a present. Usually it was a silver tea service, a punch bowl, or the like. Since the days of Secretary of the Navy Josephus Daniels (the old sourpuss who had declared liquor illegal aboard U.S. Navy vessels), punch bowls were unusual, so we guessed it would be a tea service or, perhaps, a large silver tray, suitably inscribed, from the ship's namesake city. Instead, the city presented a portrait of Margaret Mitchell, author of *Gone with the Wind*. Fine lady though she was, her portrait was not much appreciated by the ship's company. It was not long before the portrait was removed from the wardroom, along with all other combustibles, as a fire hazard. I have no idea where it was stored "for the duration." Perhaps it rests to this day in some navy "go-down," or perhaps it went back to Atlanta.

The *Atlanta* was a new kind of ship. Her purpose was to defend aircraft carriers. She was not much bigger than a modern destroyer; her armor plating was the lightest possible. She was built for speed and bristled with antiaircraft guns: four quadruple heavy machine-gun mounts and eight twin machine-gun mounts, sixteen 5-inch dual purpose ship-to-shore or antiaircraft guns—twin mounts they were, three forward, three aft, and two side mounts aft. She carried depth charges to drop over the stern and to fire by "Y" guns either side. Last, she carried two quadruple of torpedo tubes, four tubes each side. Even the most untutored eye could see that her design was graceful. To my artist's eye she was a thing of beauty and a true oceanic lady.

Now the ship's trials and training started in earnest. Going to sea for the first time unearthed many problems. There was new equipment to be broken in and new technology to understand—radar, for instance, then so hush-hush that no one even spoke the word. She was the fastest ship the Navy had ever built; no one mentioned her capability, but her crew needed to understand how she would handle at flank speed, however high that was. There was a powerful lot to learn before she would be ready to fight and so little time to learn it all.

Idle Gossip Sinks Ships

In midwinter, the *Atlanta* sailed Down East for her trial runs, to Casco Bay off Portland, Maine. Foul weather and Arctic gear was distributed to the crew; that, of course, meant North Atlantic duty. The wives were a bit apprehensive, but pleased to think the ship would put into American ports from time to time.

Jane Shaw, Stephanie Wulff, Ellie Broughton, Helen Hall, and I followed the ship to Portland. We took the train to Boston, but there was no bus or train from there to Portland until late the next morning. Nevertheless, we were determined to get rooms and be well ensconced at the Eastland Hotel before the ship got in. Not to waste a second's precious time now, Jane and I, the two who knew what we were really facing, threw caution to the wind and hired a willing cab driver for an outrageous price. We wedged five girls and all our bags into a vehicle built to ferry four people around the city and took off for Portland, a good two-hour drive, probably more. We did not care—just get us there.

Portland was asleep when we arrived. The old hotel was pretty run down and practically empty. The night clerk awoke from a doze as we excited girls burst into the lobby. He suggested that we take the top-floor rooms. "They are all equally fine, and the steam heat rises to the top so they are warmer" was his rationale. A nicety we would not have thought of on our own, it proved to be a godsend to us and our half-frozen sailormen just in from a frigid boat ride on Casco Bay.

There was not much to do in Portland. The Depression had laid the city low, but there was lots of cheap lobster to be had, and nice warm rooms in which to enjoy each other by night or for the girls to gather in by day. Of course, there were watches to stand and trial runs to be made, so not every night was blissful, but at least we were together some of the time and Van, Jim, and the other lads were still safe for a while longer.

A couple of weeks later the ship returned to Brooklyn. We headed back to New York, this time by train; but Helen and Jane left me at the hospital in Boston, for I ran into trouble with the baby I was carrying. Ellie Broughton got word, through Jack, to Van. Someone offered to take Van's watch, and Dallas Emory, the executive officer, gave Van emergency leave to come to Boston and bring me home. Van had orders from the doctor for me to stay in bed for a few days.

The whole group became involved in saving our baby. Jane, Helen, Stephanie, and Ellie took turns bringing meals to our apartment. The men took turns standing Van's watches, making it possible for him to get home every night. On Jim's nights on board, Jane would go for dinner in the wardroom and spend the evening in his cabin, vacated by his roommates so they could be alone. All the qualified officers sacrificed precious time for us, for which we were ever grateful.

Now came the hardest part thus far. The ship started intensive training in Sheepshead Bay. No one was allowed ashore, nor could the ladies go on board. We could see the ship if we traveled over to the beach at Coney Island, but that was just rubbing salt in the wound. No one knew what was going to happen next. There was speculation about the Arctic clothing. Was that a glorious hoax to keep the ship's destination a secret even from the officers, for fear someone would tell a wife who would gossip?

With just cause, the Navy had little faith in their men being able to keep a secret, even less in the wives. Rumors ran rampant on the ship, and of course the rumors got back to the wives, who whispered among themselves.

"Did you hear the ship is going to Iceland?"

"Well I think that's possible, but more likely they'll make the North Atlantic run, so I made wool socks for Dave."

"Wool socks—you're silly. Men don't know how to wash wool. They'll just throw them in the laundry to be ruined."

"It's an East Coast ship so they'll probably stay in the Atlantic, but they could get North Sea convoy duty. After all, we don't even know where 'home port' is yet, probably Norfolk."

The reserve officer's wives were used to knowing their men would be home for dinner, and they were used to talking about anything that came to mind. One of the Navy's posters bore the caption "Loose Lips Sink Ships." That seemed, in many of the wives' minds, to only apply to the men. The idea that *their* idle chatter could actually endanger all our husbands had not occurred to them.

From good authority it became clear that when the ship finally left Brooklyn it would head for Norfolk. Hearing that was to be home port, I decided to go there and maybe get one more glimpse of Van. As Mrs. Jenkins also planned to go down, I told Van I would drive her, and he approved.

That evening he came home with a change of mind. "I had lunch with Dad today and he doesn't think you should go to Norfolk," he said.

"Oh really, Van? Your Dad thinks I shouldn't go to Norfolk? Well, my dear husband, I love your Dad like my own, but I don't obey my father nor your father, nor in fact do I obey you unless you and I discuss the matter and you give me a good reason why I should or should not do something, and then if I agree with you that is what I do."

"Whoa, my little spitfire. We can talk calmly about this, can't we, Betts?"

"No, I can't talk calmly. This is very important. You told my family in Manila they could make suggestions but we'd do what we thought best on our own! Do you remember? Well, you and I discussed this trip and thought it worthwhile. Your father notwithstanding, I'm going!"

"You tickle me, Betts. You act so demure and fun-loving, but in fact you're a positive, independent, and thoroughly lovable character, and I mean character! You're right, however, we are an independent unit. Perhaps I shouldn't have said anything about Dad!"

"Yes, you should have. Our two dads have been giving us 'good advice' over a couple of martinis every evening, going the long way home from Wall Street, ever since we've been here. I don't want their advice, I want yours. Do I go to Norfolk, or don't I?"

"You go, Bunny, I agree with you. Even if I only see you for an hour, it will be worth it. Remember, it could happen I won't be able to get off the ship, but oh, Betts, I do want you there just in case."

That was the closest we had come to having a tiff, if you could even call it that.

We set up a code so Van could let me know where he would be. Mention Audie or Mrs. D. and the ship was in Honolulu. A. Mabini (our apartment in Manila) meant the far Pacific. Willow Blatchly (Van's English ex-girl-friend) meant England. The *Raleigh* (his old ship) meant the Mediterranean, and Elvira's Farm meant San Francisco. As to the dates, we could use a fictitious name. Starting with the month's first three letters and saying the day thus—"Martha's birthday is the sixteenth, please send her a card"—meant March sixteenth. We both wrote the code down in the back of our calendars to ensure I would be on hand whenever he came in, no matter what our fathers thought.

We already had a handful of code words that had passed a private message over the radio phone from Manila. I had KILUD printed on my stationery. Van often used that as a salutation when I went out to the ship the nights he was on duty. It would lack dignity to kiss me on the quarterdeck in front of the crew; hence, the word expressed the desire, and I would reply, "Kilud, Voper, over and out, Beper." If anyone overheard us they must have thought us either nuts or German spies. We became cryptologists in earnest, and this served us in good stead many times to come.

Those next few days were so hard to get through. We tried to act as we had in Manila. We decided I should keep the apartment until the ship's home port was officially changed, so I did not even have packing to keep my mind off this separation. We did manage for a bit to act somewhat normal, but at night we clung to each other, trying to say everything for a lifetime, aware that this could be our last parting but not admitting that even to ourselves. My trip to Norfolk took the sting out of our leaving Christopher Street, though for Van it meant parting with his beautiful possessions—Bini, whom he dearly loved, and his very own home—possibly for good. We did have hope of seeing each other one more time before he sailed for a war zone, although not even the officers knew which one.

Jane and Jim decided against her going to Norfolk because of the distinct possibility that no one would be allowed off the ship before they sailed for good. As it turned out for most, their own case included, Jim was right. Of the six wives who went down, only two of us saw our husbands. The skipper's wife and I were the lucky ones, but it was only a brief respite, a matter of a few short hours. We all imagined we would see our lads again in a fairly reasonable length of time, but my first letter from Van in March 1942 dispelled that pipe dream:

I miss you like fury Betsy girl. More and more in every way I love you and the fact that I am not with you is very disappointing. Betts, my own, this is turning into one voyage to which I have not and cannot give my heart. Regardless of where I am or where I go all of me that is any good remains with you.

My sweet I have practically cried with disappointment and I know you are going to feel the same way. My happy thought that we might be off on a not too extended, more or less, training cruise is way off. I still have no idea exactly where we are headed for. We know where we are heading now but from there we don't. There can be nothing gained by evading the fact that I think it will be some time—and I wouldn't want to hazard a guess as to how long—before we will be together again.

. . . The war which until now has been distant and impersonal has become acutely personal for us. It doesn't seem fair or right that this should happen to us again so soon. I have been trying to ease the bitter sting by realizing all the other people are in the same boat with us too. Some like Pat and Jim exactly the same and some not so fortunate as to be tried, proven and perhaps hardened like us.

I railed against that, for Jane and Jim had had six months together in Manila to our three weeks, and Betty and Pat McEntee had had a lot longer. I did not think we were either fortunate or hardened. I did think we had proven our ability to take adversity in a big way.

There were two big jobs of my own to do: get the baby born and keep up Van's morale with a barrage of letters. After the near miscarriage in Boston both of us were apprehensive. Van was equally disappointed at not being around, as he was worried about my health. It behooved me to suppress my own apprehension about Van and write cheerful letters:

Your letter came not as too much of a shock for despite all thoughts to the contrary I knew in my innermost being that you were going for an extended visit. Many times I know things by premonition and settle myself accordingly.

My darling wherever you have gone and no matter how long, I am with you, cheerfully and happily. I know you have a job to do and so have I. If we worry about each other, neither one of us will do our job well, I can't afford to worry about you for the baby's sake. Naturally I will worry about how you are, dear heart, but I promise you I am of good cheer. I know you will come back to us and that we will be together again as if nothing had ever happened to make us sad. I know you're on the best ship the Navy has, that you are as safe as a person can be in these times and that you are not a fool, I need not know more. I pray that God bless and keep you. Put my trust in Him and in you and there is nothing more but to wait.

If we loved each other less than we do I would have qualms, but as you said, we are tried and true. Darling, you don't know my ideas about life and death do you? I've tried to tell you but now I will define it exactly so you will know. I have no fear of death either for you or me. You can't die out of my life nor I out of yours. If I loved you less it would be different but I love you unboundedly and nothing can change how I feel. No matter what happens we are together and in a relatively short time it will be forever. . . .

All I ask is that you take reasonable care of yourself and that you remember that I love you always. . . . I keep my chin up as far as yours is and walk with you through everything. God bless you and speed you home.

A World Series

Helen stayed with me for a while after I had moved to my family's house in Greenwich. Tek Lyster joined us with little Teddy when Ted went to sea on the *Juneau*. We had quite a gang of ladies and children at Mother and Dad's house. It was a big barn of a place and could hold a large crowd, so I invited Mariah Novitski and her baby also and we had a mini-Manila reunion.

Dad, who loved babies, was delighted with young Davey Hall, little Teddy Lyster, and Beboo Novitski. Playing with them kept his mind off the trouble he was having trying to get back into the Army he had loved since his graduation from West Point. He had broken his neck in World War I, he was sixty years old, and the Army did not want him. It hurt him sorely. His classmates at West Point held most of the top posts in the Army—that was hard on him but lucky for me. He often found out things I could not have found out for myself. In particular, the president's top military advisor, General "Pa" Watson, was to be a real lifeline for all of us.

Pop Perkins was more successful than Dad. He had never been in the service, he was younger, and he had organizational skills the Navy badly needed. So off to the Navy Department he went, and with François Novitski in Washington also in the department, I had an intelligence network that covered all contingencies. Consequently, it was not hard to know that the *Atlanta* was about to go through the Panama Canal and into the Pacific. We all hoped the ship would put in to Long Beach or San Francisco, and many of the wives fled to the West Coast. I stayed home because of the baby, and Jane moved to Trenton, New Jersey, with her family now stationed there.

Both Jim and Van wrote of the long hours spent trying to get the ship in shape. They had rushed so hard to finish her ahead of schedule that she was not really ready. There were numerous unfinished bits and pieces to fix, machinery with which they needed to be more familiar, and the ever-present plumbing problems. Even the officers' mess was a mess. Van was elected mess treasurer on top of his many other duties. Fourteen-hour days on top of night watches were routine for the entire ship's company. However, all the young bucks were eager to get on with it and win the war.

As the *Atlanta* steamed into Pearl Harbor, the ship's company was confronted for the first time with the actuality of war. Although the cleanup job there, in just five short months, had been amazing, 7 December 1941 was evident wherever they looked. It made the lads heartsick and mad as hops and furthered their desire to get the Japanese. Their chance was not long coming. The men of the *Atlanta* were ready, willing, and able to test the ship and themselves.

But for now, there was the chance to stretch their legs ashore. Both Jim and Van made right for the telephone company to put in calls to Jane and me. Our first attempt to talk under censorship rules was trying and exhilarating. It was scary to be told by the operator that our calls would be monitored, that we must not mention names of people, places, or dates. Absolutely no ship movements were to be discussed. If any of the rules were disobeyed we would be cut off.

The men had to wait interminably at the phone office. I sat at home, chewed my nails, and rehearsed what I wanted to say. "Dr. Squire says I'm doing well." No, I could not say "Dr. Squire." I would have to say "the doctor." OK, I would put it this way: "The doctor says I'm fine, the baby will arrive between September 20 and October 20." No, can't say dates, scratch that, say, "Baby will arrive well before our anniversary."

When the call finally came, I just burbled, "Oh Van, I love you, how are you? I look like I swallowed a melon. Are you OK?"

Van was much calmer, but he was equally unable to say anything more than "I miss you, I'm fine, I'm tired. Oh, Rabbit, Kilud." Whoops! Mistake. Bang went the phone.

Despite the call's brevity, it was so wonderful to hear Van's voice and so crazy to get a phone call "from the war." Jane called me to tell me she had received the same kind of call from Jim, only Jim had not said a cutoff word. She had, however, by telling Jim she was going to Fort Benjamin Harrison. She had been cut off before she said Harrison and doubted Jim had an inkling where she was headed. Back to the mails for both of us.

Honolulu was not quite the liberty port of a young man's dream. The bars closed at four. Curfew came at six o'clock; consequently, nightclubs were really day clubs. Anyway, a bar full of men was hardly much fun, so Pat, Van, and

Jim decided to go to the beach for a swim. What a shock! First they had to get clearance passes. Then they came to the maze of coiled barbed wire that stretched up and down the beach as far as the eye could see in both directions, not the friendly happy sands the three had known in 1938. Only the beautiful azure water had not changed.

Their respite was over in short order as the *Atlanta* received her first assignment. She was to escort a convoy to New Caledonia and then join Task Force 16. That turned out to be an easy, very short trip. Only one exciting thing happened: the cruiser *Pensacola* lost a man overboard and *Atlanta* went to the rescue, fishing the fellow out of the water. Arriving back in Pearl Harbor, the ship remained only long enough to fuel and take on provisions. On 28 May 1942, *Atlanta* put to sea, "Destination Unknown."

The width and breadth of the land was treated to the first good news of the war: Midway. Newspapers headlined it, the radio broadcasters trumpeted it. What a sense of exhilaration prevailed for most at home! Yet for many it was tragedy.

Midway was the westernmost island in the Hawaiian chain; we had a small air and naval base there, but most of America did not know we owned such a place. Even newsmen made Midway sound as if it were a captured enemy position, when actually we were there already and had beaten off a navy, superior in force to our own, whose mission it was to establish an air base within striking distance of Pearl Harbor. For the first time patrol boats (PTs) hit the news. They were heroic in their efforts to harass the Japanese. Our aircraft flying off the carriers were the deciding factor, but it was the Army that took all the credit for defending Midway. The Army claimed Midway as their victory, but we Navy wives at home knew our men were in the midst of it. Many became widows as a result of that battle, though none whose husbands were in the *Atlanta*.

It was typical of Van to get word to me by the first possible means that he was safe. In jig time I had a letter from him mailed 8 June:

> This past week must have been a bit nerve wracking for you in spite of the tremendous headlines or perhaps because of them. It certainly was a glorious week for the country and one which we hope to finish to even greater glory. It is almost unbelievable that our own forces did what they did. Now in the months to follow we should maintain and press home our advantage.
>
> I am well and everyone else is too and that is the best news I can give you.
>
> There is so much I would like to write you, about all we've been doing this past month or so and everything that is going on, but pen hands are tied you know. Anyway, for us the excitement was nil and the tension of expectancy the maximum!

I never quite realized the amount of "chess playing" hide and seek that goes on for days. It takes time to cover and traverse great areas of ocean, always searching over the horizons. Aircraft makes the job easier but it doesn't make it fool proof.

Bettsy girl how are you? Oh I'd love to be with you, "melon" and all. I feel I am missing something—a phase or period in our lives that I very definitely would like to be on hand for. You always were wonderful, sometimes mysterious and never the same, there was always something to discover and now I'm missing something which I'd love to be able to watch develop.

Everyone asks about you, not necessarily because of the bambino but because they are all crazy about you and think you are a mighty fine person. I like my wife to be like that.

Both Jim and Van kept diaries, not as yet declared illegal. Jim's, written as letters to Jane, were to be delivered at a future date. Midway came alive from *Atlanta's* point of view in this June entry of his:

Shortly after sailing, CinCPac [commander in chief, Pacific] sent us a message wishing us well and expressing his confidence in our ability to strike hard and successfully at the enemy. This was followed by a dispatch from Admiral Spruance, CTF16 [commander, Task Force 16], stating that our mission was to deliver a flanking attack on an enemy force which was en route to deliver an attack and invasion on Midway Island. The enemy force was reputed to contain carriers, battleships, cruisers, destroyers, transports, and auxiliaries. We were to be supported by TF17 [Task Force 17] containing the carrier, YORKTOWN. We all looked uneasily about our small group; two carriers, seven cruisers, and fifteen destroyers. Now we knew what the ENTERPRISE officers meant when they said that the two task forces were the only ones fighting the war. We groused a bit because the battleships were not included in the junket, then shrugged our shoulders, and decided that if our leaders thought we could take on the whole Japanese Navy, then we probably could.

For the next few days reports kept seeping in concerning the strength and disposition of our Oriental antagonists. We drilled constantly and the carrier planes ranged far out to scout and prevent the enemy from knowing that we were in the vicinity. Finally we took station about 150 miles northeast of Midway and waited. On June third the initial skirmishes took place. The Japs made a feint to the north by attacking Dutch Harbor. Our land based planes contacted and were attacked by units of the enemy some six hundred miles west of Midway. [We had land-based planes on Midway ranging out toward Wake Island looking for the enemy fleet.] Late that day a force of Army flying fortresses attacked the enemy support force and scored two direct hits on two battleships and one near miss.

That night Midway based PBY's delivered a moonlight torpedo attack on the enemy force with considerable success.

Meanwhile in the ATLANTA we were making the final preparations for an all out battle. Life jackets were stored on station. Ammunition was made ready. Everything was carefully checked. We all searched our minds wondering what our reactions would be in the heat of the battle. The Wardroom and crew's quarters rang with conjecture as to just what was going to happen. I doubt if fear was an emotion experienced by many of the crew. Mostly it was curiosity over events to come.

At about 0745 the morning of June fourth, our first visual contact with the enemy was made when a Japanese cruiser scout plane appeared on the horizon, looked us over and then disappeared. As yet no word had been received that our forces had located the main body of the enemy striking force. We became alarmed at the possibility that the Jap carriers might know where we were and we not know where they were. That would have indeed been disastrous. However at 0800 a report came in that the enemy force had been located northwest of Midway, 200 miles from us. We turned toward the enemy, increased speed to 25 knots, went to General Quarters [battle stations], and prepared to launch our planes. Word came in that the Japs were bombing Midway. Another word came that they still did not know where we were. . . . The carrier groups had separated, the ATLANTA teaming up with the HORNET, three cruisers, and six destroyers.

We were at General Quarters while all this was going on and my only impressions of activities topside was that gleaned from words passed down to Plot by Control and the directors. . . .

At 1022 a Jap scout plane was sighted on the horizon, way out of range. I presume our combat patrol took care of him. At 1115 the Midway based planes claimed damage to one Jap carrier. At 1135 enemy planes were reported ten miles away. At 1150 eight enemy cruisers were located from the main body.

At 1200 lunch was served at our battle stations. It was interesting to note the attitudes of the men. We were all so concerned in the success of our mission that any word one way or the other would throw us into a frenzy of joy or a pall of gloom out of all proportion to the importance of the fact reported. The men found time to joke excessively and to complain vociferously about the quality of the lunch which the hard-working supply department had endeavored to make in the midst of all the excitement. Most of the men agreed that if somebody had been around to sell peanuts and pop the atmosphere could then well have been that of a World Series Baseball game. It certainly was big league stuff and definitely a "World Series!"

At 1305 [1:05 P.M.] our planes started to straggle back. At 1310 a sub periscope was sighted astern of us. At 1332 my JA telephone talker reported hearing Japanese voices over the JA circuit. I was incredulous and threw my selector switch to that circuit and sure enough there was an excited Japanese voice jabbering away at a staccato rate. I inquired and found that the radio room had put their telephone mouth piece near the radio speaker which was tuned in on the Japanese fighter plane circuits. I had the voice thrown onto all the battle telephone circuits to give the men a thrill. That Jap sounded as if he were distinctly worried about something! . . .

At 1335 a plane crashed in the water near the Hornet and disappeared almost at once, the crew being lost. At 1337 Midway reported downing eight Jap planes with AA [antiaircraft] fire. By this time most of our planes which could return, had landed but their ranks were woefully depleted. We saw no torpedo bombers at all returning and became very concerned. How was the fight going?

We commenced tracking a large group of "bandits" at about 20,000 yards. They were circling for position. At 1440 our fighters engaged this group in a dog fight. At 1440 a HORNET plane crashed off our starboard bow and was lost at once. At 1445 the Japs were coming in fast. They disappeared in the clouds as we tracked and my spirits took a drop as Director 11 reported the FD [forward deck, gun crew director number 11] radar there inoperative. Now the Japs could surprise us by dropping out of the clouds and we wouldn't be able to track them without seeing them. I remember cursing the radar roundly. Control Aft told us to stand by and we all waited tense and expectant. Something must have happened aloft about that time because the anticipated attack was never delivered. Our fighters probably drove them off before they came in range or else they decided we were too strong a force to cope with. . . .

At 1535 word came that all our planes had returned—those that were left.

. . . At 1624 a plane crashed near the HORNET and the pilot was saved. At 1626 three ships were detached to investigate flames on the horizon. At 1642 the enemy again attacked TF14. At 1647 the HORNET and ENTERPRISE sent more fighters up. A vicious dog fight ensued followed by AA fire. One Jap was hit by a direct burst of AA fire and his plane disintegrated in mid-air. We finally thought we were going to get a crack at them when one plane came into 15,500 yards, barely within gun range, so far out that it would have been a waste of ammunition to fire at him. We were sorely tempted tho'. Several Japs tried to break through the screen of AA fire around the ENTERPRISE but failed completely. None of them would come near us. . . .

At 1815 a report came in on the results of the first attack which had taken place between 1100 and 1300. The enemy force consisted of four carriers, two battleships, eight cruisers, fifteen destroyers. . . . All four carriers were reported badly damaged. Other ships were hit.

At 1900 we had our picnic lunch in Plot again, the food consisting of only sandwiches and apples, We were feeling pretty good withal a bit disappointed that we hadn't even fired a salvo.

June 5

The night of June fourth-fifth found our PBY's and shore based planes harassing the enemy continuously. Four hits were scored on enemy battleships and one on a cruiser. Fires were extensive in the Jap fleet. . . .

The HORNET planes took off on a raid at dawn, returning at 0645 with the report that a carrier, heavy cruiser, and battleship were burning. These planes made four hits on the battleship. They encountered no air opposition and all returned safely.

At 0707 a message was received from CinCPac worded about as follows: "You have written a glorious page in American history. One more day of all out battle will find the enemy defeated. I am proud to be associated with you."

June 6

. . . The battle now developed into a rout for the Japs as far as we were concerned. All of us were anxious to press the attack home and polish off the remnants with surface action. However, because of a critical fuel situation or because a bombing attack was feared, we reversed course after launching one final SBD raid at 1531.

During all these raids our ship's radio was kept tuned to the raiding plane circuit. The conversation was rich, rare and racy, with the thud of exploding bombs in the background. For example: "Wow! Sammy, you hit him right smack in the fantail. Look at those bastards run!" "Hey, look at Joe's so called objective!" "I'm going down now. Watch this!" "Where's the battleship? I'm getting low on gas. I wanna go home!" (very plaintive and repeated at frequent intervals). The whole thing sounded like a bunch of kids playing Cowboys and Indians, fantastically unreal.

Trickling Back

As soon as Van was able to get off the ship in Pearl, he called me. This time it was a thorough mess for him. He waited so long in the telephone office that he missed his dinner on board. Curfew was called, and he had to appeal to the shore patrol to carry him in their jeep over to the hotel, where he could get a snack and a bed for the night.

With it all, he said it was worth the wait. "You sound fine Betts; in fact, you sound as though you're right here. Not like in the old days when your voice would fade and return."

"Oh Van, this is wonderful, the next best thing to being there with you. Wouldn't it be wonderful if we could talk every night?"

"Well darling, that's out. We'd be broke in nothing flat. Incidentally, while we were gone one of our ushers came through, sorry I missed him. Why don't you call your friend Marge, it could be fun for you."

Amazingly, the censor let that name slip by so we were not cut off and I caught that bit of a signal. It meant the *Whipple* had made it safely out of Manila. Van was using Don Wilson, who had already gone home, to get the word to me. Marge was Don's wife and a good friend of mine. It was lovely to hear. That dear old ship had been such a part of our courtship. Thank heavens it had escaped from Manila and the Japanese.

In his letter in late June 1942, Van also wrote other decipherable passages: "The fellow who ran our reception sallied forth in his Nazi uniform as soon as it was declared 'an open city' by his Nibs. The populace immediately hung him from a lamppost and left him there to rot." Easily interpreted, this meant Mr. David, the manager of the Army-Navy Club in Manila, who had arranged our wedding reception with Van, including the embarrassingly tall wedding cake, was a Nazi spy in a perfect place to glean Navy information. It gave me a cold shiver down my spine. "His Nibs" was General MacArthur, whose "open city" declaration had been reported in the newspapers long past. As usual Van had managed to tell me something important that the enemy could not interpret.

Van was able to get one more helpful message to me over the phone: "You know the trouble I have with my bottom? Well I'm going to get it fixed and hope it will be better well before Nane's birthday." As Van had never had any trouble with his bottom, that could only mean they were going into dry dock to get the ship's bottom scraped and would get out before July 12, Nane's birthday. That gave me a nice three weeks, or thereabouts, to be free of worry about Van. I also longed to go out to the West Coast in case the ship might go into the yard there, or that Van would get there for another reason—aviation training.

Van and Jim had been discussing this in their letters home, to get our reactions. Their own reasoning was that, as Jim had written to Jane, aviation is so closely linked with surface operations in the Navy these days that being an aviator is, while not a necessity, a very definite advantage for any line officer. Neither Jane nor I had any objections to the idea. Certainly we had no reason to believe that naval aviation was any more hazardous than what they were presently facing, and at least they would get home after flying a few missions. They both eventually found a doctor qualified to give them aviation physicals; both passed with no trouble, but they were turned down as they were considered essential as experienced regular line officers, who were still in short supply.

Living in an Army household, I felt cut off and lonesome. When Van phoned in July, as usual I was so excited I hardly told him anything. I did not know it was going to be eons before I heard from him again, but I did not think they would scrape the ship's bottom and get her ready for sea for nothing, and I wanted him to know about my progress with the baby business and how I felt about him once again before he got in another scrap. And here I had muffed the phone call saying nothing of importance.

After the call, I wrote what I meant to say over the phone:

How lovely to talk with you. I am still in a vacant haze over it darling. It is so exciting to hear your beloved voice and know you are well. I feel so reassured and comfortable and talking to you is just as though you had never been away at all and that we were just having a chat while you had the duty. . . .

I am so afraid of breaking the censorship rules that I say nothing but trivial things because I can't think fast enough on a phone to determine whether what I'm about to say is or is not censurable where in a letter I can stop and think first.

The censor and I are now good friends and this time she merely said "Mrs. Perkins, you are familiar with the censorship rules aren't you?" and I said, "Yes indeed I am."

So that made it doubly important that I not break the rules. When I know I'm going to talk to you I try to plan what I will say but darling the minute you say hello I get so excited I forget all my plans and just say, "How are you darling— I love you—what are you doing? etc."

I went to see Dr. Squire today and I am fine. I still have two crazy measurements which I guess aren't going to change and he says consequently I will have a fairly long labor but that he doesn't intend that I will know anything about it all. . . . My desire to have it short was so that I could do it without too much dope and know what was going on but if it's to be longer I think it is best for me not to know. . . .

There is nothing really amazing about people all telling me how fine and wonderful they think you are. Your character is written all over your face. You have the strongest and at the same time, gentlest face I've ever seen.

. . . Darling the first time you came down here to the house before you went to China I was impressed with the direct manner in which you approached everything. When we were in Manila my first thought was that you were the most delightful combination of being worldly and at the same time naive. Later I discovered it was not naiveté at all but a very true sense of balance by which I mean that you had kept unspoiled in your own mind all the fine things of life and at the same time, knew and accepted short comings. . . .

Being your wife is a never ending joy. You do so many great and small things for me. You show me something new about you that I never suspected, and it's always another lovable quality. I've yet to see a mean or hateful streak in you.

A Floury Mess

Life at home was unrealistically war-conscious. The populace knew so little about military strategy and tactics that their efforts to participate in the war became antics.

There was not one military installation in Greenwich, Connecticut. In fact, there was only one factory of any kind at that time that could be called a military target, the Electrolux Vacuum Cleaner Company. They were making something useful to the services but hardly worthy of a German air raid. Notwithstanding, the town went into a flap, which gave me a splendid subject to describe to Van:

> Fourth of July was celebrated by a mock air raid, complete with planes and bombs. I was up here [at Craggy] so I missed it but I understand it was quite a floury mess as the planes dropped bags of flour to denote a bomb, while huge firecrackers were set off for realism. . . . The Air Raid Wardens put out the "incendiaries," got the people to their shelters (I'm not sure what that proved as we haven't dug up our lawns to make same yet) and had the streets clear of traffic for an hour and a half.
>
> The Beach Club was all agog about it at their annual dance which Wood took me to. They were practically frothing at the mouth about how well the people had acted and how well the Wardens had performed their duties.

The whole episode was written up in the local paper, which I clipped to send to Van, knowing he would get a good chuckle out of Greenwich's first, last, and only "air raid." In such fashion did I attempt to make my letters fun for Van.

I did a lot of dreaming about how Van looked: his clear blue eyes that sparkled with amusement, his beguiling smile that showed his white teeth, his full underlip and what remained of a dimple—now elongating. I thought of his great long legs and how his walk was so enthusiastic he almost skipped. Dreaming kept my chin up.

Still, it was hard to just sit around waiting for the baby to come. I had joined the Civil Air Patrol before Van came back from Manila, but now I could not even button my uniform. Long gaps came between letters. Obviously the ship had gone to faraway places once again, and I began to chafe at the lack of communications. With little to report, I found it increasingly hard to think of interesting topics to write about. I took to studying the maps Van had given me to fill the void. I became familiar with every island in the Pacific on my big map. My favorite pastimes were letter writing and figuring out where the ship was from the meager news in the papers and nightly broadcasts.

My letter from Van written 9 August arrived in late September. It was simple to know where he was by one statement alone: "Names and places I've barely noticed in print actually exist." We knew the Aleutians, so he was not there. The other theater of war was reported as the Solomon Islands, so that was it. His letter continued:

> As I write this Jack is writing Stephanie and we are both wishing we could say which war we were in. We thought it would be easy for you to guess but we have just learned there is fighting going on in two wildly separated spots so that makes your guessing game harder. Personally I'd like to read a newspaper and find out just what is going on. I am sure I don't have a very clear picture of all the little details.
>
> The important thing is that we are all alright. Gosh how I wish I could write an intelligent letter to you, a long one in detail about everything. At least I am keeping up my diary with daily interesting happenings. . . .
>
> By this time darling, bambino's birthday should about be set, or as nearly so as can be the first time. I hope I am some place when the time arrives that will be near to a phone.
>
> I want to be with you so much but most of all I would like to be among the first instead of the last, to receive the news.
>
> We have our good times and our little groups of closer friends. Each with his own particular sense of humor or conversation. Jim Shaw is one of those rare people who doesn't say much but what he does is original and often very funny and both Drs. Garver and Erdman are good company. Dingy is fun to be with and we five guys sit together for meals which are always enjoyable for the company if not for the food. Of course once you get started talking about the people on board, things are all pretty interesting, except when I get annoyed once in a while at one or two of the J.O.'s [junior officers], and they are reserve J.O.'s without the training and background they might have acquired at the Academy. Academy training isn't completely necessary because one of my closest friends among the J.O.'s and a capable one too is just out of Harvard.
>
> I wonder how I got started on this subject of personalities. Life on board isn't too dull or monotonous. We have enough watches to stand and some work to do to keep us busy, then something turns up to take our interest for a while and we aren't too serious. Mostly everyone talks about when they will get back to the States and that is natural enough. I've yet to find a sea going man that doesn't someday hope to settle down on a farm.

Jim Shaw kept his diary wrapped in oiled silk and strapped it to himself whenever they went into battle. His entries about this period were specific:

July 19, 1942

Here we are across the equator again on the prowl for trouble—and having an excellent chance of finding that trouble. . . .

Our immediate destination is the Island of Tonga Tabu of the Friendly Islands or Tonga Group. . . . Immediately the Captain announced that we were going to Tonga, all hands posed the question of why. I took a look at the chart and saw the islands lying along our line of communications to Australia, some four or five hundred miles southeast of Fiji, almost due east of New Caledonia, south east of the Solomon's. I think the answer lies in the Solomon's. The Japs are on the move again and have taken over the most easterly of the Solomon's, an island called Guatacanal. [No one knew how to spell Guadalcanal at that time. My big chart spelled it Guatacanar, and I officiously wrote Van to correct his spelling, which was as poor as Jim's.]

Their flying boats have been seen over New Caledonia. So we're going down to clean out the islands. I don't know but I'll wager we find Army transports and Marine landing vessels assembled on Tonga ready to embark a landing force for somewhere. It will be the start of the long road back, retaking all that the Japs have won from us. We should have plenty of land based as well as carrier based air power for the job. And [the USS] North Carolina is an aggressive weapon in any operations despite the current scream about obsolete battleships.

I wonder if the Japs and Germans lighten their war effort with any levity at all. It's a cinch the Americans couldn't go to war without some humor—and I believe the same is true of the British and Chinese. At any rate we have as much fun as our wartime condition will permit us. On watch in control with me is Dave Hall and three sailors. We while away the hours with the most incredible nonsense. And over the main battery telephone circuit we have debates, long discussions, wisecracks, and the like. Far from decreasing our battle efficiency, I think the relaxation is good for the watch standees. When anything happens, we wipe smiles off our faces in nothing flat and are ready to blast anything from a sub to a plane. My sailor assistants on watch consist of one gunner's mate, one storekeeper, and one seaman. The gunner's mate is what would be known in rural circles as a "kidder" I guess. At any rate, I enjoy turning the tables on him to confound him. The storekeeper is a "feather merchant"—reserve—whose ignorance of Navy ways aside from storekeeping is most appalling. The seaman is one of my super intelligent F division boys. I have appointed a "beefeater" watch after the fashion of the Tower of London, one of the talkers being on as beefeater at all times which means he must watch all our ships and listen for broadcasts on the warning net. So we perch up there, the five of us in a little world of our own, eight hours a day, rain, shine, heat or cold. Most of the time I sit on a broken down stepladder leaning against the splinter shield. Once in a while when a plane comes over, I order the main battery to simulate action on the plane and the turrets come swinging out at my command.

I think probably too much of you Jane, for my own good since it just gives me an attack of homesickness when I do too much thinking. I'll warrant I could write almost a day by day biography of our life together, the details of our brief happy unions are so vivid in my mind. Happiest time of all was in Washington. Separation seemed so distant then. In Brooklyn we had the specter of it over our heads. In Manila it was the same way. In Tsingtao we were really just becoming acquainted. Memories are a poor diet for the nourishment of a love such as I feel for you. Honestly, darling— [interrupted]

Jim was interrupted by a call to general quarters. He took up the narrative on 5 August:

The eve of another big battle and me not quite caught up on my sleep! What a calamity! If the battle holds off for a couple of days, I might be able to squeeze in a few hours. . . . Right now we're cruising around in the Coral Sea not very far from the site of the last big battle if one can call a spot on the ocean a "site." . . .

Yesterday the Commander let us in on the secret of what it's all about. Our objective IS the Solomons, specifically the port of Tulagi, the islands of Florida and Guadacanal. [Not much later Jim used the new accepted way to spell Guadalcanal.] The Japs have built themselves an air base there and established some two thousand troops. We have about fifteen thousand troops. The Japs have about 150 planes in the area or readily available as against about three hundred for us. They have four or five heavy cruisers and a squadron of destroyers. It would appear, off hand, that we possess numerical superiority in every sense. I'm a little skeptical about this being a push-over tho! The Japs had numerical superiority at Midway and look what happened to them! However, we will have some support from the Army. We saw two flying fortresses and two B-26's the other day. The sailors are all joking about how the Army with four planes (against our 300) will claim a great victory over the Japs just as they did at Midway. Childish jealousy. . . . MacArthur has nothing to do with it other than give us his Army bombers to do with what we may. . . .

August 12, 1942

. . . I suppose one could say that this is being written in the lull in the battle, although we've not yet fired a gun, the battle has been going on for some days now, ever since the eighth. It's rather hard to feel a part of an act when the movements of the actors are known only through what we read in the papers. Yet that's the way it's been.

Last Friday we slipped up to the Solomon Islands with our carriers and transports and loosed the fury of our attack against the completely surprised Japs at Tulagi, Guadalcanal, and a couple of other islands. So little of the battle pertained to us that I didn't even bother to make a chronology of it.

. . . We could hear the fighter planes and bombers talking over their radios and sometimes hear the whine of high powered engines in power dives but that was as close as the battle came to us. We stayed at General Quarters all day, had a few false alarms and that was all. It was nowhere near as exciting as the Battle of Midway.

That night we steamed around in the darkness waiting for daybreak to renew the attack. The previous day's pattern followed fairly closely. Forty Japanese torpedo planes arrived at Tulagi at 1300; some fifteen of them were shot down. What success they had we do not know. We had expected them to attack us but apparently the Japs still didn't know the whereabouts of our carriers. Again we stayed at General Quarters all day with no action.

Sunday found us steaming off to the south to refuel leaving the transport and landing force in the islands. We steamed to within 190 miles of New Caledonia and some six or seven hundred miles from the war theater, arriving yesterday afternoon at a rendezvous with a tanker—or was it the afternoon before that—time is so fleeting.

This morning's press came out with the startling announcement that we had lost one cruiser, had two more damaged, two destroyers damaged, and one transport damaged in the battle. This came as a complete surprise to all hands from the Captain on down. Criticism of the conduct of the battle which had been half formed broke out in full fury and bitterness; so much so that the Captain felt called upon to deliver a warning to us to watch our words lest we taint the morale of the crew and undermine their confidence.

On 17 August an AllNav order came out to the fleet prohibiting any further keeping of diaries; consequently, posterity lost valuable personal accounts of some of the fiercest battles of World War II.

Devotedly, Daddy

Now that the ship was out in the far Pacific more than seven thousand miles from the West Coast, mail in both directions slowed to a trickle. The *Atlanta* was operating almost continuously, seldom seeing any shooting action. The mail seemed never to catch up with them. When I did get a letter it was almost never about what Van was thinking; in fact, it seemed to be about two things:

the various island clubs Van visited ashore, no name of the islands of course, and worry about our baby's imminent arrival. Apparently he was missing a lot of my letters, and both he and Jim never failed to mention how terrible it was to go into one of the islands, dog tired from constant tension of not knowing what was going to happen, four hours on watch, four hours off, right around the clock, and terribly homesick—only to find no mail. V-mail was a flop as far as time was concerned, and it was unsatisfactory from the personal point of view. We used it to back up a regular letter, but that was all.

With the baby's birth getting closer, I decided to try another tack, a registered letter I wrote in August. Wow, what a success! Van was elated:

> I've been thinking about you and the coming baby a lot these days. I'd so like to be with you and be there when the bambino arrives. I hope I don't have to wait too long to find out whether it's a boy or girl and how you both are. . . .
>
> I think I will probably pass out cigars or something when I hear from you.
>
> I guess I am quite calm, cool and collected because I don't know exactly when the bambino is coming and it wouldn't do any good to get upset anyway.
>
> . . . I've asked mother to go shopping for me and get you a little present. I told her about what I wanted to give you and I'm sure she can find it for me.
>
> Anything I give you though Betts darling can't compare with what you are about to give me. I love you so much darling and I am so happy that you're my wife. Nothing you do though and no number of babies will ever change my love for you. You are my wife, the girl I love. . . .
>
> P.S. Betts beloved: Your registered letter came through in three days which certainly is very speedy. I love to get them hot off the griddle. Any news is good but fresh news is best—Right?

Then came a long dissertation on how to get word to him about the baby's birth. He doubted the Navy would clutter the airways with a message about a baby. He thought his father might be able to help from the Navy Department in Washington. If all else failed, maybe my father's pal General Pa Watkins, the aide-de-camp to President Roosevelt, could help. At any rate, he wanted to know as soon as possible.

All during August and into September, the *Atlanta* had been embroiled in the battles of the Solomon Islands. The ship was used to bombard the shore wherever a Jap battery was spotted by an overhead plane pilot. She had reason to use her antiaircraft batteries, too. During one fight that lasted more than forty-eight hours, the crew remained continuously at general quarters until, from sheer exhaustion, they dropped to the steel deck for a minute or two of shut-eye and then climbed back to their feet.

I did not get much in the mailbox, but I heard a lot on the radio news broadcasts or from our friends in Washington. I received one brief letter in early October that worried me a good bit:

I love you more than anything else in the world, for myself I care little but for you I want no hurt or unhappiness. I am happy when I know you are. Always be happy and keep the sun in the sky.

I don't expect that anything is going to happen to me but I feel that the immediate future is not going to be the snap it has been in the past and I think we are about to be tested. As a Nation we have bitten off a mouthful and now it must be chewed and swallowed.

Don't worry dearest and don't be upset, remember the Bambino. I'll write of course when possible but I'll never stop loving you.

By the time I read this letter, I was in the hospital, having had Pam. I had been thirty-six hours in labor, had received a lot of medication, and was in a fuzzy, euphoric frame of mind. I was aware that Van was telling me he was in harm's way and was trying to give me something special to read "just in case," but I was so doped up it did not sink in until much later. As usual I had lovely flowers from Van along with a beautiful aquamarine ring, which staggered me.

All my family and friends came to see me, including Van's brother Woodie, who came at night when only a small light was on in the room. For one brief moment I thought he was Van. Poor dear man, he had been so good to me all during the four years Van and I had been separated, and now as he came into the room, I was holding Pam in my arms. I should have smiled and instead I cried. I think he knew I mistook him for Van, but he never let on and did his best to comfort me.

As it turned out, Pop Perkins got a bare-bones message to Van that merely stated, "Pamela Ann born Oct. 11th both well." Van's first letter to his daughter was necessarily brief:

My Darling Bettsy and Pamela,

Yesterday, the seventeenth, was a great day because I received the dispatch which told of Pamela's arrival. I felt so proud and pleased and I am very happy. How lucky I am to have two girls to love now. Pamela, your Mother is the most wonderful person in the world and if you grow up to be like her I will be a very satisfied and pleased Father. Bettsy I wish I could have been with you and been the first to greet little Pam. I am so very anxious to get home and see you both. I am a very happy man and I am extremely proud of all three of us. I love you both with all my heart, Bettsy my wife and Pamela my daughter.

Devotedly, Daddy.

Being a V-mail letter, it came rather quickly, and right on its heels came a letter he had started writing on 10 October in which he described going ashore with Jim Shaw, Dave Hall, and Jack Wulff and drinking all of some poor man's beer. The next day he experienced bad stomach cramps, which he attributed to the beer. I thought it more likely that he had had sympathetic labor pains—anyway, I like to think that. Later, *Atlanta's* doctor told me he agreed with me, as Van had not had symptoms of any kind, just a gut ache, hardly caused by beer.

Van received a letter from Mother and Dad telling him about the baby's birth. He became thoroughly excited and expansive, writing them a nice answer on 31 October:

> I was so pleased to get your nice newsy letter. I very much like the idea of being a father and having a daughter. I am very proud of Bettsy and think she is the most wonderful person in the world. How I wish I could have been with her when the baby arrived. I would so like to be home with Betts and see the baby. I hate to miss any of the fun or the trials which there are. I am most anxious to have the letters arrive which will give me a fuller account of everything and particularly how Bettsy is.
>
> All my friends on board were just about as enthusiastic as I was when they learned of Pamela's arrival. The Commander and the Captain gave congratulations and some of the others kidded me by calling me Pop. So it was an event even for those not directly concerned. I am tickled to death with my new position as a father. I am so pleased and proud of both Betts and myself and our young daughter.

That day, now anchored at Espiritu Santo, Van got Bowdoin Craighill, the ship's legal officer, to write up a new will leaving everything to me and then our children (with even a little embellishment, our grandchildren), and if none of these, then brother Wood. He chose as witnesses to the will Jim Shaw, Jack Wulff, and Jack Broughton. That important document he sent home for safe keeping.

On 1 November the crew of the *Atlanta* was busy loading ammunition and supplies, going over everything preparatory to going back into battle. The ship had acquired Admiral Scott and his staff, so Van and Jack Wulff had to move out of their airy, comfortable quarters and back into their old room. Jim and Pat McEntee vacated that room and returned to their old cabin. A general shakeup to accommodate a lot of extra officers doubtless meant a big effort coming up. Van's letter of 7 November described Admiral Scott, whom he admired. Then he told me how to handle his finances. As clearly as daylight, he was telling me he was heading for something big, and soon.

On 19 October 1942, Pam (aged eight days) wrote a letter to her father with my help:

Dear Daddy,

I can hardly wait for you to come home. Presently I am putting up with the most awful indignities because Mother and Mrs. Major act perfectly ga-ga about me.

Yesterday, for instance, they spent a lot of time oohing and aahing over my duff.

"Have you ever seen such a cute little duff in all your life?" my Mother said.

"Most certainly it is the cutest I have ever seen," Mrs. Major replied.

Mrs. Major tells me about taking care of you when you were sick a long time ago. She says you are a super fellow. Mum agrees. . . .

Obviously, I not only love you already I also need you to protect me from these foolish women. You won't act sappy the way they do, but I hope you will love me very much.

Pamela Ann [two ink footprints]

Her dad's reply showed he was still very excited about his child, for on 8 November Van took time out from a trying and busy schedule to send his daughter a letter:

Pamela Dearest,

I received the sweetest, most wonderful letter the other day, it was the one you wrote to me with Mummy's help. I'll always treasure your very first letter because it was so full of love. It was signed in such a sweet way with your two tiny footprints but I loved it ever so much because only you have used that signature, it was something all your own. Pam I've read your letter many times and I'm so proud of it and your tiny footprints. I've showed it to a few of my friends and they think you are very clever.

Dear one I am so glad that you have come to live with Mummy and me. We have been waiting a long time for you and are very, very happy now. I am so proud of my daughter and your Mother is just as proud. We think we are pretty lucky parents.

Pam I'm so pleased you are such a wonderful person. I love you very much.

I am so sorry that I couldn't be on hand to greet you and that I can't be home with you now. I'm very very anxious to hold you and let you make noises and faces at me.

About this time the young officers and men were getting fed up with what was being said in the press and what they were hearing from home.

On 6 November 1942, Jim wrote Jane of his disgust shortly before going into battle:

> We're heading for something big this time and the men are wondering as to how they're going to act and feel under all circumstances. Each man confronted with a new trying situation can shrug the worry off with "Well it can't be any worse than last time and I felt all right then." So the very few that were going to crack did so before the ship ever left Brooklyn.
>
> What is going to be a wonder to behold (and a nightmare for any civilians within five miles) is going to be the reaction of this crew when we hit a civilized port. Emotions pent up for months will break down the walls of inhibition and the sky will be the limit. And let one, just one civilian comment to me about "wild sailors" and said civilian had better run for his life!
>
> The officers and men feel very strongly on most subjects touching the war. We all feel we've been giving quite a lot and therefore are quite arbitrary in our demands as to how others should act and let us act. Gallup wouldn't need to take a poll here to learn how we feel. . . .
>
> We hate the petty bickering of politics that seem to have been bred with the election. We hate the disunity between labor and capital. We look with a sort of contemptuous tolerance on such organizations as the USO. [All their time out there they never saw a USO show, but the Salvation Army was there for them.] We eye askance and critically the opinions aired by the press. As for the "Military commentators" who learn their strategy out of books, we writhe in disgust at their positive statements as to how the actual combat should be carried on. . . .
>
> After the war is over the fighting man is going to demand a kind of peace and a kind of government that will be some slight remuneration for the blood and toil and anguish of the war. The gladdest sight we see these days are new guns, ships, planes, men and equipment. . . .
>
> I love thee dearest girl and look forward only to the day when we're in each other's arms again. It's so hard to be separated from you.

Van and me at my fourth birthday fancy dress party at 44 Mayo. My mother-in-law wrote on her copy of the photograph, "The tallest and the smallest." Van was the Pie Man, and I was the Queen of Hearts. I am marked by an *X* at my feet, Van by an *X* on his hat.

Belle Haven House (Van called it "44 Mayo"), where I grew up and Van attended my fourth birthday party.

My safe haven. Craggy, Van's home, was prerevolutionary. I so loved it.

Ens. VanOstrand Perkins. "Mother, the minute Betts gets home please give her one of those good pictures of me—that's important."

My engagement photograph.

My wedding photograph, taken in Belle Haven just before I left home, 1940.

The embarrassingly large cake Van chose from a drawing. General MacArthur's wife Jean (*over Van's left shoulder*), as promised, attended the wedding.

Jane, Jim's bride, was always beautifully dressed. Washington, D.C., January 1943.

Jane Elizabeth Holt-Shaw and Lt. (jg) James C. Shaw at their wedding, 22 June 1940.

Jane and Jim at their house in Tsingtao, China, June 1940.

Jane, Jane's mother, and Jim the day Jane was evacuated from Manila, 1 January 1941, six months after Jane and Jim were married.

Van on Christmas Day 1940. Our first married holiday halfway around the world, alone.

The USS *Atlanta* after the battle in the Solomon Islands area, 14 November 1942. The wounded are being readied to send ashore to the Naval Hospital in Guadalcanal.

While recovering from their wounds, Van and Jim fished in the New Zealand Alps.

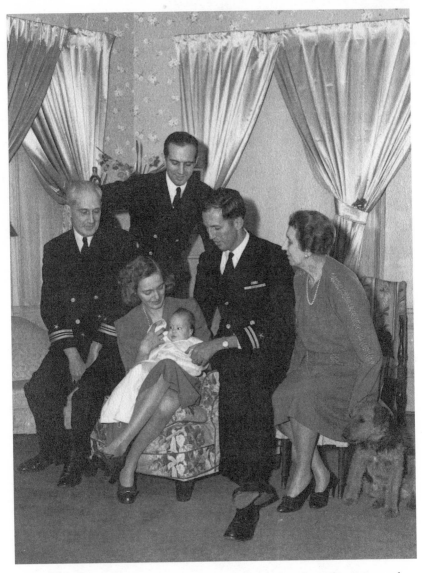

Van, just home from the hospital in New Zealand after the *Atlanta* was sunk, poses for a family portrait with Van's father, brother, mother, Pam, and me. Even our dog Bini joined us.

While serving on the USS *Bunker Hill,* June 1943, both Van and Jim (*pictured*) received their Silver Stars for "conspicuous gallantry" on the *Atlanta.*

Lt. Cdr. VanOstrand Perkins receiving the Silver Star aboard the USS *Birmingham,* Honolulu, May 1943. Van is the only one wearing full uniform with cap.

Pam, me, and our dog Ginger at Craggy.

On leave in Napa, California, 1944. Our knees were level even though Van's foot was a whole step down.

Posing with a Civil Air Patrol plane in 1944. Although "dogeared," it was one of the very few pictures returned to me from the USS *Birmingham*.

Right: On 11 May 1945, after two and a half years in battle, a lone kamikaze plunged through cloud cover and attacked Jim's aircraft carrier, the *Bunker Hill*. The Japanese reported, "Our bombers successfully laid a chicken on a plane carrier and made a heavenly hash out of it."

Taking Van's sword to cut the cake, Jim quietly said, "Thank you, dear friend."

Lovely Lady, Goodbye

NOVEMBER 1942—FEBRUARY 1943

By 12 November 1942, the *Atlanta* took up station about three miles out from the U.S. beachhead on Guadalcanal to give antisubmarine protection to transports unloading troops and supplies. About six o'clock that evening, there was submarine contact, and the ships of the screen launched numerous depth charges. Though they failed to make a kill, the experience served to heighten the tension and put the lads in *Atlanta* on the alert. Shortly, they became aware that they were heading for a scrap, as they changed course northward toward "the Slot."

There were all manner of reactions: braggadocio from a few, stoicism from others, exhilaration all around at the prospect of getting a whack at the Japs again. Only fools would have no apprehension, and there were few fools in this ship.

That night was one of the strangest of the war. St. Elmo's fire, a sailor's sign of trouble ahead, danced eerily on the mast and rigging. The new moon had disappeared over the horizon, and the stars were out directly above; at the same time, lightning flashed fitfully, illuminating low-lying clouds hanging over Guadalcanal as the "Lucky A" glided gracefully toward her fate. Some men, knowing that in a matter of hours it would be 13 November, wondered if thirteen would be their lucky or unlucky number.

Oddly, the admiral in command of Task Group 6.7.4 flew his flag in the USS *San Francisco,* a ship with only air search radar. Admiral Scott, the junior flag officer, and his staff were in the *Atlanta,* directly ahead of the *San Fran-*

cisco. They had better radar equipment. The *Helena* and the *Juneau,* to the rear of the *San Francisco,* had the most modern radar then extant. The ships were steaming in one long column heading toward Savo Sound, with the Japs in two columns closing fast. Communications were crackling over voice radio at such a rate, and from so many sources, that those listening were utterly confused by the jumble.

At one point, the *Atlanta* had to swing hard to port.

"What are you doing?" barked Admiral Callaghan aboard the *San Francisco.*

"Avoiding our own destroyers," answered Captain Jenkins in the *Atlanta.*

Such was the confusion as the ships maneuvered in the area soon to be dubbed "Iron Bottom Bay."

Jim's battle station was in the plotting room five decks below the bridge—not a happy place to be, as he could see nothing. Van's battle station was directly behind the bridge. Needless to say, all ships were sailing "darkened ship." Eerily, the shadowy forms of men moved about the decks; they spoke in whispers for fear any noise would give their presence away.

They knew the enemy was no longer ahead of them but virtually in their midst. Jim, receiving a barrage of information, and with his radar showing the Japs closing fast, was bewildered that no one had given the order to fire. Van, from his vantage point, could now see the dark outlines of the enemy ships against the inky sky. Why no order to fire? They waited, every nerve tensed. Still no order to fire. Six whole minutes elapsed. Suddenly, the Japanese turned on their search lights, illuminating the American ships and simultaneously opening fire. Without waiting for orders, Commander Nicholson, the gunnery boss, shouted, "Open fire!" In seconds all hell broke loose.

The *Atlanta* was hit again and again—with shells from enemy ships and from at least one of our own ships. Admiral Scott and most of his staff; the navigator, Cdr. Phil Smith; and many more were killed by direct hits on the bridge, first on one side and then the other. By a miracle, Captain Jenkins, though wounded, and Cdr. Dallas Emory survived the dreadful destruction of those salvos.

Jim had no clear picture of what was happening topside. Water was cascading through the overhead. It seemed as though they might already be sinking. A mighty explosion lifted the ship bodily out of the water. As she settled back down, a shudder went through her that the men felt like a wound to themselves. A torpedo had struck the forward engine room, aft of the plotting room, breaking the watertight integrity of the bulkhead, and water now gushed through into "plot."

Years later, Jim recounted that time for his son, Allan:

I was thrown against the bulkhead, smashing my right hand. Seeing the danger of their position, I ordered two of the men to leave the compartment, as I and the two remaining men attempted to secure the space. I contacted Cdr. Nicholson to report we were flooding and asked for orders. His reply didn't help. "Stick a pillow in it," then the phone went dead and I was on my own.

There was only one way of egress from "plot" to the Quarter-deck. That was through the trunk—a sort of tunnel straight up. The first two lads climbed the ladder, reaching the Quarter-deck just in time to receive the full force of a salvo, killing both men outright.

Now, my hand useless, I ordered the two remaining men to get topside, as water swirled higher around us.

"Dear God," I prayed. "Get us out of here before we drown."

The men started up the ladder, but then realized I couldn't maneuver it one-handed. They reached down grabbing me by my left arm, they hauled me up the trunk. Another terrible explosion threw me through the air full force across the space into the bulkhead, knocking me out. My helmet saving my life. How long I was out I don't know, but shortly I picked myself up and proceeded out to the Quarter-deck. I tripped over the two lads I'd sent ahead, dead on the deck. For a brief moment, I sagged against the bulkhead fighting back nausea, holding my wounded hand to my chest to assuage both my pain and grief, feeling the awful weight of command and choking back a scream I couldn't allow myself to utter.

"God Bless Them," I said to myself.

As Jim struggled to gain his composure, he became aware of someone speaking to him. Boatswain Leighton Spadone's letter recalls,

About 10 to 15 minutes after the incoming shell fire ceased I left the mount and climbed down to the Quarter-deck area since our phones to machine gun control were dead. I was scouting around to determine as best I could what action should be taken. Upon reaching the vicinity of the Quarterdeck I noticed Lieutenant Jim Shaw just inside the door leading to the engineering spaces below the starboard lifeboat—he was holding his arm which apparently had been wounded and he seemed to be in a somewhat dazed condition but 100% mentally functional. He was the only officer in the vicinity and I asked him what he thought we should do.

"Suggest we get the lifeboat lowered to the deck level and load the wounded personnel on board," Jim said. "Then secure same alongside, the men will have a better chance of making it in the boat."

Jim remained in the area while the boat was loaded and secured alongside. I have always felt that, in spite of his condition he retained the ingrained qualities of leadership expected of a good Naval Officer—we shared an unforgettable experience.

Leighton Spadone worked miracles that night helping wounded when he could, dousing fires with no thought for his own wounds or well-being. As dawn came up and the ship was still afloat, he helped the wounded in the boat back aboard, later to be taken ashore by Guadalcanal-based boat pool from the American sector recently wrested from the Japanese.

Meanwhile, Jim made his way through raging fires, burning amidships, through smoke and debris to the after part of the ship. He found the doctor, just up from sick bay, where he had been working furiously over the wounded. He was smoking a cigarette and taking a quick break. Diffidently, Jim asked, "Hey Doc, could you splint my hand? I think it's broken."

"Stuff it in your life jacket. I haven't time to care for it now," the Doc replied. Jim took the suggestion. His hand was hurting fiercely now, as well as his head, but he was determined to keep going.

Part of the salvo that hit the bridge and killed Admiral Scott and his staff caught Van, stationed behind the bridge, shattering his kneecap and cutting his face from his lip over his chin and down his neck. Somehow he managed to slide down a guywire to the 0-1 deck and take a swab from a locker. Turning it upside down, he made himself a usable crutch.

Charles Dodd's letter told me what went on in his vicinity. "At the time of the action I was fireman 1st class," he wrote. "I was the hoist operator for the No. 1 and No. 2–1.1 Machine Guns. After numerous shell hits in the vicinity of my battle station, I, and other survivors from this area, proceeded down the starboard outside ladder to the main deck. It was shortly thereafter that I observed Lieutenant Perkins. He was on the starboard side of the 0-1 deck just above where I was standing. He had apparently been wounded and he was using either a swab or a broom handle as a crutch. I could not hear what he was saying, but it appeared he was organizing the personnel in his immediate area."

Once Van had done what he could to get the men fighting fires and helping the wounded, he made his way aft through choking smoke and fire, hobbling on the makeshift crutch. His knee burning with pain, he stopped a minute. He put his hand to his face and it came away sticky with blood, the first he knew his face had been hit. He heard someone sob but could not locate the man. A lad not hurt was hurling colorful invectives at the retreating Japs, as he worked at releasing a pal from under debris in which he was trapped.

Stumbling and slipping on the oil, blood, and debris that littered the deck, including the contents of the potato locker, which had burst open, causing an additional hazard, Van had a profound feeling of desolation as though he alone of his brother officers was alive. Sick at heart, he hobbled on. His relief was immense when, through the smoke, in the flickering light of the fires, he found Jim. His elation was such that he cracked wise when Jim, none too dexterously, gave him a shot of morphine with his left hand. "Son of a gun! That hurts more than my leg does." Van in turn gave Jim a shot of morphine, which took care of the pain in his hand until morning, when he saw it was as big as a ham. Not until then had he realized how seriously he had been injured.

They worked on together. Jim's calm, efficient help was invaluable to Van. They made a fine pair: three usable hands, three working legs, and two outstanding minds. Cut off by fire from the forward part of the ship—no power, no communications, they had to take matters into their own hands, solving horrendous problems as they found them. Van directed fire-fighting parties and other damage-control matters and Jim, using his good legs, carried messages and delivered orders. Both helped wounded when they could with their morphine, which only officers could carry.

Van's face and neck wounds kept breaking open, dripping blood down his neck and inside his life jacket; his leg was numb by now, but with a cane someone brought him to take the place of the swab, he kept going. Once, he felt inside his life jacket to see if his packet of letters was all right. It was, and so was his little silver folding picture frame with my picture in it. He realized that the folding frame had saved his life, for it had a large dent in it, having deflected a piece of shrapnel headed right for his heart.

"Thank you, Betts," he said, giving it a pat before he started once again to do all he could to save the ship.

Lord knows, Jim and Van were not alone in their efforts. All the men were splendid, the less-wounded doing all they could. They worked the best way they knew how, often without orders for lack of communications. Some of them, unaware that there were any officers to turn to, used their long months of training to good account and made a valiant effort to save their fine ship. They all but succeeded.

The battle was over as suddenly as it had begun. As dawn crept up in the sky and the fires no longer gave light to silhouette the men, the eerie gray shadows turned into living beings. Out from the American base came a boat to take off the wounded. The captain ordered Jim and Van to go with the wounded. They both took exception to the order, but Captain Jenkins prevailed.

For their outstanding efforts, the captain recommended both men for the Navy Cross, but the review board reduced their awards to Silver Stars. Their citations best describe what both men did that night:

The President of the United States takes pleasure in presenting
The SILVER STAR MEDAL TO LIEUTENANT JAMES C. SHAW,
UNITED STATES NAVY
for service as set forth in the following
CITATION:

"For conspicuous gallantry and intrepidity aboard the U.S.S. ATLANTA during action against enemy Japanese naval forces in the Solomon Island Area on November 13, 1942. After his ship was badly damaged in the course of the engagement, Lieutenant Shaw, although suffering from a broken hand bravely assisted in transferring wounded personnel from the stricken vessel to rescue boats alongside. Unwilling to abandon his efforts and submit to medical treatment, he requested permission to remain aboard, but was ordered to be evacuated with the others. His game endurance and unselfish devotion to duty were in keeping with the highest traditions of the United States Naval Services."

For the President
Frank Knox, Secretary of the Navy

The President of the United States takes pleasure in presenting
The SILVER STAR MEDAL TO LIEUTENANT VANOSTRAND PERKINS,
UNITED STATES NAVY
for service as set forth in the following
CITATION:

"For conspicuous gallantry and intrepidity aboard the U.S.S. ATLANTA during action against enemy Japanese naval forces in the Solomon Island Area on November 13, 1942. Although severely wounded during the course of the engagement, Lieutenant Perkins, despite acute pain and waning strength, continued his direction of fire-fighting parties and other damage control activities. Unwilling to abandon his efforts and submit to medical treatment, he requested permission to remain aboard after injured personnel had been removed, but was ordered to be evacuated. His sturdy endurance and unselfish devotion to duty were in keeping with the highest traditions of the United States Naval Service."

For the President
Frank Knox, Secretary of the Navy

As Van and Jim left the *Atlanta* for the last time, it was as though some part of them was being torn out. Good friends, friends they would never see again, had been killed, and they would never again see their beautiful ship. She was special—very special! She lies at the bottom of Iron Bottom Bay, and with her the 131 killed and 14 missing. Seventy-eight were wounded. In silence, Van and Jim looked at the ship as long as they could, then collapsed from utter physical and emotional exhaustion.

Once ashore, Jim and Van were separated. Jim was still walking. Van was on a stretcher tagged with his name and the nature of his wounds, including the legend "leg must be removed." Van was in a lethargic state when a good friend of ours, Ed Dissette, spotted him and stopped to talk. Van asked him to call me, as Ed was on his way to the States, and then Van dozed off.

Ed caught hold of a doctor who told him, "He's smashed his knee cap and he'll probably lose his leg. We'll air-vac him to Espiritu Santo where a final determination will be made, but I doubt they can save his leg. He's lost too much blood to do much for him here, except keep him comfortable."

Jim was disconsolate, for he had lost everything in his room; worst of all were all his letters from Jane and his sword. At least he had his diary still strapped to his leg. Van's diary, however, went down with the ship. Still ambulatory, but with his hand and arm broken, Jim was fitted with a temporary splint, which made him more comfortable, but by early evening he was told the Japs were about to launch a counteroffensive and he was ordered to get himself into a foxhole.

An officer asked him, "Do you have a pistol?"

Raising his eyebrows in astonishment, Jim said, "Affirmative, but my right hand is broken, what in the hell am I supposed to do with my pistol?"

The answer was, to put it mildly, curt: "You'll learn in a helluva hurry to use your left hand."

That was another tense night without sleep, and Jim thanked his lucky stars he was in the Navy and did not usually spend nights in foxholes.

The next morning Jim was told to join a group of wounded in a tumbrel-like cart drawn by a tractor to be ferried out through the jungle to the airstrip from which they would be evacuated. Halfway through the jungle the cart stopped. They could hear explosions ahead and were told the airstrip was under attack and they must wait until the Japs quit shelling.

Out of the gloom of the jungle a Marine officer, in grimy garb, stepped smartly. He came over to the cart, leaned against it, and asked, "Anyone here out of the class of '36?"

Jim replied, "Shaw here, who is it?"

So there in the jungle, with an unholy noise up ahead, they held a very mini reunion. The Marine jumped into the tumbrel with Jim for the ride to the airfield. Presently, as the noise of shelling ceased, the cart bumped forward, and Jim was on his way to the base hospital in New Zealand. There he and Van were reunited and spent the next three months together, talking about feelings and family, Van's baby, times in Manila before and after they were married, the grand time when we had all been together in New York, and all the friends they had in common. They spoke very little about the *Atlanta*. That was almost more than they could stand to mention.

It would be some time before they could talk about "That Night," November the thirteenth. It was never to be forgotten by the devoted crew of the "Lucky A." Friday the thirteenth, thirteen ships in column, and all of them sunk or badly damaged, except the thirteenth ship, the last one in the column. The USS *Fletcher*, destroyer number 445. Add that number up: 4 + 4 + 5 = 13! For so very many thirteen was tragedy; for others, it was a lucky number. For all the men who lived through one of the most violent sea battles of the war, that night was written indelibly in their memories for the rest of their lives.

Even the Ship's Mascot

We at home knew within twenty-four hours that the *Atlanta* had been hit seriously during the battle of Guadalcanal. Our husbands had told us about the ship's mascot, Lucky. "After getting to sea we discovered a stowaway, a little mongrel puppy," Jim wrote Jane. "It seems this puppy crawled under a sailors jumper while the sailor was ashore and the sailor didn't even know it was there until he returned to the ship—at any rate the dog's on board, sad faced, waggle tailed and being completely spoiled. The sailmaker made him a lifejacket, the sickbay made him an I.D. tag, the carpenter made him a bed and the office prepared him a service record—he's been named 'The Lucky A' or 'Lucky' for short."

So when the reporter on board got a story through about a ship that had been hit and the numerous casualties on board, he added, "Even the ship's mascot, the little dog Lucky, died at his post—not a scratch on him, probably concussion killed him." Seeing the story in the *New York Herald Tribune* had alerted everyone connected with the ship that the *Atlanta* was in deep trouble. I do not think I can ever forget the sick feeling I had that morning, reading the papers at the breakfast table. Of course, I knew that Van was in danger anytime he was at sea, but this was both Van and beyond. It was the whole ship. That beautiful, graceful vessel that had seemed so invulnerable, and all the splendid young men who were our friends.

For the first time, I was struck with horror at the brutality of war. To build a thing of beauty, to fill her with the finest young men the Navy could muster, and to send them out to kill and be killed or maimed! How fruitless, how unconscionable—the ultimate stupidity of mankind, the ultimate horror of womankind. I came to hate, unconditionally, for the first time in my life. The Japanese were the focus of my hate.

Young people cannot long sustain such philosophical thoughts without taking some action, so I went upstairs to our baby and she and I did some praying. Then I wrote Van, knowing I was sending a letter that might wander around the Pacific and never catch up with him. If it did reach him, I wanted it to be upbeat, something fun for him to read, so I wrote about the baby and I added a note, "So sorry to hear about Lucky," so he would know I was aware of the battle. It was hard to write that letter.

Though I knew for a certain that Van was in some deep trouble, I did not doubt for a minute I would see him again. In fact, I had supreme confidence that my husband would manage somehow to find his way home. I read over his letters and so often they would say, "We're going to have such fun when we're together again." Holding that thought in mind drove back panic. I was pretty good at being dramatic in the best of times. In these bad times I sensed that if I let myself go, the dramatics would turn to hysteria, so I forced myself to act as though nothing was amiss.

Every morning now I tried to get down for breakfast in time to grab the *Tribune* before Dad got hold of it. On 28 November I found what I had been searching for. The headline read "Detailed Story of U.S. Victory Over Jap Fleet in Solomons." The subtitle read "Naval Officers Describe 3 Day Battle of Sea and Air Forces." There was a brief description of the Japanese losses, and then came a tally of our fleet: "A United States Navy task force opened the battle, outnumbered, out-weighed and out-gunned and emerged with a great victory. It was dead black at 1:48 A.M. on November 13 when the American task force of light cruisers and destroyers went in against a Japanese formation headed by a battleship. 'It was like a scene in the movies when somebody turns out the lights in the barroom and everybody starts shooting at once,' Lieut. VanO Perkins of Greenwich Conn., one of the participants, said."

I read no further. I just whooped at the top of my lungs, "He's alive! He's alive! Oh, thank God, he's all right. Mum, Dad, come quickly! He's alive!"

Dad took up the newspaper and read out loud more about the battle. One phrase caught my attention: "For the first time America has gone on the offense; it is doubtful if the Japanese Navy will ever be able to move forward again for despite our heavy losses we turned back the enemy who were unable to reinforce their troops. This is the turning point of the war."

What that meant was a bit obscure to me. Did the writer think we were going to chase the Japanese Navy right back to Japan? It was too much for me to take in at that moment, but it sounded grand, and with the news that Van was alive it became a moment of jubilation. Mum kissed me, Dad patted me on the back, and I jabbered, "Oh, whoopee! Wow! Whoopee!" In short order I sobered up, for if Lucky had been killed, so had some of our friends.

We had no "support groups" then, except those the wives made for themselves. Not too long after my own good news, Grace Smith called. "Can you come," she pleaded. "Phil has been killed!"

"Oh Dear God, Grace, I'll be right there, probably half an hour to get to Mt. Vernon. Hold on, lady!"

"I'm all right," she said in a voice that made me think she had not yet grasped the full import of her news.

I grabbed my coat, yelled to Mum where I was going, and drove as fast as I dared. Just as I arrived, Grace was talking on the telephone to Mrs. McDermott, Jack Pierce's mother. I heard Grace say, "Oh God, Jack has been killed!" Whirling, she flung her arms around me, sobbing, "Van—oh—Van, what of Van? That's Jack Pierce—is Van? Oh Jesus, Mary, Mother of God!"

"Come on, Grace, don't worry about Van, he's all right. We need to get to Mrs. McDermott."

Not until Grace saw Jack's mother did she realize the enormity of her own loss. Mrs. McDermott, who was trying to cope with the loss of a son before he had time to realize his potential—the ultimate crusher—was wonderfully kind to Grace. I do not know how she mustered so much courage.

The next few days were a nightmare of phone calls. Elly Broughton was the hub of the West Coast network of wives, and we soon knew who was wounded, killed, or all right. I don't think the AP News had anything to do with our finding out casualties. Going to memorial services became a painful part of my existence. I ached for the brave women whose lives were shattered, and I said my own silent prayer of thanks that my Van was alive. There were so many tragedies happening to my friends.

Then came a call from our friend Ed, who had seen Van on Guadalcanal, and I dashed to New York to see him. When he told me Van was losing his leg, I was overjoyed, for that meant no more war for Van. Yet I felt guilty for feeling happy in the face of so much tragedy. Ed made me feel selfish to boot when he said, "You know, Betts, Van will hate being beached when all his friends are fighting. You're going to have your hands full keeping up his morale."

Two of my closest friends, Wirt Cates and Scotty McLennon, were reported "Killed in Action." There were so many blows, and there were more to come. Certainly my own concerns took a back seat, including my baby, not yet six weeks old, whom I had turned over to Mrs. Major and my family, knowing that she would be in loving hands. My family was splendid. They chipped in their gas rations so I could get back and forth. Dad and Pop Perkins tried to check out and verify every report we received.

Finally, I got through to Jane Shaw. She had received a grotesquely censored letter from Jim, written almost illegibly with his left hand. Her answer to Jim on 30 November 1942 was written from Fort Benjamin Harrison, where Colonel Holt was stationed:

> Your letter arrived this morning, and sort of knocked the pins out from under me. All I can think of is to thank God that you came through, how very, very lucky I am! Your letter was cut to ribbons, and I only get the idea that you "got off all right and that you are in a 'safe' and comfortable place and feel like a pampered gold brick." Judging by the writing your right arm must be injured, but they cut out all the part about what your injuries are, so I can only guess. I was completely unprepared for this, if there is anything, it hasn't been told here, and I haven't received any "brief note" that you speak of. Betty Lou didn't know anything about you either, she called and said that they hadn't told her anything about you at the office, but we both have a feeling that there may be a family reunion within some time. I don't know, that is just a guess along with everything else. Just so you are all right, my Jimmy, nothing else matters. So many things fade into insignificance in the face of something like this. It is hard, knowing that you are hurt, and I don't know where you are, or how much you are hurt or anything else. Darling, you are so much a part of me that it seems to make me suffer too, not only mentally with worry and wonder, but physically. I hope that by the time you get this you will be up and well again, providing the address reaches you. No matter what has happened, just the mere fact that you are safe and able to write a note to me is the only thing that matters at all. Try and get well soon, and if they will let you, come home for a while. . . .
>
> Everything else has skipped out of my mind, dear, it is completely absorbed with you, so I'll get this off on a chance that it may reach you. Now remember, no matter what has happened, we still have each other, and we can still fight together for the future we want so badly. We'll have it too! I just thank God every minute that you are safe, what more could I ask of life?

The Red Cross censors had totally blackened out with ink, or cut out with scissors, any mention of our husbands' wounds. That sort of censorship was not only foolish, it was cruel. Despite phrases such as "I'm fine, don't worry about me," the mere fact that the paper on which letters were written had "Red Cross" in red stamped across the top and large cut-out phrases made one's imagination run wild. Certainly, anything the men said could not have given "aid and comfort to the enemy." It took Betty Lou and Colonel Holt some finagling to get a report on Jim's hand. Both Jane and I had the same thankful reaction: our husbands were wounded, not killed. Possibly they might even come home, though we had heard some of the men were reassigned to duty in the Pacific. I wrote Van on 1 December:

I received parts of your letter of Nov. 17th. I say parts because some darn censor had ripped it to pieces. Obviously you were telling me all about yourself and not a thing that hasn't been headlined in about umpteen papers over the country. All the other girls are now possessing full information as to what their husbands "minor wounds" consist of. I hope darling that yours didn't hurt too awfully much. The one and only thing I would really hate for you is if you were blind, which I know you aren't, because everything else you can overcome and you're the lad that can overcome anything you put your mind to. I'm so terribly thankful that you're safe and am about to bust I'm so proud of you. . . . Maizie's husband told me about what it is said is wrong with you. If it's so, I'm sorry only because I know it must have hurt like hell and I don't like you to be hurt. Anyway, you know I know if it's true and if it isn't, I'll know soon enough that it isn't. . . . The point, in my mind, is that you're alive and you're the same man you were before only more so, and don't you forget that's what I think. Don't you dare go worrying about me and what I do or don't think is wrong with you. . . .

Darling, this is three days later, I have been having an awful time trying to write this. You see I've thought you were minus a leg which makes no difference to me but I've thought perhaps it would to you. At this point Aunt Kate has had your letter so that I feel a little more certain from that and the girls in Coronado have told me their side of the story. . . . If by chance it is true I say just what I did in the beginning of this letter and add that much again, we start on a new life which will present just as few adjustments as all our other starts have. We are far too close to each other not to be able to take anything in our stride, in fact I sort of look forward to something new to conquer.

You know we've had knocks here and there and we've gotten pretty big because of them. If we continue to get knocks we'll be busting our seams one of these days. Everything with you is fun and that's how I look at this. If it's true, we have so many new things to plan, like where we're going to live and I'll want to hear all about what kind of business you're going into. I hope it's ship building, or even yacht gas stations. [A pipe dream of my own, as marinas did not yet exist.] Oh my, there's so much to think about. If it's not true then we have all the speculation about what you'll be doing next, and I'm wondering if you'll get home for a short leave and perhaps be able to see Pam long enough to realize she's yours and not just a baby. All our lives together have been one long speculation, if's and but's. . . .

Dearest, I have to go to Phil Smith's funeral tomorrow, it will be kind of trying I guess and I think some sleep might stand me in good stead, so for now I will dream such wonderful dreams of you.

Not Ever to Know

Not long after the memorial services were over, I had a tragic call from my dear friend and bridesmaid Tek Lyster. Ted was missing in action. The *Juneau* had gone down with a mighty explosion on her way south after the battle of Guadalcanal. No one knew what happened. Could Pop Perkins find out anything? She and Ted were two of our closest friends, and there was so little I could do, with Tek way out in Oregon.

Van's dad did all he could to find out what had happened, which was precious little, for not even the Navy could be sure who had lived through that hellish tragedy. He tried to discover Ted's status, but the only answer he received was "Missing in Action, presumed dead but not officially." That left Tek on a roller coaster of hope and despair. I think she knew in her heart what had happened to Ted, but until she was officially notified, she prayed and hoped. He was not one of the ten survivors. I wrote Van at the end of a letter:

P.S. Precious Tekla just called me, Teddy is missing, Oh Lord, this is an awful world, if it'd only stop. Poor Tek, not to know, not ever to know. I love the girl like I would a sister and it hurts to have her so sad. She's wonderful too, her chin so sky high and she's sure Ted will come home sometime. You know for all these girls, the war is over. Thank the Lord they have children for they have something anyway. Gosh I can't help saying all this, but with so much tragedy going on around me I wonder why I'm so lucky. You know there were two "lovely ladies" and now they are gone. How very incredible and how very sad. . . .

The most important thing in all of life to me is that we love each other, for nothing bad has ever come from that and over and over again something good has been the result.

Jane and I compared notes whenever we got letters from New Zealand, where our husbands were hospitalized. Young bones heal quickly, and by Christmas Van and Jim had left the hospital long enough to play a ridiculous game of golf, Jim one-handed and Van stiff-legged and still using a crutch. They were unable to manage more than four holes. The course was totally flat or

Van could not have managed at all. Neither fellow reported the score in their letters, if score there was, merely that it was great to get some exercise and fresh air.

Van wrote that New Zealanders were allowed three gallons of gas a month and asked how we were getting along with rationing. I wrote back in early January 1943:

> We are faring well enough in view of the fact we have NO GAS at all! The Metropolitan area ran very short so now only essential vehicles get gas (despite the fact we're in the country with no bus service we are part of the shortage). It is a bit rough riding a bicycle in six inches of snow when you can't sit down comfortably in a soft chair. [My coccyx was broken when Pam was born, and it had not as yet totally healed.]
>
> The rest of rationing is a bit of a challenge. No canned goods to be had. Nothing rubber, no silk or nylon stockings (I hoarded a few and wear cotton until you come home). Sugar, coffee, butter, meat, cigarettes, liquor all are in very short supply and rationed to boot. I smoke a little lady's pipe Doc Squire gave me, it helps. Shoes are hardly obtainable but I am a centipede according to my shoe rack, so unless the war lasts ten years I shouldn't have to buy shoes. Well, everybody thinks this isn't much of a sacrifice, it's more a challenge really. Keeping the house warm is impossible so we keep everything closed up except the living room where we keep a fire burning. Mother bought some horrible material with which to make curtains to cut off the big hall. It helps.

The whole rationing business was a constant sleight of hand trick. Three gallons a week was plenty for city dwellers, but for those in the country with no public transportation, we dusted off our old bikes and prayed the tires did not give out because new ones were not available. Meat, butter, sugar, and coffee all took "red points" (little stamps in the ration books), so a few of our neighbor's pooled red stamps to buy a large roast, then we cut it up so each family had a small roast. Cigarettes were rationed, so I smoked my little ladies pipe and gave Mum my cigarette coupon.

I guess oil rationing was the hardest on most people. Our house had several fireplaces. We learned to burn canal coal, which was available, and we burned any wood we could get our hands on. Shoes, stockings, and anything elastic like panty girdles were severely rationed or just plain not available. We seemed to spend a lot of time making do, but it was a challenge and we deemed it our patriotic duty. Maybe others had a hard time with all this, but our neighborhood seemed to find it a bit of a game. Who saved the most foil? How far could you stretch the red points? How far could you ride the bike up hill before you had to get off and push? The heavier your groceries (carried in the bike basket), the sooner you had to get off and push. It could have been drudgery or fun. We chose fun.

Days went by. More wounded poured into the hospital where Van and Jim were. The wards became so crowded that the two men were told to get out on their own for a few days. They made plans and took off for the New Zealand Alps, where Jim wrote Jane in January 1943:

> We're off to go fishing where Zane Grey used to fish. . . . When we arrived at the resort we were greeted by an old guide. "Yanks, by God," he chortled. "I been waiting the 'ole war to see you. Do you know my sister who lives in Brooklyn?"
>
> We assured him that we hadn't as yet had that pleasure but would certainly rectify that if ever we got back to the States. He, in turn, assured us he would guide us to the best fishing spots. Sure enough he did, boy did we catch fish. He even took pictures of Van and me with our biggest fish, which pictures I'll send home for you to put in our album (better yet I'll bring them). The Maoris smoked the fish we didn't eat and we brought back enough to feed the entire ward.

Both Van and Jim sent home the photographs of their giant trout, four of which weighed more than six pounds. The photos were shown with pride and a bit of a boast.

With all the sad things I had to report to Van, I was delighted to have something comical to write:

> Yesterday afternoon I was honored by a call from Mr. Robert Chute, late of the *Atlanta,* now home on leave. He was both amusing and pathetically glad to talk. Full of the usual horror stories and equally full of scathing remarks for the *San Francisco.*
>
> "Mind you, Mrs. Perkins. I ain't talking about this ship to no one but you, but a guy's gotta blow off some steam to someone and all this Hero Ship stuff is the bunk. It gives me the pip and I can't shoot me mouth about it to no one, and seein' as you're in the Regs, I guess you know the score and I can squawk an' get it outa my system, cause if it don't come out now I'll bust some one of these days."
>
> Then he launched into a dissertation about you—
>
> "Now Mr. Perkins, he's a fine Officer, he knows his job. Of course he's awful military and strict and some of the men didn't like him because he was like that. But that's the way you gotta be if you want good men, an' he's fair. He never gets you fouled up like so many of them Officers do. Now if you tell him sometime to give the men a smile once in a while he'd be an Ace, he would. It's only he's a bit too Military but then you gotta be Military to get anywhere and that's no

lie. Now I'm telling you true Mrs. Perkins because this husband of yours is a fine Officer and if it was I could do so I'd like to serve him again and though he don't know me from Adam and I don't know him so good, I know he's a snappy Officer and I like him and would like to serve with him as I says before."

Sister Nane and I were almost in tears over him. He was so in earnest and so desirous of putting his ideas across. The bit about Van not smiling somewhat amazed me, for I had seen him smile at the men many times. I thought, perhaps, his insistence on excellence from his men might have annoyed the lazy. In any event, I relayed the message for what it was worth.

My friends in Washington kept assuring me that Van would soon be coming home, but nothing Van heard in New Zealand gave him any encouragement. He could not understand why he was being held there. Both he and Jim were getting along so well they were going shopping and to the movies, even swimming. I could see in the photographs that Van's knee had something bulky on it; if he could swim, it was probably an ace bandage. He had talked of going dancing one night, which annoyed me. I saw no reason why he could not be home dancing with me. He felt the same way, telling me it was nice to be able to do something as removed from the war as going dancing (albeit with a cane in hand) but that he wanted to dance with me and he wanted to meet his baby girl and he was *damn mad* about being held there when he could be mending at home much better.

Finally, the two were given orders to sail on the troopship *West Point.* They were just part of the troops. They were fed breakfast at 5:00 in the morning and then had nothing to do all day until supper at 5:00 in the afternoon. Two meals a day and pretty awful at that.

Then came a message from the ship's captain to report to the bridge. "You are both qualified watch standers aren't you?" he asked.

"Yes, sir," they replied enthusiastically.

"From now on you will be put on the duty list and stand watches with the ship's officers," said the captain.

"Oh good," Jim answered. "We'll eat three meals a day in the wardroom, that'll be great."

"Certainly not, you will remain as you are—supernumeraries," the captain replied.

Van took up the discussion. "I guess we won't be able to help you out, sir, as we are not officially members of your crew. Request permission to return to our quarters."

"Permission granted," the captain said, glowering his displeasure.

So Jim and Van returned below decks, chortling over getting the best of the captain but sorry not to get three square meals a day for the rest of the voyage.

They spent the remaining time talking as they had all this past year and a half, only this time Van talked a lot about his ideals and ambitions for his baby daughter, and how he longed to have a home of his very own where he would know I was when he was away. Jim talked for the first time about his longing to have a child and how he hoped Jane would be in San Francisco to meet him this time. They made plans for all four of us to go out tea dancing together their second night home.

Somehow, Jim's letter to Jane telling her to meet him in San Francisco never reached her. When I called to tell her I was going out and asked her to meet me in Chicago, Jane said, "I think I better wait here. I haven't heard what Jim wants me to do. I'm not even sure he knows Dad has been transferred to Fort Benjamin Harrison. Oh yes, of course he knows that but I just think I better stay here."

Once again Jim was bitterly disappointed. He wrote Jane a wistful note:

Bettsy Perkins is here with Van, their baby girl and nursemaid. I do so wish you were here also, and can't imagine why my letter never reached you.

Never mind, it won't be long now before that glorious moment comes when I can take you in my arms. My precious Tumble, I love you.

Pam's nursemaid, a high school girl named Agnes Magnus, the baby, and I were ensconced at the Fairmont Hotel, waiting for Van's arrival. He was not sure when he would arrive so had not told me to go west, but I went just the same. The phone rang. It was Mother, saying, "Van just called. He's on his way up to the Fairmont, I'll get off the phone. Dear love to you both."

I quickly hung up and hastily combed my hair, no lipstick this time, and told Agnes, "Go away, go anywhere for at least an hour. Go on, scram!" Minutes later came a knock on the door and there was Van.

Poor darling, he looked so thin and his eyes showed the hurt more clearly than the livid scar that ran from his lip over his chin and down his neck. I buried my head on his shoulder afraid that kissing him might hurt. In a second he disabused me of that notion. The flowers he had brought me were forgotten on the floor.

Taking him by the hand, I led Van into the other room, where, for the first time, he looked down at his daughter, fast asleep in her crib. Slowly he sank to one knee, his face level with hers, and kissed her. Then he looked up at me. "Oh, Betts, oh, Betts," he whispered.

He stretched out his hand for me to hold and put his finger in Pamie's little hand. When she curled her fingers around his and opened her eyes, he said, "Oh, Lord, oh, Lord, I have my little family all together—how I've prayed for this day." Picking up his daughter for the first time, he held her close in his arms and rocked her back and forth, crooning, "Little Pamela, little girl, my child, my daughter. Oh Betts, our daughter. At long last, I am well content."

We played with the baby, sprawled out on the bed in our room. Finally, Van said, "I really have to eat. My last meal, which was lousy, I had at five this morning and it's six P.M. now. We'll be here for three days, then Greenwich, here we come. Jim and I made a date to go out together, but other than that I just want to stay by ourselves. I'm so glad you brought the baby."

We headed home by train this time. No need to hurry. We were together and that was all that mattered.

Star-Crossed

MARCH 1943–MAY 1943

What fun Van and I had when we reached Greenwich. Pop Perkins took a few days leave, and he and Mom came up from Washington. So did Van's brother, Wood, who was by then a Navy doctor. My two brothers came home from college. Only sister Nane and Joe could not get to Greenwich. Despite rationing, Mother rolled out the "fatted calf," and Dad depleted his dwindling stock of scotch. The "court photographer" was called in to take numerous pictures of Van and his family, which would delight us for years to come.

Van's orders were to take ten days leave and then report to Washington, D.C., for temporary duty. We were in high good humor over this, for it was unusual for a man who had been wounded and was changing station to get such a short leave, and we thought this meant that Van was to have a choice of duty. Maybe flight training or maybe command of a destroyer escort, which he really wanted. Maybe even shore duty, for by now he had served more than seven years overseas. We spent a joyous time with our baby and going to see friends, or relaxing up at Craggy, where Van totally enjoyed himself romping with Bini II in the snow and stretching out full length in the big sleigh bed, a luxury his short bunk on board ship had not allowed him.

Ten days flashed by in a twinkling, and off to Washington we went, anticipating at long last being able to have some sort of normal married life. That night we stayed with Van's family at their apartment, and the following morning Van reported to the Bureau of Personnel. I waited eagerly for his return.

Late in the afternoon a thoroughly dejected Van arrived; his first words dashed our hopes. "It couldn't be worse, Betts. I've been asked for, by Captain Wilkes, to be assistant damage control officer on the *Birmingham,* a new cruiser already operating. Because of my expertise on *Atlanta,* I have a couple of days here reporting on my theories as to why her sister ship *Juneau* sank, then we're off to Norfolk."

"Van, surely you can object to that," I said. "Everyone else from the *Atlanta* has managed to get what they wanted. Jack Wulff and Lloyd Mustin have a ship that is months from completion, neither commissioned nor even launched! They'll be home till next winter at least. Jim Shaw's ship won't be ready for trial runs until May. Dave Hall and Jack Broughton won't leave until fall, if then. Yet here you are, no leave to speak of, going to a ship you said is already operating? Don't we count for anything? Jack simply refused his first orders, why can't you?"

Unfortunately, my adored mother-in-law, for the only time in her association with me, chose that moment to interfere. Before I could say more or Van could answer my questions, she said, "Bettsy, you are being very selfish. You are only thinking of yourself and what you want. Not about Van and what is good for his career." Amazed that she should not understand, I turned to Van expectantly, waiting for him to speak up on my behalf. He did not. He just sat slumped down in his chair. He did not even look up at me, so I had no idea what he was thinking. My eyes filled with tears and I fled to the bedroom and paced up and down, trying to reason this out and calm myself down.

After what seemed like an hour, Van came in and started to put his arms around me. I brushed him off, saying, "Don't touch me right now. I want to understand what has happened in an unemotional way. If you touch me, I'll cry. That's no way for us to figure this out. Do you think I am selfish and am thinking only of my needs?"

"Oh, Betts, don't," he said. "Don't make a mountain out of a molehill. Mother shouldn't have spoken up, I grant you, but I shouldn't have discussed this in front of her. When you're asked for, it is very hard to get such orders changed. Come on now, smile, it could be worse. I could have been ordered to sea from New Zealand." Laughing, Van put his arms around me the way you would comfort a small child, which was the way I felt, unsure of myself and wanting to please him at any cost.

Three days later we drove to Norfolk, to a dingy room in a small hotel. Trying to create a sense of home, the first things I unpacked were our Ming vase, which Van had bought for me in China, and our wedding picture. We started combing the newspapers for rentals. Van called the yard and found that the *Birmingham* was already at sea "training" and would not be back for three weeks. At least that gave us more unexpected time together, though wartime Norfolk was hardly a vacation spot.

Through a friend of my Dad, we found a cottage for rent—two bedrooms, a living room with dining ell, and a small but nice kitchen. Perfect for Pam and her nursemaid, Bini II, Van, and me. There was even a large sitting room upstairs, with pullout couch and bath, in what had been the attic, and an attractive back yard. We took it and sent for the baby, and in two days we were all together with several days to just enjoy our little family.

Finally the ship came in and I drove Van down to report. A cold shiver hit me as I looked at the ship for the first time. It did not have the graceful raked bow of the *Atlanta*. Bigger, snub-nosed, it was artistically out of proportion. Ugly! I said to myself. Van kissed me and said he would call me when he needed to be picked up. Then he patted my shoulder, looked at me a long minute, grabbed his bag, and walked down the dock to the USS *Birmingham*.

My apprehension grew as I began to meet the wives. Our call on the captain was nice enough. I liked Mrs. Wilkes very much. Captain Wilkes was a powerful, stern man who had been in Manila and was obviously comfortable with his command. That helped. Most of the girls I met were wives of reserves and were standoffish with me. Of course, I hardly knew their husbands, as only the regulars were accustomed to make the social calls that drew the ship together as a family.

Immediately the ship started operating in a very strange manner. All weekend they would go to sea, come in for a day or two, and then anchor way out in the bay, training in sight of the shore. Morale on board was low, as there was seldom liberty for the crew and they had no idea why they were being driven so hard. The officers had the duty one day out of three when they were in port. They were almost never in for more than two days, which meant husbands and wives were lucky to spend more than one night together.

One of Van's junior officers was unable to find a place to live. Van asked me how I felt about letting Jack and Marge have the big room upstairs. That, of course, would mean sharing the kitchen. It would be cramped and we would not have our privacy, which both of us so dearly needed, but I agreed that we could not be selfish and keep a young couple apart. Unfortunately, this relationship proved to be unsatisfactory, as so many young couples found when they tried to double up due to lack of housing. In our case, there was the additional strain of the baby and her nurse, plus the fact that Van was fairly senior while our guests were young and childless. They failed as guests, in fact, for they did not keep to their quarters. Our privacy was vastly invaded. They moved into our living space—not just the kitchen but all of the downstairs, which was not what we had offered them. Marge's belongings were frequently underfoot, and she did not abide by the refrigerator or cooking rules we had agreed upon. It was most unhappy for Van and me. The situation added to my instinctive feeling that the *Birmingham* was star-crossed.

Poor Silent Guy

Van and I seldom had a weekend or a holiday together. Van had seen to it that flowers arrived on my doorstep early on 25 March, the morning of my birthday, which we had hoped to spend together. The day was sparkling bright with a promise of real heat by noon.

The phone jangled, and I ran to it thinking maybe Van was back and we could celebrate. Instead a strange voice said, "Is Lieutenant Perkins home?"

"This is Mrs. Perkins. May I take the message? Lieutenant Perkins is unavailable at present."

"Oh Bettsy, this is Bud Mack. Jim Shaw wanted Van to know that Jane died day before yesterday."

"Dear God! What happened? Oh how terrible. Give Jim my love. I'll tell Van and Helen and Steph and Ellie. What else can I do?"

"Nothing Betts, just tell anyone else you think of. Can you get in touch with Mrs. Jenkins or the captain? If so, tell them." He continued to tell me the circumstances of Jane's death.

My birthday had turned to tragedy.

The first thing to do was write Van and hope one of the ship's flyers would come in for the mail. Flyers flew planes that were catapulted off the stern of the *Birmingham,* often carrying personal as well as official mail.

There was no gentle way to break such news about our close friend: "The most awful news—Jane Shaw died last Tuesday. She got a strep throat which developed into scarlet fever and later pneumonia set in and she died very suddenly. Oh Lord, poor Jim. It just busts me up to think of that poor silent guy having to take that—it's too much."

Later Jim told me of this terrible time in his life after he came back from New Zealand to San Francisco with Van. He was bitterly disappointed that Jane had not come out to meet him. He and his sister had a nice visit and they had drinks with Van and me. Again Betty Lou did not take much to me, but by now Jane and Jim and Van and I had become good friends in New York and Jim knew a great deal more about me through Van's eyes. He liked what he knew and what he had heard and admired my spunk.

Jim had finally cleared San Francisco several days after landing, with orders in hand to report to the aircraft carrier *Bunker Hill,* to be commissioned at the

Charlestown Navy Yard in Boston. He and Van hoped to go to flight training. Van, on his way to Washington to report on what he thought had happened to the *Juneau,* would see what he could find out about flight school and let Jim know. With high hopes, Jim's mission was to get to Jane and thirty days leave.

First to Fort Benjamin Harrison, where Colonel Holt had Jim's hand rebroken and set properly, for it had been badly set. He spent most of his leave in therapy for his hand. Then to Malden, outside Boston, to settle into an apartment as near the Navy yard as they could get while the *Bunker Hill* was being readied. It certainly looked like the break they needed. Commander Nicholson, the gun boss on the *Atlanta,* had asked for Jim as his assistant. Bud Mack, another *Atlanta* shipmate, was also to be aboard the huge aircraft carrier.

There followed an interlude of normal life—Jim to the ship by day, evenings with Jane. In mid-March they went south for a little R&R in New York. On the way back Jane complained of a sore throat. It began to snow as they passed through Connecticut, and by the time they got to Providence, Rhode Island, the snow had turned into a blizzard. It was late, and Jane felt worse. They saw a banner hanging across the road: "Providence Welcomes Servicemen."

"We'll stop here and spend the night and get you to bed," Jim said. "In the morning I'll get you home. If you're not better, we'll call a doctor."

They tried the best hotel first. "Full up—absolutely no rooms, all reserved." They tried the second and the third. "Full up—absolutely no rooms to be had in Providence." Jim's temper began to flare. He stepped to a phone and called the mayor, who had conveniently signed the "Providence Welcomes Servicemen" banner. He got the poor man out of bed and said, "This serviceman and his sick wife have not been welcomed in Providence by anyone!" When Jim was mad his voice was icy and clearly commanding.

"Just hold on, young man, I will find you a room," the mayor replied. "If I can't, you'll stay with me. What number are you calling from? Hang up and I will call you back in five minutes."

Jim started "pacing the bridge," a watch officer's habit of a lifetime, twelve paces, turn, twelve paces back, turn. After five minutes of this the phone rang.

Cheerily the mayor instructed Jim to return to hotel number one; they would have a room for the Shaws. And so they did—the bridal suite, paid for by the mayor. Jim and Jane were delighted, though because Jane was sick they could not rightly enjoy the rooms. They were most grateful to the mayor, and that evening composed an open letter of thanks to the city of Providence, the mayor in particular, which they posted to the newspaper the next day.

Morning found Jane somewhat better, her throat still sore but the fever broken. She no longer felt dizzy, so off they headed for home. Two and a half hours later they arrived and unpacked the car. Jane quickly went to the food shop to stock the apartment and get some throat lozenges. Upon returning she assured Jim she would be all right and would take it easy. Jim headed for the ship.

By nightfall, when Jim came home, he found Jane considerably worse. Her temperature had gone up again and she was having trouble breathing. Jim called a doctor, who, on hearing her symptoms, directed Jim to take her to the hospital. The malady was diagnosed as pneumonia with possible strep throat. The hospital was the place for her to be. Jim stayed with Jane as long as he was allowed and then went back to a lonely apartment.

The next afternoon he was phoned on board the ship and told that Jane was being transferred to a contagion hospital with scarlet fever. Jim was frantic and got permission to leave the ship early. Dressed in a hospital gown and mask, he visited with Jane and they talked about how awful it was to waste three weeks of their precious time together with Jane in quarantine. There was one happy note, however. Jane told Jim she thought she was pregnant. He was delighted at the news. He urged Jane not to worry, telling her that they would spend all the time together the Navy and the hospital would allow.

He came back the next day after work and they talked a bit, but Jane was tired so Jim left to let her sleep. The doctor stopped him in the hall to tell him Jane was a very sick girl, but he hoped the crisis would soon be over. Jim called Colonel Holt, his Army doctor father-in-law, and reported on Jane. Colonel Holt said he would come as soon as he could get transportation, and that he would try to shake some penicillin loose from the Fort Benjamin Harrison Army Hospital.

The following morning Jim went to the ship as usual. Later he was summoned by the captain, who told him he was to go to the hospital immediately; an officer would accompany him. He did not wait to get his coat. He tore off the ship and sped to the hospital, praying that this was just the "crisis" yet fearing it was worse than that. When he arrived in Jane's room she was in a coma, and shortly, as he held her hand and pleaded with her to come back, he realized she had died. He had lost his Dearest Jane.

How long he sat there holding Jane's hand, his body wracked with great sobs, he had no idea. What happened next he could not remember. He only remembered the doctor gently releasing his hand and leading him into another room, where he told Jim that Jane's heart had given out. They had been unable to bring her temperature down. He was terribly sorry.

Jim said his reply sounded foolish, even to him. "I'm sorry too!" he said. Then he began to cry while the doctor stood there patting his shoulder, saying over and over, "There, there, son—there, there, son."

At last a calmness came over him and he was able to sign the necessary papers. He called his parents-in-law and Betty Lou, who said she would come as soon as she could get a leave of absence from her Naval Intelligence job. Finally, the officer drove Jim home and stayed with him, giving him a drink on top of the sedative the doctor had given him. He became drowsy but wanted to get to the funeral parlor; so he drank some coffee and they went to see about arrangements.

When Jim chose a plain bronze casket, the funeral director said, "Why, you don't want to insult your position by getting that cheap casket, and you an officer burying your wife in Arlington Cemetery." Jim nearly hit the man. He would have, had not his fellow officer restrained him. Leaving the officer to make his own way back to the ship, Jim got in his car and drove. Where he went, he never knew. He did know the car had traveled over a hundred miles and was almost out of gas when he returned to the apartment.

Somehow Jim survived the grim trip with Jane's casket to Washington, where she was buried in Arlington Cemetery. It all became a blur in his mind that he never was able to verbalize.

Jim returned to the apartment in Malden, where Betty Lou joined him until he could move aboard the ship. He went back to work. To work hard was a solace. The ship's company were wonderful to him. A few were unable to look him straight in the eye because they did not know how to handle a young wife's death. Most tried to show their sympathy by doing everything he wanted in short order or by asking him and Betty Lou to dine, go to the movies, or, later, go dancing.

Men in war expect that they can be killed. They do not expect to come home from war to watch their young bride die. It was so hard to accept Jane's death, but somehow he had to.

Jim was deluged with letters from his old shipmates, his former skippers, and his many friends. All of them he answered himself. In the mail was a letter from Van:

I've just heard of Jane's illness and your great loss. A letter can hardly explain how badly I feel and how sorry I am. I was very fond of Jane and I count you as one of my closest friends. I too will miss her.

I regret that there is so little comfort and so little help that I can offer you Jim, but if there is anything I can do, now or later on, please let me try.

Jim answered:

I guess I'm on here for the duration but it doesn't make much difference now where I go. Mainly I want to get this war over. I'm just tired of the whole thing.

Thanks so much for your kind letter about Jane's death. Van, it helps to know your good friends want to help even though they can't. I will look forward to seeing you out there, which will be great help indeed.

At the same time, he had letters from all the *Atlanta* wives who had been part of our crowd in New York. The first of these to arrive was from me:

The news of Jane has just reached me. Jim, when there is something important to say, I can't do so because it's too deep inside me to put in words. I only know that Van and I want you to know that our thoughts are all with you now and for always to come.

Van is at sea so please understand why it is that I write without him. He will write as soon as possible.

Before closing, I want to make mention of my affection for Jane which during our brief friendship became a firm one.

Jim answered my letter also:

Our dear, good friend, thank you for your kind letters to Betty Lou and me. I am sure Col. and Mrs. Holt would appreciate a letter from you also. . . .

You ask Betty Lou if there is something you can do—I will answer that there is: namely I would appreciate it if you would write once in a while as I will get very little mail from home and particularly, I want to keep in touch with you, Van and our close group from the Atlanta. Of course you and Van have so many other things in common with me that it seems doubly necessary to keep in touch.

He was wrong about very little mail from home. In fact, he was swamped with letters from girls he met after Jane died. He was a prime target for the affections of the youth and beauty in Boston, tall and handsome in his new lieutenant commander's uniform, a tragic figure, a youthful widower just about to turn thirty years old. Betty Lou warned him that he was vulnerable as well as being a "good catch."

June saw Jim at sea heading for the Pacific on the aircraft carrier *Bunker Hill*. He was glad to get back where the routine and training of his men kept him busy enough to distract his mind from his tragedy. He started writing stories as well as letters, which kept him occupied during slack times.

Complying with his request, I started writing Jim newsy letters. In his replies, he told me about Jane, about things she had never mentioned to me. He said she was a fine poet, that her friend Merrill Moore, who though a medical doctor was the poet laureate of Massachusetts, had considered Jane one of the up-and-coming poets of the young generation. He also wrote, "Jane loved her cats. Now me, I like dogs best and cats second. That was one difference we had—hardly major."

If You Are Gone

Meanwhile, Van and I were facing our own problems once again, pale in comparison to Jim's, but nevertheless upsetting to us. Poor Van's immediate boss had been disciplinary officer at the Naval Academy, variously known as the "Galloping Ghost," "Winnie the Poop," the "Scoutmaster," and other uncomplimentary names. Van soon found they must have been deserved. More serious than that, the man knew nothing about damage control or first-lieutenanting. It wasn't long before Van was spending our few evenings indignantly objecting to the man's inadequacies. That was unlike Van, who usually liked people and seldom talked about others in a derogatory manner. I began to worry about him. Moreover, we were both concerned about having another baby and wanted to keep that news to ourselves for a while until we were certain I would not have another episode as I had experienced with Pam.

The ship took off as usual. Van sent me a note back in with one of the flyers. "I've no idea where we're going nor how long but suppose you'll figure it out as you usually do," he wrote. "I love you my dearest, this last while has been heaven indeed. Take care of Pamie, darling, and remember, you have something important to do for us. I shall think of my two and a half girls constantly and love you more than ever before. You are my perfect one. No man ever had a better wife than I my darling little Betts."

On one of the days while the ship was off on this training cruise or possible departure, I had three of the wives over for luncheon. We were playing bridge after lunch when the doorbell rang. I excused myself and went to the vestibule, just off the living room, to open the door. There was no one there.

I started to turn away when Van, who had flattened himself against the building out of sight, stepped into view, whacking me on the backside. Unaware there were others in the house, he commanded, "To bed, Mrs. Perkins!" Guffaws from the living room, embarrassed giggles from us. Then Van said, "You ladies better get home in a hurry, where you'll probably get the same order. We had no way to let you know we were coming in. You best get a move on." In an aside to me Van mumbled, "Boy that joke, for your ears only, sure backfired." As the ladies left, I complied with Van's command, laughing uproariously at his discomfiture.

Many times the ship went out and we ladies sat on the beach waiting to see if it would suddenly reappear. It was not surprising that I tucked a note in Van's pocket as he left the following morning, just in case:

If you are gone for one day I will miss you a thousand years worth. If more 'twill be a million years I miss you. If it is another surprise trip, for good! I will miss you more than words alone can say, and love you as much.

A pleasant Easter to you my precious, I will say a prayer in church for you.
Your own,
[I drew a wistful rabbit as my signature.]

This time I thought it was the real thing. Marge and I had driven out to Virginia Beach to see what we could see, which was nothing, not even a tramp steamer. Later that evening I wrote about it:

Today has been very sad for me. I hated to see you go so! Even though I thought it for a short time. Then Mrs. C. called and said you wouldn't be in for a long time and when you did come in, it would be only briefly. She's so morbid that I don't know what to think.

Oh my darling, I am so lonesome tonight. Perhaps it's wrong of me to tell you but I'm no good at making believe. I'm weary to death of war and worry. All I want, and that with all my heart, is to live in peace with you. Just to be able to love you at leisure. Never have we felt that we had forever ahead of us, it's fever pitch and cramming a lifetime into a few days. It can go on indefinitely, I suppose, but I sincerely hope it's all over soon and we are together for always.

The ship was out a good three weeks. Then Van came in just long enough to spend the night. We stayed out in the car all day to have some privacy from Marge and Jack. The next afternoon, 2 May 1943, the ship was off again for another long week in Chesapeake Bay. This time Van sent some wonderful news:

The big news is of course that I am a Lt. Commander now. We received the dispatch in its completed form this afternoon. Isn't that something, your Pappy a big shot. . . .

We used to say there were three kinds of Officers. Young bucks, old fuds and Lt. Commanders, and I guess I'm no longer a young buck. Being a Lt. Cmdr has its advantages, but it's got disadvantages too. Young Ensigns, Jgs. [Lt. (jg)] and Lts. will take longer to get to know me. I'll have a harder time getting next to the men, and other such little items as the half stripe will awe them. There will be more responsibility and the higher you go, I find, the more one feels he should devote, perhaps, a little extra time to the ship and his job. I mean as a Lt. and below it is easier to drop your tools at four-thirty and say I'll finish tomorrow. Also as a Lt. and below, it is easy to get people to swap watches or stand by for you. Now if I am on the Head of Dept. Watch list, I'd probably only have one Watch in five or six but I'd have to remain aboard when I had the duty as there will be no one to take it for me. All other Dept. heads being married and equally anxious to get home. . . .

Gee it was fun to get home for the night and then spend the wonderful day with you. I enjoyed every minute of it even though we spent a good deal of our time just sitting in the car. It is so wonderful darling when I am with you. The time passes quickly however. I wish the same as you do, that we knew we were going to have a year or two undisturbed together. That would be so very delight-ful and peaceful. I never stop hoping and believing that someday in the not too distant future we will have all that we want. . . .

I hear all you girls are going to have a party at the club tonight. I wish that I could be there and we could celebrate.

It became evident that the lack of cohesion among the wives was having an effect on the officers. All the bickering they indulged in had created a schism among the husbands aboard ship. Van and I thought this could be because so many were reservists who did not comprehend the esprit de corps that existed among the regulars and the wives did not understand that their petty complaints could affect the absolutely necessary team spirit of the ship if she was to become a well-oiled fighting machine.

The party for the wives turned out to be another shunning of Marge, and I too was treated oddly. I had regard for several of the girls but was not about to put up with out-and-out rudeness to someone living under my roof. At the same time I thought it imperative that the wives' petty jealousies not embroil the men, something that was already happening. There seemed to be no easy solution. Certainly the wives' party had made matters worse.

On 8 May 1943, Van wrote me:

Special Delivery just so you will get this sooner.

It was so wonderful to get home to you last night. I always love coming home, being with you and Pam and fooling around the house. But oh this morning how I have that blue Monday feeling. Darling I hate to come back to the ship and get underway and leave you, even for a minute. I so feel I should stay around home and I want to. I love being an old "home body" 'cause it is always so much fun.

I do hope that this week will be less hectic, that Agnes is up and around more and can not only take care of herself but help you too. I hope too that Pam is a good girl and sleeps and eats like she should, and you darling, I want you to eat and sleep and get fat like a wabbitt should be fat. . . . I'd much rather have you have roast beef and steak and liver three or four times a week than save your points for me.

If you are going to have another bambino I insist that you take extra special care of yourself . . . resting and not working too hard, because it is soon after Pam and I don't feel that you have had long enough time to have gotten yourself back in shape or have completely gotten your strength back. In other words some of the energy which should be going into your own system will be sidetracked to take care of the new bambino.

That's why I wanted to wait a while. To get you all fat and sassy and strong like an ox again before starting to make babies once more. I don't want you to be sick or have a hard time or be poorly afterwards because of having two bambinos in rapid succession. You probably feel that you'd rather give me the bambinos, but I'd rather keep you strong and healthy. . . .

Gee I hope this week you gals can get together where necessary and remove some more of that misunderstanding that might still exist. It is bad enough to have a situation like that but I hate having you mixed up in it.

Van was justifiably worried about the baby I was carrying. I was losing weight instead of gaining, and it was true that I was saving my ration stamps in order to feed him super meals when he got ashore. We were not given stamps for men aboard ship when they came home, which certainly presented a problem, for of course we all wanted to make life delightful for our husbands the short times we were together.

Trying to relax, I planned a backyard picnic with Marge. We asked a handful of the girls and their husbands whom I liked and set about getting beer and some sort of punch, enough to have a good promotion celebration Friday for Van. Then Saturday I could spend the afternoon and evening on board ship, where Van and I could at least talk in his room without Jack and Marge underfoot.

What an awful week that was. Little Bini managed to sneak into the back of the car while I was washing it; I found him three hours later dead of heat prostration. Poor little mite, he had become violently jealous of Pam. He had nipped her once when Van was holding her and had bitten our next door neighbor, who got between Van and the pup. I blamed myself for his death and thought Van would too.

Then our nursemaid Agnes had to be hauled to the hospital with a high fever. She turned out to have something contagious and had to be sent home to Greenwich. Pamie, Marge, and I were tested but the results were negative. We kept Ginger, the dog Agnes had rescued, hoping he would take Bini's place.

Van wrote a lovely letter about Bini II and then changed the subject to a very new idea of his:

Our great inspection by the other cruiser was a success, at least they all said afterwards how good we seemed to be at damage control and how fast we got fire hoses to fires and so forth. I think we are pretty good although I am far from satisfied. I can think of so many things I want the repair parties to know.

By golly the Navy ought to set up a damage control school ashore. They have school ashore for just about every other job in the Navy but that one. The course should include the fire fighters course plus a lot besides, it should teach officers and men what to look for, teach them the little tricks you can only learn from experience and what is important and why. The only reason I know anything about the subject is because I'm interested in it. I've had over a year of good schooling and experience and I talk to everybody I can whoever has had anything to do with it and collect other people's ideas and experiences. It wouldn't surprise me in the least to be stuck with damage control jobs for the duration because there are so few trained officers that know anything about it. It is a relatively new subject, or at least no one took it seriously except for the last four or five years. My boss man knows of 10 new ships, only three of which have experienced DC officers. We are superbly well-off here. Personally I'd like to get command of a D.E though.

. . . I am sorry we disappointed you this weekend but the ship got detailed unexpectedly and here we sit. I'd much rather be at home with you. You are more fun than ANYTHING, OH BOY!

With the imminent departure of the ship looming over us for the umpteenth time, we made contingency plans. I would send all our personal belongings, the things that made a house a home, to Greenwich: sheets, towels, favorite pots and pans, silver, and bric-a-brac. The heat and humidity were doing Pam in with prickly heat and eczema, so we made arrangements to send her and her new nurse, Katherin, home by air to Mother. When Van actually left, I would drive the car to Washington and leave it. Once in Greenwich, by train, I would wait until Van came home, if he did. Then if he could get leave he would fly up to Washington, I would meet him there, and we would drive to Greenwich together. We had one more false alarm. On June first, I wrote Van:

Oh Lord how I hated leaving you this morning. I can't describe the lost empty feeling I've had all day and still have. I knew it would be sort of like this, but darling, every meeting is more wonderful, I know, so I guess it's reasonable that each parting is more horrible than the first. At any rate I know this one is the worst to date. Not that I cried more, I didn't cry as much, outwardly, but I've wept bitterly to myself the whole day long. It's like having the dry sobs. You just turn cold all over and quiver like a race horse but nothing else happens. Somehow it's worse than if you could really cry and get it over and done with.

Lord but it was heaven just to sit and hold your hand or have your arm around me. Not that we did anything so different but it was just that I was so terribly conscious of how much I appreciated all these things of which life will be barren for the next little while. . . . I kept thinking things like "Van has his arm around me, it will be a long time before this happens again. Appreciate it to the utmost while you can" and other such thoughts. I stored up a lot of memories this time, darling. You and the baby together this morning will last me a long time by itself. That was one of the loveliest pictures of all time when Pam was lying with her head on your shoulder smiling and you smiling with your arm around her. Nothing could have been sweeter than my Van and his daughter being so contented together.

My first mission in life now is to get healthy and that fast. I am going to eat and sleep and bask in the sun and gain back all the weight I've lost down here, so that when you come back I will again be your bouncing bride and not the old hag I am now. Really today I looked at myself and was ashamed to call myself your wife. I'm thin and all sort of shriveled up and I'm not going to stand for it. . . .

Darling this time I'm scared. to death of what will happen. Please Lord, bring you home safe and sound to your wife and daughter.

Van wrote me at the same time. He also was almost certain that this was the final goodbye:

Dearest, I've had such an empty feeling missing you all day. I get so I depend on you and count on coming home to you every night. You really are everything to me precious. Love is a wonderful thing, a happy bubbly time when we are together, but hollow and dismal when we are not. Oh but I love you my darling wife.

I'm so glad that I was able to reach you on the phone. It was good to be able to have a few words with you and to know you were all right.

This evening, it is delightful and cool outside, but inside the ship it is still hot. I expect it will cool off some shortly as the blowers start blowing the cool fresh air into the ship and the sun doesn't heat things up anymore. . . .

With all the ring and watch leaving at home we did, it didn't seem too widespread an idea. The only other person I noticed besides Pat O'leary was the Captain, who I understand makes it a habit. [One more sign that not many on board were battle-wise. Those few who had been in battle and had lost their prize possessions left such things at home. Van's rings and watch had gone down with the *Atlanta*. It was also his way of telling me they were heading for war.]

At this point I know of nothing to add to our already meager supply of information so I guess you go right ahead with your plans. . . .

Sweetheart I love you with all my heart and all my soul. You are everything to me. My wonderful wife, my little girl, my pride, my entire world.

The Other Shoe

JUNE 1943–AUGUST 1944

We had said goodbye so many times that we were about wrung out. We had sent the baby home, and that had cut us up, for it was breaking up our family, and we had been together only briefly. Again we went over contingency plans, sorted out finances, and, as always, forgot to cover all questions. We had been expecting "the other shoe to drop" for so long that this time was an anticlimax. We said goodbye almost casually. I guess we both knew deep down the other shoe had dropped. We wrote simultaneously on 7 June 1943:

> Thanks so much for calling this morning, I appreciated it no end, both the first and the second time. Of course if you hadn't called me the second time I'd probably be befuddled about just what to do. I am, at this point, going to wait this afternoon at the club till six thirty. In fact I'm going to have dinner there, and if no word from you by twelve noon tomorrow I will leave for Washington and on to New York on Wednesday morning arriving in Greenwich around four.
>
> Everything is packed at this point and the house is getting that unused appearance. You know, a little too neat to have Mrs. Perkins living there. So I will be glad to get out of it as I like to have our things around. I like to see your shoes and socks on the floor, your pocket pickings on the dresser, your picture in full view and I like the ice box to be full for my family, the silver to be in evidence and feeling that you and I belong. When it's time to be alone again it's best to just clear out . . . and think in the past, or the future, not the present. So darling, with no future in the house I wish to leave as soon as possible when I'm sure you're gone.

Please take care of yourself and God Bless you and take care of you Van my boy. I adore you now and always,

Bettsy

P.S. Don't forget about Edith Orion and Willow and Dorothy.

This last was important, as Edith was in Panama and Willow and Dorothy had been Van's girls when he was stationed in the Mediterranean. These names would be the code words to tell me where he was. Van wrote,

Today has been a hectic one for us all. We left the dock at ten thirty and anchored out which you undoubtedly saw. There was no word about liberty or our departure or anything, so I couldn't think of anything for you to do except hope we could get ashore in the afternoon and meet you at the club.

Well, I imagine you came down to the base Tuesday morning, that's tomorrow as I write, and if it was late enough in the morning found that we had left. Anyway, this afternoon late we are leaving. I presume and hope you and Marge get off all right. I shall be anxious to hear about your trip. I don't mean I will be anxious about you because that would be foolish. I just want to hear about the trip.

Darling I don't know what arrangements you and Marge have made beyond the two week visit in Greenwich but why don't you see if you can avoid committing yourself or making definite plans to share the house in Norfolk. . . . With the whole house to ourselves Pam and the nurse could be more comfortable and we'd have more privacy or time to ourselves this next time. . . . There is no reason why you should be a self-appointed guardian and helper, with our coming baby. I won't say anything to Jack yet until I've heard from you. I think it should be fairly easy and natural to have it happen that we need the whole house when we return.

Sweet Bettsy I miss you. Saying all these good-byes has sort of deflated (or is that the word I want) me. I almost feel that I will be back any minute. However knowing that I am off this time makes it easier in a way because I can put on my little "being away from you suit" button it up and start trying to get used to the situation again.

I guess you are doing the same thing, going about doing things and realizing that you must fill in the gap caused by me not being with you.

I try to keep busy and occupied but I never can busy myself enough not to have moments of loneliness and great pangs of yearning for you. The hardest times of course are in the evenings and in the morning when I wake up and realize I must get up and start another day without seeing you. I'm so glad I've got so many lovely pictures of you and of Pam and that I've got my K. Bunny. . . . I think it's wonderful to have K. Bunny. He is my little mascot that is you.

Together we have a sweet and charming daughter who is the apple of her Poppy's eye to say the least. Gosh but I think Pam is a precious wonderful little person. Daddy sends special love and kiss for her. He certainly hated to see her leave on that plane too.

Bettsy, don't forget to eat and sleep a lot so that you will become a butter-ball bunny.

There had been much speculation that the ship's home port would be New York. Norfolk was probably not her permanent assignment. We all sincerely hoped the Atlantic Fleet needed our cruiser. If that was the case it would be logical to put into New York long enough to arrange for families, household goods, bank accounts, allotments, and so forth, all of which needed our husbands' signatures. The only time women were "in the Navy" was when the Navy wanted to evacuate us or anything detrimental to family life. The seagoing Navy families were always on their own—no quarters, no housing assistance, nothing. The Navy washed their hands of families. Assuredly, if they could have gotten away with it, the bigwigs would have preferred to impose celibacy.

We thought and prayed that the ship's home port would be New York, for then, when she needed an overhaul or repairs, she would go into the Brooklyn Navy Yard. Also, I thought fighting the Germans would be a sight easier, for their logic was Western and comprehensible. The Japanese were enigmatic; they scared most of us who knew them, with just cause. Some of us had witnessed the Japanese Navy, losing dear friends at their hands, and by now we were aware that the seagoing conventions of war were not being upheld by the Japanese. They had no respect for individual life—either theirs or their captives'.

Following in His Footsteps

I wrote Van about our trip home to Greenwich, which was only thirty miles from New York and handy to the Brooklyn Navy Yard:

Here we are in Greenwich after a perfectly mad trip up here. . . . Arrived in Washington without mishap about seven o'clock. Had a nice visit with the family and started up here, on the eleven o'clock, yesterday morning.

Miss Kate drove our car down and left us at the station with Ginger and then went right home. We of course, had made no provision for Ginger thinking we could blithely just throw him in the baggage car.

We waltzed up to the Conductor and said, "Where's the baggage car?"

"Lady, there is no baggage car, there's no mail car and you may not take your dog on board."

I pulled a dramatic, you know, poor little girl how should I know the train rules. What was I going to do with my dog whom I loved so dearly. Oh Lordy, Lordy, couldn't I get a compartment for him. Well of course I could but there wasn't one. Well, I finally persuaded him that somebody would be kind and keep Ginger in their compartment if the conductor would only let me on board. He did, and I dashed into the first compartment I could find. There sat a couple with their baby and DOG. I told them briefly our trouble and they said "Oh sure." Just as the train was starting we got aboard. The conductor came up and said there was a compartment available so it all ended happily ever after. But, oh boy, what a time.

Pam looks wonderful. The roses have come back in her cheeks and she's sleeping almost all day long and all night to boot. Just making up for lost time. . . . She is so much better now she's up here. She eats and sleeps and that's about all.

Quite a considerable amount of time elapsed before I had a letter solving all our speculation. Instead of using our "name of ladies he had known" code, Van talked in riddles no censor could fathom but I could decipher most easily:

The New York deal is definitely out as is now painfully obvious, for the time being anyway. Maybe later but that is one of those things one can't count on.

I hated to watch us standing out of the harbor. It was sort of a lost feeling, realizing I was leaving you behind. I must say I was well prepared for this departure and strangely enough didn't get all down in the dumps and low, like I have before when I left in the Atlanta and even several times when we went out for what proved only to be a weekly trip. . . .

I couldn't have wanted more during the last two weekends or the last four or five days we had together while the ship was in. We did just about everything from picnicking to partying, had each other and had a crowd around. That was our first picnic together you know.

. . . "My Day" started at sun rise which by juggling the clocks was around six. [Of course this meant five so he must be going east.] I had planned to catch 40 winks during the morning but got too interested in a fueling operation, so I spent all the time trying to straighten out all these people who had never done it before. Then a watch after lunch and after the watch a little relaxing in the sun topside but I never got around to a nap which I'd planned.

After supper a radio message caused another job to be necessary right away which took all the C & R [control and repair] people until ten-thirty to do, and now I've mid-watch. [My guess was that they were taking on special ammunition way out at sea for secrecy's sake.] But that's the way it goes when we are at sea and as you can imagine it takes a little time to get accustomed to. . . .

Red Price was kidding me about getting my other ribbon before he will. We both have the same ones and of course are trying to get something different. But my room is forward of his and my watch station is forward of his so I will cross the boundary line first unless Red finds out ahead of time when we will cross and runs way up to the bow of the ship to beat me. [Again a signal: he was going to get an Atlantic theater ribbon.]

We have had a "sea bat" on board for the last day or so. Some humorous character took a small empty box and punched a few holes in the top of it for air. He then put the box on the quarter-deck in the sun and began to watch. Pretty soon a curious person came along and wanted to know what was in the box. A "sea bat" he was informed. When the curious one leaned over to peek in the box a couple more funny guys would whale him across the fanny with brooms. Even one of the ship's cooks was laid upon when he came out with a small piece of meat to feed the "sea bat."

In a day or so "this here rabbit" should be following in his footsteps. We only know that we will get some kind of liberty when we arrive at our destination, how much and how long remains to be seen.

I knew both Van and Red Price had China Service and Pacific Theater ribbons, so when Van wrote of how Red was trying to get a new ribbon first, I knew they were going to get Atlantic Theater ribbons as soon as they crossed the longitude that would put them in that war zone.

"Following in his footsteps" referred to Van's tour aboard the *Raleigh*, stationed in France and operating in the Mediterranean. According to one of Van's old "day books," which were at Craggy, he was once again in the Mediterranean. He had gone to Algeria from Villefranche a couple of times. He had gone to Gibraltar several times. As France was now in German hands, the French coast was out. No doubt their landfall was Gibraltar, with Algeria as the place they would anchor and get liberty.

We Have Been That Busy

Once the war was well under way, government agents came to my family's house and demanded that Mother's German cook and waitress remove themselves inland, as they were aliens and someone was reporting on the convoys proceeding up Long Island Sound to German U-boats waiting to sink them as they came out into the Atlantic. Dad had made a large button that read "I am a Filipino" for Iraneo, who was our butler and married to the German cook. He, poor dear, was hauled to the police station as a Japanese spy every time he went downtown. All three of them had been part of the family for so long that we were heartbroken at their departure, and it left Mother, who was not too well, unable to cope. It fell to me, the only grown child at home, to fill in some of the gaps, and doing so kept me so busy there was no time to fret. Mother finally got a refugee couple to do the cooking and housework, and I went down to be with Van's family in Washington.

There had been no mail after the letter from Algeria, but the invasion of Sicily was headlined in every paper in the country and I knew for certain that Van was involved in that. On 15 July I wrote from Washington:

> Just a very hurried note. I am here with the family and all of our very kind friends have me dated up for every minute of my time for the next couple of days. Today I had lunch with Hazel Jenkins—mind you I'm calling her Hazel these days. . . .
>
> Incidentally, Capt. Jenkins wanted your address for his files. Guess that means one of two things, he's either going to make certain you get your cross [Navy Cross] or he's going to request you for duty with him again, either case it would be a pleasure, eh? To be continued. . . .
>
> Darling, such news as I have for you from this end. I had lunch with Mrs. Jenkins yesterday and she said, "Well how does it feel to be the wife of a damage control officer" and I said, "I don't know. Van's only an assistant" at which she hit the ceiling. Then she said, "When did he get his cross, while you were together I hope." I said, "He hasn't it" and "no he hasn't his purple heart either." Well she said she knew the Captain thought you had same and would be furious and would see what went on and she said the Captain had said this, "There were officers whom I liked before the big moment who fell down when the time came and there were officers whom I thought not so good who showed up beautifully in a crisis. Perkins was both a good officer in normal times and splendid when the time came." Plenty nice compliment from him. Also, Mrs. Jenkins said the Captain had found that the ship was to be allowed to wear the [Presidential Unit] citation ribbon and I think that's pretty special. I'm going to see Captain Jenkins tomorrow and confirm same but these were all things that Mrs. Jenkins was pretty positive about. I mean she wasn't asking me questions for the heck of it. She was verifying what the Captain had told her. She thought you had picked a plum when you got your present job and when I told her it was a nice green lemon she said, "Sam will fix that." My goodness, she was emphatic about it.

Two days later I had more good news to report:

> I am so proud of you I'm about to bust. Yesterday you were awarded the Silver Star and I am just beyond myself with excitement for you. Your citation is certainly a mighty fine tribute. . . . Enclosed is a copy of the citation which Pop copied out of the Buper Inf. Bulletin. He was unable to get a copy of the Bulletin for us today as the offices were closed down but promises one for us tomor-

row. The family is so excited and proud of you. Lord, everyone is. What a nifty thing. Darling you once said that the only medal you really wanted was the [Navy] cross and you came mighty near getting it but this is, in my opinion, just as nice a medal and really more appropriate for what you were cited for and it leaves you something still to be desired which is, after all, the reason for existing. What's more, this Silver Star is the second highest award issued by the Navy. . . . I greatly prefer you to be gallant and intrepid than heroic, for heroes are either fools or madmen and you're neither. If they have occasion to give you another citation your Cross will be in the bag so to speak.

What Captain Jenkins said was this: He wrote your citation and gave it to some guy out in the Pacific who wrote the recommendation for Navy Cross on the citation. It was then sent to Washington where it was out of Captain Jenkins hands completely and they gave you the Silver Star. I can't get over your citation. I think it is such a lovely one. Nor can I get over what Captain Jenkins had to say about you.

We had dinner with the Jenkins' last night and the Captain said things that were enough coming from him to be equivalent of a two hour dissertation on the merits of Perkins by F. D. R. Namely that you are "the best bridge officer I have met in my career" and that you are above all else completely qualified for your own command and that he is going to do his darndest to get you a destroyer no less. Can you imagine? Captain Jenkins asked me exactly what you are doing now so I told him you were again asst. D. control in a dept. of ten Officers, that you are no longer standing bridge watches and that you seem to be without much of anything to do. He snorted like an enraged horse and said (and I quote exactly) "outrageous waste of good material, not proving a thing, wasting his time, terrible. I'll see to that." . . . Why I even told Captain J. that it would be nice to get new construction so we could have time together, he said he'd see what he could do. The destroyer business is all his own idea and I'm pleased about it. My lord, you a skipper. Well, to get on with my news, last week it came out as a definite order that all men on board a ship at the time that it is cited for the *first time* are entitled to wear a citation medal with star and your purple heart you are entitled to wear. . . .

This is the first time I've ever had a husband who's been awarded a medal for personal merit and I'm pretty darn well staggered by it all. Sweetie, aren't you glad we got married before you had any medals because now you know I didn't marry you for your medals (on the outside that is. Those on the inside that no one can see I did marry you for).

It was months before Van had his Silver Star officially pinned on him, a ceremony I would have loved to have seen. By that time he had more ribbons on his chest than anyone else on board his ship, including the new captain, who was serving his first World War II sea duty and his first combatant ship command.

I wrote Van on 21 July. Our letters crossed:

The news in your direction is so unspectacular that I am beginning to worry. To date we have admitted the loss of one Hospital Ship. There has been no damage reported. You know it is all so utterly ridiculous. First of all they advertise that the taking of Sicily is "The beginning of the end." The greatest thing we've done so far. Wonderful! Wonderful! The war is almost over. Tonight they announce Sicily is only an out post. Why is everyone excited? The war won't be over until '49. Then Knox says in small print "that is if labor starts laying down on the job."

Keeping quiet about our losses may possibly hinder the enemy tho' I doubt how much. On the other hand if you tell our people what our losses are they become more determined. Catastrophes always bring out the best in people.

Much as I'm enjoying it down here I'm missing Pam no end. She's such a cute little monkey and she's so much like you. What's more she represents everything that is wonderful in our lives. . . . Should anything happen to you, my world would be you in Pam. Do you see what I mean?

Sweetheart, you said in your letter "If anything should happen to me at least I will be doing something big." —Well dear one, I am glad that you have that feeling. I'm glad you have any feeling one way or the other about what will happen to you. It means you are thinking and not being impulsive, and for me, if you have a reason, that suffices.

On 21 July, Van wrote what little he could about Sicily without violating censorship:

This is the first chance I've had to write to you Betts since the beginning of the month. "We have been that busy." I hope that when we get in I will find some mail from you and be able to answer your letters. There hasn't been a single drop of mail, official or otherwise, since we left the States so that is why you may have some unanswered questions. By now the mail man ought to know where we are though.

I am fine and in excellent health, as a matter of fact we all are, and that is about the most important thing there is to say.

After reading some of the axis press releases, I couldn't blame you if you worried, but I hope you didn't. Even in my wildest dreams I never would have thought we could do what we did and as easily. Some jobs undoubtedly were tough but none like we expected. . . . Anyway, all is well with us and all I lost was a lot of sleep and had a few tense moments.

I wrote you a V-mail today also and in it suggested that you continue to sit tight in Greenwich until we see what is up. . . . I certainly wish I could help you with any decisions you have to make. The only thing I am sure of is that I would greatly prefer not to get involved with Marge and Jack or any other family again. Whatever we have, I'd like to have it ourselves. I imagine it depends on how quickly things go and how much more work there is.

Oh my darling I miss you so and miss being with you. If we weren't so much in love and you weren't such a wonderful wife the things I think at times would be very bad indeed. . . . As I look back, even to Manila, I know that each time we are together the flame gets brighter and fiercer. If we were to measure things by the periods we have been together, each one has been much much better than the last.

As I heard later, the trip over was peaceful enough once they had finished a realistic war game way out at sea. Algeria was wild for the men. Van had drawn on his letter a picture of a rabbit heading for a bar in a great hurry. That's just what the men did, neither wisely nor well. The French police and the shore patrol rounded up a considerable number of the crew, returning them to the ship in what is termed, in polite society, a "deplorable condition." Van had his hands full conducting summary courts for the malefactors.

From 23 June to 5 July 1943 the ship was involved in gunnery practice and back in the port of Algeria long enough to take on all the ammunition they could hold, plus other needed supplies. Again Van's duties kept him busy, as he had to oversee that operation as well as refueling. On 5 July they headed for Sicily, arriving in the area the night of 9 July in foul weather. Not only was it raining but "the wind was blowing harder from an odder direction than it had in two hundred years." I was told this by the navigator of one of the ships that was supposed to be the beacon marker of the designated area. His ship was blown off course, and with great difficulty it made its way to the area in time for the *Birmingham* to pick up the beacon and take up her designated position.

Just before five o'clock, when it was still dark, the *Birmingham* fired her first battle salvo on schedule. The ship fired at the targets on shore and, as she was constantly under attack, continued to maneuver. Her planes spotted shore batteries, which the ship then knocked out. By nine o'clock the Italian flag flying over the castle at Licata came down, and up went the Stars and Stripes. One young airman spotting for the ship had been mortally wounded, the only fatality the *Birmingham* suffered in the Sicily campaign.

During the following days the ship continually bombarded the shore batteries, German troop concentrations, a railroad terminal—anything the Army asked them to knock out. Porto Empedocle was captured at three o'clock in the morning on 17 July, the same day that Agrigento fell. Almost exactly one week after the *Birmingham* had fired her first salvo, she fired her last salvos, disposing of a small troop concentration near Empedocle. At last the ship was no longer needed, as General Patton's army headed inland way ahead of schedule. She returned to Algeria to refuel and take on stores, then headed for home.

Captain Wilkes received the Legion of Merit for his brilliant maneuvering of the ship at flank speed, dodging in and out of harm's way, never getting a single scratch. Only the planes were hit, and the flyers, too, were rewarded for their performances. Van, who had told me how he loved nighttime high-speed maneuvers out in China, said that Wilkes's was one of the most beautiful pieces of ship handling he had ever experienced; this confirmed my confidence in Captain Wilkes. Despite his rather austere bearing and all the sadness he had caused us, I felt him a true and able leader.

Whispering in Your Heart

The rumors flew that the *Birmingham* would be back late in July. It did not take much figuring on my part to conclude that if Van's letter of 21 July said that they were in Algeria for several days, and it took more than a week to cross the Atlantic from the Mediterranean, it would be early August before the crew arrived. I returned to Washington, where I had left the car on my way north and where my intelligence network would inform me when the ship would get back.

I called on our friend and my Navy Department informant, François Novitski, who told me to get down to Norfolk fairly soon as the ship would come in August sixth. "I'm sorry to have to give you this news," he told me, "but better you know it now. Van won't be in any length of time at all, so don't try to move the baby down. Van probably gets a short leave."

"How long do we have, François?" I pleaded. "Six weeks, two months, how long?"

"Oh Betts, I'm sorry, dear girl, neither of those. Two weeks, give or take a day."

What a blow that was. Here we were once again with no time to be together. I had thought at least the ship would go into the yard for an overhaul. My whole being turned over, my mouth watered, and I knew I was going to be sick to my stomach. I dropped the phone and ran to the bathroom. It was worse than that: I lost the baby boy I had so wanted to give Van. And I had tried so hard to stay calm enough to give him a good start. Well, maybe, just maybe, I thought, I would have another chance, though I knew that was a fairly futile hope. But perhaps Van would ask for a transfer when he got in; that would give us another chance.

A few days later, after I pulled myself together, I drove down to Norfolk to wait for the *Birmingham*. Each day I went out to the beach to look for the ship. Finally, a speck on the horizon grew into a warship, not a tanker or a freighter. As she came closer, I knew it was the *Birmingham*. The only reason I at last thought her a pretty sight was because my Van was aboard and coming home to me, if only very briefly.

Jumping in the car, I dashed to the Navy yard, beating the ship by quite some time. When I could see where she was going to berth, I got out of the car and paced up and down, waiting for Van to come ashore. The wait seemed interminable. Finally he came down the accommodation ladder. I flew to him. Breaking all conventions, I threw myself at him, laughing and crying at the same time. He just held me tightly, dancing me around, as oblivious to being in uniform as I was.

At last he let go of me, saying, "I dropped my bag when I saw you. Let me get it, then we're off on leave. I made plane reservations to New York for both of us. We'll have to hurry to make it."

I trotted along beside him, asking a thousand questions. "How are you? Was it awful? Did you get any rest on the way home?"

He laughed, "Come on, darling. We'll have time to talk on the plane. Right now, where are your bags? Do we have to pick them up? I only have five days of leave, could you do without them?"

I stopped cold in my tracks. "Five days? How can they be so rotten?"

"Betts, don't spoil it, darling. We're lucky to get the first section. Come on now, we must hurry."

We flew to La Guardia Airport, and by late afternoon we were home. Van jumped out of the car and ran across the lawn to his baby daughter, who was tottering on her feet. It was the first time he had seen her walk. He tossed her above his head then cradled her in one arm. Wrapping me with his other arm, he said, "How I've dreamed of holding my two girls. My whole world encircled in my arms. I want just this forever!" He smiled wistfully down at me; it tore at my heart.

Four days fled by, which we spent mostly playing with Pamie. Too soon the moment to say goodbye came. Van held his daughter close and tried to sing for her, but he choked up and was unable to go on. His eyes were brimming over with tears as he handed her to her nurse for the last time, and turning his back, he headed for the door in deep despair. We flew back to Norfolk, barely able to talk to each other.

Captain Wilkes had been promoted to admiral and was turning over his command to a new captain. The new captain seemed nice enough, but hardly a strong enough character to inspire much confidence in me. Dad's friends, who molded my idea of a leader, were men like General Wainwright, General Patton, General Milling, and General Richardson. They possessed a combination of toughness and compassion, and they were imposing figures. Their wives were equally outstanding, as was Mrs. Wilkes. The new skipper and his wife seemed nice, but I did not feel at ease about them as I had immediately about Captain and Mrs. Jenkins, whom I adored, or Captain Wilkes, whom I admired, and Winnie Wilkes, whom I had come to know as a friend to look up to in the same way I looked up to Hazel Jenkins.

Van was no sooner back on the ship than he caught the flu. He kept on working, but for the first time he became depressed, nervous about where he was going and not enthusiastic about his immediate boss. Not once since coming back from Sicily had he said, "We're going to have such fun."

I was no help either. Despite my recent miscarriage, I was determined to have another child. My own tension was obvious to Van, and he was very upset over losing the baby, as he was at my weight loss. When I heard the ship was going to sail on the twenty-eighth, I cried bitterly. I begged Van to ask for a transfer. He said he wanted to, but he did not know what he wanted or where he wanted to go. Maybe the Naval War College and then his own command. He had been overseas for nearly eight years, and he desperately wanted his well-earned tour ashore.

Finally, Tuesday, 18 August, our last night together, came. God only knew when we would meet again, or where.

Before he sailed, Van sent a letter ashore:

First of all I love you so very, very much. Even when I am not at your side to tell you so my spirit is there whispering in your heart and telling you that you are the most perfectly wonderful wife there ever was and that I can't do enough or say all I want to make you happy. I am always happiest and most contented when I know you are too.

Such fun it was Bepe to be with you. It was too short, much too short but I don't think we wasted a minute. I enjoyed the evening at the Carriks, perhaps too much, but it was restful to get over there and get slugged with a couple of scotches before going to bed. I just didn't tell you enough after we jumped into bed how very much I do love you.

I hate going off again and leaving you because there is so much we have to do together. Complete though our time always is, when I leave you I feel there is so much I have left undone and unsaid. I just want more time with you. We have so much fun and every minute with you is so delightful and I'm so much in love with you that I'm convinced you are the most wonderful person in the world.

I love you, I love you, I love you. Lonely for you, Rabbit.

In Words of One Syllable

Our cottage in Norfolk had been sold while Van was in Sicily, so I had taken a room with the other wives who were staying at the Chamberlain Hotel across the bay from Norfolk. It was a tall old building, within the Army post, which was used for transient personnel; hence, the girls who had given up their living arrangements before Sicily were able to get rooms there, Marge among them.

After I took Van to the boat landing to go out to the ship this last time, I drove over the bridge and joined Marge and Sophie Lou, the chaplain's wife, to watch the ship depart. Not to watch it go totally out of sight, for that would be bad luck. We wanted to make sure they were really leaving, however, and the Chamberlain was a grandstand seat from which to watch the proceedings.

I wrote Van about watching his ship leave and our trip to Washington:

This will slay you—we watched for hours it seemed while the ship picked up the planes and washed down the decks, we could see everything so plainly and were enjoying ourselves so much. Then finally you went by and I watched you in your greys (very clever of you darling as I spotted you instantly) walk half way back from the forecastle and pull out your hanky. I wonder if you saw me. Well, I was so excited I practically jumped out of the window with the binoculars in my hand. A very little while after you left and Marge and I were putting away the binoculars, in walked an Army Intelligence Captain and a Shore Patrol gent, and you have never seen two more surprised and confused young ladies than we were.

Apparently you are not allowed to look at the harbor with binoculars. I knew cameras were out, but I'd heard nothing about binoculars. Well, they asked our names and addresses, about our husbands, what ship they were on, did we know what ship we were looking at and if so which one. We told them the exact truth and they then became sympathetic and nice. In fact they couldn't have been nicer and they assured us it meant nothing, that it would not go in your records or ours. That there was nothing to worry about and that all it was, was a routine affair that they had to do, no matter how distasteful, as General Drum had ordered no binoculars about a week ago.

I had the good sense to say c/o Col. J. W. Riley in giving my address and as all of General Drum's office knows Dad, I'm sure there will be nothing to it. But we were two plenty scared young chickens before they got out of the room.

Sophie Lou Brocklebank fortunately stepped out of the room shortly before they came in and returned right in the middle of it, but they didn't question her at all and we shut her up before she could make a break about being with us. Isn't it typical of us to get in a mess. We are sure you must have seen us. After all the Coast Guard did so you must have too. We certainly had enough junk hanging out the window, a pillow case and a mirror to say nothing of ourselves. When Peyton Moss arrived we told him all about it and he is sure it proved nothing.

I am utterly sunk at your leaving again so soon. . . . From time to time I have to pull myself together and get out of my slump. Lord knows what's eating me. Maybe Tuesday night took right away, and you are to be presented with another child. I almost act that way.

Darling I keep wondering if you really knew what you were saying Tuesday night, or more accurately, Wednesday morning, apropos of having another baby. In a sense it seems to me you said it in an off hand manner. Then again, perhaps it has been in the back of your mind for sometime. I couldn't tell, and now I wonder if we are having another one, if you will be provoked with the idea, mildly surprised, or glad, or has the whole thing slipped from your mind? You know we even went so far as to discuss a girls name in case we have another girl. This is a true example of counting your chickens before they're even conceived but then. . . .

Tuesday night I felt too maternal towards you to act like a little girl and get things out of my system. I felt like there was far too much to be gotten out of your system. I hated seeing you like you were the last couple of days and having you go off that way. All tense and unhappy and therefore unwell. You getting potted was wonderful and I'm glad you did, and if you made me no pretty speeches you certainly gave me a good round loving and you pleased me no end by forgetting everything except us and the world we were in at the minute.

Van told me of his side of the binocular episode:

Darling it was so very hard to leave you again. Each time it gets harder and each time I become more and more convinced I'm not doing what I want to most. I have tried to analyze my feelings and have concluded that what I mainly want is not so much to get off this particular ship as it is to get ashore. . . . Something in which there is more security for both of us. The next best condition is of course one in which I am satisfied and pleased with things. . . .

. . . How I ever became such an ardent family man I don't know but you had lots to do with it. I told Ed Ryan that this time had just about broken the camels back and I was all for getting a farm in Connecticut and humbling my pride to ask my father's friends to give me a job after the war is over. He congratulated me and said he was glad to see the Navy hadn't taken my initiative away.

. . . I want to be with you and I want security and permanence. Furthermore, I know that is just what you want too. There is no kidding ourselves. This going off to war isn't bad because of separation of time and distance, it's the worry about the future or rather whether there will be any future or not! . . .

I still don't know our ultimate destination and neither does Al. We have simply been told that our next port will be Panama which is and was most obvious. Chances are we won't know either until we get to sea again which won't be much help. (22 August destination still?)

You know Betts, the more I wear my wedding ring and see it on my finger, the more pleased and glad I am that I have it. You are such a good person to think of all these things.

It was not customary in 1940 for men to wear wedding rings, nor was it usual to have double-ring services. I had been thinking for a long time that Van should have such a ring, for he had married me, for certain, with a ring. While he was in Sicily, I bought him a wedding ring. When he came home, I put it on his finger, saying, "With this ring, I thee wed." He was a little startled by my thought—that I had not married him as thoroughly as he had me—but it pleased him so much that he remarked on it in his letter. Then he continued: "I saw both my boss and the Exec about this request and explained somewhat how I wanted my own ship etc. Now I wonder what sort of endorsement I'll get. The course [at the Naval War College, a prerequisite for command] is only about 5–6 months long and they take only 15 regular Lt. Cdrs, Comdrs and Captains so it is a long chance. The way I look at it is, if I get it I'll get back home fairly soon and be able to be around for a while and if I don't get it at least I have a request, an official one, in for a destroyer. . . . If nothing comes of this I'll ask for something else, out and out shore duty. We will see what time will bring."

I was now in a terrible frame of mind. Once again I miscarried. Twice in a very short time, and Pam not yet a year old. Van had gone straight to Hawaii, so my trip to the West Coast would be pointless as far as seeing Van was concerned. I had written, urging him to put in his request for the Naval War College and subsequent command of a destroyer. He had made a quick stop in Washington to see if that was a possibility during our five-day leave. I was amazed that the new captain had not taken action on that right away, but he had not.

My decision about going west was settled for me by my father, who, noting my depression, insisted I take the trip anyway. I wrote Van, telling him that I was going to visit my dear friend Tek for a week or so and then the Rosses on the chicken farm in the Napa Valley, where I intended to join the "land army" for a bit, thereby doing something for the war, I thought. Indeed, I found fifteen thousand chickens of war work all right! Stupidly, I did not tell Van that I had lost the baby because I did not want to worry him. He had me all stirred up about his wanting to get out from under his immediate boss. How amazed I was that Van had not put in a second request. I berated him for allowing what other men on the ship might think to influence his decision not to ask for what he wanted. The other *Atlanta* survivors had done so successfully.

Van often used pat phrases when he was writing: "I'll put all my cards on the table" or "We'll cross that bridge when we come to it" or "Don't count your chickens before they've hatched." This time he answered my diatribe with yet more such phrases. His letter was filled with comments such as "I have to do things in my own good time" and "Men have two worlds, women only have one." All very understandable for someone who had lived in a man's world for almost twelve years, but then he used a pat phrase that sent me skyrocketing. He wrote, "In words of one syllable, for the time being, no transfer and don't think I will get to the States soon."

"In words of one syllable"—the phrase my father had used on me as a child, the one that went along with "Because I say so." In my mind it was belittling and insulting. Poor Van did not know that when he wrote. He also made another mistake: he told me his latest version of the difference between men and women. I say latest version, for it was diametrically opposed to all that we had discussed previously. He had said he admired my independence, my sculpting, and my numerous interests outside my home—all of which made me a good Navy wife. But his letter said,

> Sweetheart, you know I love you and miss you and don't mean to do things which bring down the roof. My letters have no subtle or hidden meaning in their sentences.
>
> Take what is written and don't try to make it into something I didn't intend it to mean. Also perhaps it is hard for a woman to understand, although I am sure you do, but any man who is anybody or is at all worthwhile has two sides to him, a Dr. Jekyll and Mr. Hyde complex as far as wives are concerned. He can love his wife and family and want to be with them and think of no one else but them. But at the same time have his business or professional interests. Family and business are his two loves and in neither does he want to be a failure.
>
> Sometimes the two can be mixed and sometimes they can't. More often I guess they can't. But because a man likes or wants to do his job it doesn't mean he loves his wife any the less. I guess that is a man for you. A woman is different because her whole being is wrapped up in her man and her family and she cares little for

anything else. Knowing that I do have another interest besides my family in which you can't entirely share is something illusive in your husband's life. Because you are as you are, I can understand how you feel and how much you want to share everything with me and darling as far as I am able I try to have you do so. I hope all this coming from me will go to help you understand man in general and me in particular a little more. Remember too, when the time comes, when you have a son and he grows up, he will go off and make his own life and be independent. That is mankind, they feel they must do something in the world and be successful in more than just a family way. So whether I'm in the Navy or growing apples on a farm, I will have a business I'm interested in and trying to be successful at.

Reading the part about how my only interest in life was my husband and my child and explaining this as though I were a simpleminded teenager distressed me. He had never written or said anything like that to me before, and besides, it was not true and he knew it full well. In fact, he had shared all his troubles with me in the past. He had told me over and over how he wanted to get off the ship because he was desperately unhappy. I wondered from whence such maledictory thoughts were coming. Maybe he had started reading some of Freud's hogwash about women.

When he told me about my having a boy who would grow up and leave to make his own life, I became indignant, for I had fought hard to leave my home and become independent. I had insisted on saying "Love, honor and cherish" instead of "Love, honor and obey" when we were married. The minister had remonstrated, but Van had been in complete accord. He now seemed to be rejecting all the qualities I had that formerly he had said he admired. It was not like him at all. I struggled with the problem and finally wrote to Van.

At great length I told him about my distress over the lack of camaraderie on the ship and his unhappiness, so eloquently written in previous letters from him. I went on to say that if he could not tell me his thoughts anymore I would adjust myself accordingly. I had plenty of interests aside from my husband, and if that is what he wanted, I would gladly go back to them if it would make him happy. Nothing was worth breaking up our beautiful marriage, and we best talk this over in person when we got back together. "I'm glad you are over your fear of the Pacific," I continued. "I hated for you to be so unhappy. I still have a horror of that Ocean, a foreboding I can't seem to shake. Perhaps in time I will achieve a complacency once again." It seemed necessary to add one little bit about the phrase that annoyed me so he would not use it again:

PLEASE don't ever use the phrase, "in words of one syllable" when talking to me. You might as well have slapped me in the face as use such an utterly degrading remark to me. I can't stand it from anyone at all. It is one of my phobias and best remembered.

Whatever happens, I love you, I want us to be more than common place which I know we can be.

As soon as Van received this letter he sent me a long cable, in care of Mother, who phoned me at Tek's and read it to me. I remember it vividly:

My darling you are right and I am wrong, can you forgive me for hurting you. We always have had, always will have, something special. Have said before, say again, we were made for each other. Kilud Voper

That ended our squabble, and we both resumed our former informative way of writing to each other. On 31 August I wrote,

I have only a short while to myself. I don't like to write obviously to you as it might make Tek feel badly. . . . Darling old Tek, she is the most wonderful gal. She is still certain that someday Ted will come back. Who knows, perhaps she is right. The rest of the girls are, and were, certain that the ship is gone for good and their guys with it, but Tek says she has never felt that way about Ted, and that she has been convinced from the word go that he is still alive.

Before seeing Tek I couldn't see what she was going on, but now I have talked to her I understand. First of all Chuck Wang told her there were over 125 men in the water after the ship went down because he counted them to amuse himself. He said you couldn't tell who any of them were because they were black with grease and muck. He told Tek enough to make her mad a bit which is a good reaction to have and then the Navy Dept. has been so perfectly awful that she turned all her excess energies into hating them. As she said, for people like ourselves, it makes no difference, but for people whose income is dependent on the Navy it is a stark tragedy and for the boys who are now fighting to have the knowledge that the Navy does not keep its promise of supporting their family for a year after they are gone and do not give them their just travel claims and in fact get out of the whole thing as cheaply as possible is terrible for their morale. Tek has never been reimbursed for their original trip to the East Coast, nor for her return here. Her household goods are still in New York and the Navy has just said in effect, "Lady, you were never part of this organization and you have no claims on us."

As Tek says, for us, that's not so bad but what about some little seaman's wife who had nothing to start with and her husband goes. She expects a short time to recuperate from the shock, but, no! For bang! The Navy Dept. says, sorry gals, your boys are legally dead as of today and so we're giving you no more money. Bango! Socko!—and what's more gals, your husbands had not put in for transportation to your home and as you are no longer part of the service and have no one to stand up on your behalf, we'll just ignore any claims you may claim to have as the books are conveniently at the bottom of the sea and you can't get at us, period.

Personally I think Admiral J. should be court-martialed because of it and I guess if the *Juneau* wives have their say, he will be as they are all going to their Congressmen and Senators making as much fuss as possible. Not so much for themselves as for future young widows who will have the same mess to face unless something is done about it.

Pamela had seven teeth on Friday when I left and it still looked as though more were on the way. She may have taken a long time getting them but now they've started coming with a vengeance. . . . You know leaving home must be twice as hard as it used to be for you. . . .

Darling this trip is doing me worlds of good. First I have no responsibility at all. Next being here with Tek so utterly minimizes any trouble we have.

When I left Portland in September 1943, I went back to San Francisco, visiting with all the girls from the *Atlanta* days and getting a chance to see Jack Broughton and Dave Hall, whose ship, a sister of the *Atlanta,* was still not operational almost a year later:

I knew when I first got out here that the people on board the Atlanta had had a unique experience and I could observe first hand that all the other wives were as unhappy as I about their present ships. I now see that I had a love for the Atlanta like that you afford a human being and that ships are after all just floating offices and as warm as a dead fish. I will never forget the Atlanta. She taught me a lesson. I won't ever try to love another ship. I'll just take them for what they are worth which is nothing. The Atlanta is dead and buried. She got buried in my heart which was perhaps the wrong place for her, but she got there, and now I realize that she was unique and that I must not try to hold up other ships to her standards which means that I must become more tolerant towards other ships because I cannot judge all by the exceptional.

We'll Be Home Free

As so often happened, there was another coincidence in Jim's and Van's lives. Jim's ship had arrived in Pearl Harbor in October, and the two men received their Silver Stars simultaneously. They were pinned on them aboard their respective ships, in front of the ship's company, and their citations were read over the loudspeaker by their captains. It was a proud moment for both of them, and they told me how pleased they were, though Van once again wrote that the only medal he cared about was the Navy Cross.

Now that Jim's ship was in the Pacific, Van and Jim were often in port at the same time. Jim's job was vastly different from Van's. The man who had asked for him to be assistant gun boss was not only his friend but his gun boss on the *Atlanta*. Having chosen his own relief, he was later transferred, leaving Jim as the head of the department.

Van's case was totally different. He was asked for by Captain Wilkes, who had known him slightly in China, largely because of Van's fitness report. The man assigned to be the head of the Damage Control Department had no knowledge or experience, either in damage control or as a first lieutenant. Van was extremely capable in both capacities, and Captain Wilkes needed the best to make up for the C&R boss's lack of experience. When Captain Wilkes was relieved by a new captain, Van's fate was sealed. He would go on stooging for this boss for a long time to come. That had been bad enough through Sicily, but he had hoped to get transferred before they headed for the Pacific. That was not allowed; Van was considered indispensable.

He and Jim were heading for something big, which Van told me about in his letter of 15 October describing their dinner aboard Jim's ship:

It has been old home week around the Officer's Club these last few days. I've run into several more classmates and some of my China friends.

Yesterday at the Club I met Jim Shaw, Bud Mack, Bob Graff who asked all about you and Pam. We had dinner on Jim's ship. It certainly was nice to see them all again and exchange news. They all asked about you, and I told them how you had been visiting on the West Coast and been with all the ex "A" people there. I told Jim how sorry I was about Jane, in as natural a way as I could which I think was alright. He looked well and from what I could tell seemed to be O.K.

I wish, sweetheart, I could be with you for our third anniversary. Think of it, married three years. Three most wonderful years while I've been with you. Three lonely ones when I haven't. When I'm not with you though I have something to live for. I am so very glad darling that I found you. . . .

The only thing which I would not do, if I had these last few years to do over again, is spend so much time away from you. My only improvement would be to do some of the things we have failed to do through lack of time together. . . .

I had a nice afternoon swimming with Joe [Nane's husband had finally left the States and they made contact] and a couple of his cronies. Then after a drink or so we had dinner in town, which was very nice. They took me back to the dock at eight-thirty but as there was no boat until ten I walked a little ways down to where Bob Graff's ship was tied up and went aboard to talk with him for an hour or so.

I haven't seen so many people I know in ages. Joe is working with the Marines and knows all about what we are going to do, but he doesn't talk and I don't ask him. Things like this, the less people who know the better. Too many people know things as it is.

Later on Jim told me that at the dinner aboard his ship, Van met Shane King, *Bunker Hill*'s damage control officer. They hit it off right away, both of them having been oarsmen on the crew at Annapolis and now in the same department. He was extremely interested in Van's expertise, so Van sent him the new plan he had drawn up for the *Birmingham,* which Shane adopted as part of his plan for the *Bunker Hill.* Shane told Jim years later that Van's plan saved the *Bunker Hill.* He thanked Jim for getting him together with Van, saying, "That was a lucky day for us, m'boy, there were so few who had experience and I picked Van's brains the few times we met."

My real anniversary message came thanks to Joe, who put in a personal call from his quarters to Nane. They let Van talk to me. Navy personnel were no longer able to make calls, so it was sheer heaven to have Van tell me he loved me in his own beloved voice. He said that though it was our third anniversary, it was really our fifth, as we both knew, having considered ourselves married since the day Van said "I'd marry you of course" that spring of 1939. It was wonderful!

The ships set sail for the far Pacific again, heading for the Solomon Islands, and it was once more November. Van started a letter on 3 November 1943:

I hardly know how I feel, whether it is excitement, apprehension or the sort of home coming feeling you get when you return to someplace you know well, and will never forget. I can't really decide. . . .

Ed Corboy dropped in for a minute last night and asked me if it didn't seem strange to be in this part again, so I guess he must feel the same as I do. We are underway and following a familiar road which in a way does seem friendly as I recognize land marks and so forth. I told the Exec that if he wanted a good pilot I was his man.

Of course there are three or four others who are old hands here too but none with the time I have spent except Helweg.

You will probably want to worry like anything, but Ed said last night and I've thought, if we get by the thirteenth, everything will be O.K.

When the ships rendezvoused, prior to the upcoming battle on 9 November at Bougainville, Van wrote,

I want to write you a note tonight and tell you of the interesting day I had. Practically one year ago today I was here but you would never recognize the place at all. It is so changed I can't even find familiar land marks ashore. This morning Pat O'Day and I spent a couple of hours running about in a downpour trying to round up some supplies and get them sent out to the ship. Why there are more cars and trucks on the roads than go up and down the Boston Post Rd. . . .

We haven't had any mail now for going on five weeks. Mainly because we've been on the go and never gone to the right place where our mail is. It is like old times in that respect. . . .

I can't imagine what Pam is like now at 13 months. Is she big and talkative? Does she walk all around or what? I've a pretty good idea what a baby from 4 to 8 months is like but I'm lost when I get over a year. Gosh how I want to get back to you and Pam. I want to watch Pam grow up and I just want you.

P.S. If we get through Nov. 13th this year, I reckon we'll be home free. [They were at Guadalcanal.]

Van added to his letter of 14 November,

A world of things have happened and I've been as busy as a whole colony of beavers these past few days. I've thought of you a lot too. I've wanted to write a line or two also but besides being busy, I hardly dared breathe easily until today. We were not at sea on the anniversary but nevertheless I was a nervous wreck. There were good and ample reasons for me to mutter "it would be just my luck." . . . I am fine, however, except for being a little tired as a result of working more than my usual easy going amount. . . .

We made a fancy light weight diving outfit which consists of simply the face piece of a gas mask hooked to an air hose and a belt with lead weights. We connected the air hose to a big bottle of oxygen and the thing was ready for use. I tried it out first, not so much to see if it worked but because I wanted to go swimming and play around. I never got more than about 20 feet below the surface but as it was so comfortable and easy to use I had a lot of fun. Alan Reed helped me test it out so we paddled about in the water off the ship for a while and felt greatly refreshed.

I don't know why we don't swim off the ship. Even when it is safe, it is rarely done.

Jumping from "it would be just my luck," which was a signal the ship had been hit just as the *Atlanta* had been one year earlier almost to the day, he continued, "but because I wanted to go swimming and play around." Change the word "play" to "look around" and making such a rig made some sense. He said they had "paddled about in the water off the ship for a while, and felt greatly refreshed." That was silly—you did not need a diving outfit with air hose to feel refreshed. By substituting "encouraged" for "refreshed," I began to get the picture. Unable to tell me at the time what this was all about, Van did his best to let me know in his letter, telling me of the device he rigged to look at the damage done by the torpedo that had hit the ship, tearing a gaping hole in its bow, during the battle at Bougainville on 8 and 9 November.

An article from the ship's newspaper, quoted in Adm. S. E. Morison's *History of the Navy in World War II,* describes what Van did to make *Birmingham's* trip across the Pacific possible: "On the passage home for repairs, *Birmingham's* Assistant Damage Control Officer, Lt. Cdr. Van O. Perkins devised a trunk leading up to the main deck from compartments open to the sea, so that water could vent and relieve pressure from the shored-up bulkheads. Geysers spouted from the trunk whenever the cruiser pitched, earning her the nickname, 'Old Faithful.'"

The next day Tokyo Rose admitted the loss of fifteen planes but claimed the sinking of three American battleships, two aircraft carriers, seven cruisers, thirteen destroyers, and many transports. The *Birmingham,* the only ship even damaged, thus became equal to a whole task force.

Van had written, "It will be a couple or three weeks before I can write again." Did that mean a trip eastward for him? It would take that length of time to reach Honolulu from the Solomons, particularly if she was damaged. If my interpretation was right, the ship probably needed major repairs, and that could mean San Francisco. I thought I had better make plans right away for another trip to the West Coast.

I wrote Van about my November thirteenth:

Saturday was a pretty grim day for me as I went to New Rochelle to be with Mrs. McDermott (Jack Pierce's mother) and Grace Smith. They sent their regards to you.

When I got home, Nane brought Pam and David to the station to meet me and we all four went to church to offer thanks for your being alive.

Saturday night the Wulffs and Mustins called and we drank a toast "To all who sailed the 'Mighty A'" and another "To our own great good fortune." This was somewhat pre-arranged so I had a drink waiting to accommodate the call. It was nice to hear them and to know that all of us were sort of thinking with one accord though we're scattered all over the world. They sent much love to you and were sore as hen's teeth that you were never transferred to their little bucket.

Later on Van was able to send a personal report to his family about 8 and 9 November, when the night seemed to explode around him:

The ships we were with one night tangled with some Jap torpedo planes off Bougainville. It was the longest night I ever went through, I think it was harder than our battle a year ago. The Atlanta's battle was relatively quick and all the shooting was over within an hour, and once it stopped I didn't worry much about the Japs returning, at least not until daylight the next day when we were afraid of an air attack and were helpless. . . .

This last deal continued off and on all night. The planes kept flying around out of gun range heckling us and every now and then would come in to attack. We were the only ship to be hit but the formation shot down ten planes that we know of and undoubtedly got more but we couldn't see them fall because of the darkness.

I doubt if the Japs know they hit us because we never slowed down, stopped shooting or in any way indicated we had been hit. It was just luck to take torpedoes in no vital parts of the ship together with having a well-built ship and a red hot Damage Control organization, and to make things interesting, they dropped a bomb on us too but everyone treats that hit more or less lightly. In all this, only three men were killed so you see someone was looking over us. It was an exhausting and harrowing time and the next few days were awfully tense ones too.

Old Faithful Returns

As soon as Van got back to Pearl he got Joe to phone sister Nane, asking her to tell me he was all right. I had been nervous about him for the past two weeks. Maybe, just maybe, he was coming home, and if he was, surely this time he would be relieved and come ashore.

What confusion now occurred. Van went back to his old trick of trying to protect me from disappointment. He never totally understood that I knew all about his happenings within days, often hours, of an event. He knew I did not gossip about matters military, but he certainly should have known by now that I had a network. Other people told their wives, via codes like ours, and the wives who knew me called asking if I was going to the coast. Van had no concept of the present difficulties of civilian travel across country but should have known I would act on my own.

On 10 December 1943, Van's thirtieth birthday, I wrote,

A very hurried note to tell you that I am going to try and get out to the farm.

I have reservations on the 14th as far as Chicago but cannot get anything beyond that until Jan. 17th, so I am going to Chicago and take my chances with getting beyond there. You have no idea how ghastly the traveling problem has become. I am not going to take Pam with me as there is a Flu epidemic raging and I don't want to take any chances traveling with her. Later perhaps I can send for her. . . . She will have to have reservations for certain before I want her traveling.

I know you will want to kill me for going off like this just before Christmas but you see if I am to get to the farm at all I must go now and take my chances. . . . Guess you better start writing me duplicate letters for the next three weeks so that I will get them if I get to the farm or have to turn back and come home to Mother's.

Van also wrote me on the tenth:

Today I am the Birthday B. and I hate to think of how old I am. It is almost depressing to realize it. I feel young enough and hope I look young and act not like an old fud. I still like to think of you as my bride and myself just as a young buck.

I have been having the time of my life this last week. . . . The Pooh took over the job as Exec and got so busy and buried in work he has left me to run the C & R dept. completely. . . . I work with the yard jobs, with ships work, my big effort of the moment is scraping the bottom which is a hard job because you have to keep pushing and spurring on the men. The job will be completed in four days which isn't bad to my way of thinking.

I went over to the Commissary today with Joe and we both bought a lot of things. Joe for his quarters and me to save ration coupons. I will go back a couple of more times so when I am through my room will look like the A & P in better days. It was fun going marketing but I felt sort of foolish at first pushing one of those little carts, with a basket in it, around. In this Commissary however there were only a couple of women but many men handling oranges and picking out their canned goods—quite a turn about. . . .

Thank you my darling for your little B'day cards, particularly the big one you drew and the poem. I am glad you sent me the chin straps, they were a pleasant surprise and needed too.

Betty King, Patsy Reed, and I had made our way to Chicago with actual reservations. We had boarded the train to San Francisco with two upper berth reservations between the three of us. Thanks to a kindly conductor, I was allowed to spend the first night sleeping on the transom in the men's room, much to the chagrin of the male passengers next morning. Fortunately, the occupants of compartment B debarked somewhere around noon and Betty and I, having whiled away the morning in the smoking car, were installed in our own quarters.

Betty had a pet phrase with which she liberally larded her conversation. "Oh shit" she would say at the drop of a hat. I, who had my mouth washed out with soap for using such innocuous words as "gosh" and "darn," unconsciously began to be just as salty.

Arriving in San Francisco, we went directly to the manager at the Fairmont

Hotel and told him of our plight. He took pity on us and gave us one of the display rooms with cots set up between the glass cases and a promise that he would get each of us a room as soon as they became available. Blessed man, he was as good as his word and had us comfortably housed in our own rooms by the time the ship came in.

The *Birmingham* left Pearl Harbor on 18 December, after spending seventeen days being patched up sufficiently to make it to San Francisco, a record that Van described to his family in a letter of 19 December 1943:

> Every now and then something happens to prove the Navy does have a heart and can take time out from the whole to think of little things. That is how we happen to be getting to the States in time for Christmas. Originally we wouldn't have left Pearl Harbor until the 20th or 21st at the earliest and could never have made it but Admiral Nimitz and everyone else involved with us pushed.
>
> I've been in many Navy Yards but never one in which the men working on the ship showed so much enthusiasm and energy in their work. They knew we were trying to get the repair jobs done quickly so the ship could get back for Xmas and every man of them worked. . . . After watching them tear out great sections of the hull and rebuild it I can see how we build ships in a matter of days and break all kinds of records. . . . Our workers went so fast they caught the destroyers flatfooted and the destroyer people had to put the pressure on to finish when we did so as not to hold up the flooding of the dry dock.
>
> . . . The Navy you know is very cozy about information concerning ships that get damaged. Particularly about how badly damaged, and how long to repair the damage to ships is vital. Of course the public hears about ships that are sunk but never about those damaged. . . .
>
> I need not caution you about discussing this.

While Van was on his way home from Honolulu, I had everyone looking for an apartment for us. Neither my San Francisco nor my Oakland friends turned up anything. Bill and Elvira Ross found one at Stag's Leap in the Napa Valley, thirty-five miles north of Mare Island. I told them to pin it down; Van would find some way to get back and forth.

This time there was no getting information about the arrival of the ship from Dad's friend at the Presidio, for censorship had clamped down on the West Coast. Patsy, Betty, and I just waited as time dragged by. About the twentieth, the hotel gave each of us separate rooms. None of us dared to go out for more than a few minutes, and then never all together. We let the hotel operators know what room we were in to make sure we did not miss a phone call. By 22 December we were nervous wrecks. Then Elvira Ross called me to say she had spoken to Van. This time Van had called Elvira, who told him where I was, and in jig time he arrived, just after Patsy and Betty flew out of my room. I quickly combed my hair and was at the door when Van's knock came. There was a double-lock contraption on the door, and try as I would, I could not get both locks to turn and open. "Oh shit," I said, using Betty's favorite word. "Oh shit and double shit," I said, this time beginning to shake with frustration.

Inexplicably the door locks opened, and in a second I was in Van's arms. All the horror of the past year was wiped out of our minds. He had made it home in time for Christmas! I had disobeyed him and come to the West Coast, but he was pleased and kept telling me so. "I'm so glad you paid no attention and took matters into your own hands. I wasn't sure you'd be here. Oh, you're a true wonder."

Finally I said, "Oh hush, you're making me blush. What I need is to kiss you."

After a while we went down for luncheon and talked over how we would deal with the commute from Mare Island to Stag's Leap. I larded my suggestions with Betty King's pet word, and finally Van gave me a big smile, put his finger over my lips, and in his most beguiling voice asked me, "Betts, if you must use that word, would you kindly give it the French pronunciation and say Shee-tay?" Van was certainly no prude, but he had a more than adequate vocabulary and found four-letter words distasteful from anyone, most certainly from his wife. As was his way, he made a joke of it and totally disarmed me. I have never used the word to this day, except to tell the story, and then I usually only spell it. Once in a while, however, "Shee-tay" slips out.

After New Year's, Van wrote his family about our Christmas:

First of all Christmas was grand. We had a little tree about three feet high and got a few real ornaments from friends of Betts and improvised others so that it was well decorated. We hung a wreath in the window and tied a few red bows here and there to give the hotel room a Christmas look. Then it was lots of fun opening all our packages together. I seemed to have a million what with yours, the Rileys' and Betts'. . . . It was a very satisfactory Christmas for me and Betts and of course one of the best I've ever had.

I received Dad's letter with the bill which you wanted me to use buying our Xmas dinner. I didn't buy the dinner but it was handy later on. Thanks so much.

Betts and I went to Omar Khayyam's our favorite restaurant run by a character named George Mardikian. . . . Well, George gave us a very good Christmas dinner and when I asked for the check he said it was on the house and wouldn't let me pay. He knew I had just returned from the wars, etc. and said it was the least he could do for Betts and me. We thought it was pretty darn nice. . . .

A couple of days after Xmas we went out to Napa to visit the Rosses for a day and a half. The country air and life worked wonders for us both as the city and hotel food was beginning to pale. While visiting the Rosses, I made a deal with a very nice Napa automobile agency to get a car, and we got rooms and a housekeeping arrangement at a place called Stag's Leap, where I'm writing this as Betts is cooking supper.

. . . What I have done is in effect bought the car because it is registered and insured in my name and pay the man $125.00 each month. He agreed to service it, keep it in good condition and take it back when I am through. It is a lot of money but one just can't get around without a car and for a couple of months it is worth it. . . .

Stag's Leap is 11 miles out of Napa, which is a little country town, 25 miles from the Navy Yard at Mare Island and about 70 from Frisco. . . . Stag's Leap is about half way up the Valley and right at the base of the mountains in wild rugged country and yet only a whoop and a holler from the flat country. The place is properly named and Betts and I saw five deer the other night.

I am sold on this country as it seems to have everything I've ever looked for. Good farm land, easy to work, and excellent climate. It rains for three months; Dec., Jan., Feb. and is dry the rest of the year, not too cold and not too warm, mountains and rolling land, near enough to a big city and everybody I've met has been grand. . . . I would seriously consider buying land here and building a home after the war. . . .

. . . I dislike intensely stooging for my immediate boss and would go to almost any extreme to get away from him. Of course the ideal berth would be a nice shore job here in the States someplace. Next to that, or rather if I have to go to sea, I'd just as soon stay on a new cruiser. Small ships are O.K. but I've lost my enthusiasm for DD's during wartime. Perhaps I'm foolish, but I think it should be the bigger the better. I don't know, it is all pretty risky business and when you are safe from torpedoes you are wide open for shells or bombs.

After Van worked the miracle car deal, we headed for the ration board accompanied by the Ford agency man, where Van did it again: big, shy smile, uniform with more medals then the clerk had previously seen. We came away with an unlimited gas allowance and an unlimited meat allowance—sugar, butter, cigarettes, anything he asked for. Napa went all out for us. The only thing they could not find for him was scotch. I had scrounged two bottles at home for him, but we were going to live at Stag's Leap, which was a famous winery. No scotch but plenty of brandy if Van wanted hard liquor. Beer was his preference, and that too was readily available.

Stag's Leap was delightful. We were given a huge combination bed-room–living room at one end of the second floor hall complete with fireplace and two big, comfy chairs. At the far end from that there was a strange kitchen built over the front porch in an ell shape with a stove, sink, and refrigerator in the foot of the ell and a small table with two chairs in the leg part. All the windows were old, it had a leaky tin roof when it rained, and this was the rainy season.

Our co-apartment dwellers were Mrs. Grange and her son, Freddy, who owned and ran the place, Commander and Doris Archer, doing the same as we, and Uncle Stanley. I never knew him by any other name, but he was a delight, a funny lush. He never drew a sober breath, nor was he ever really drunk; he just tippled all the time and was great fun, particularly in the culinary department. He had been the maitre d' of the Monkey Bar at the Elysee Hotel in New York. This crew of strangely assorted people soon informed us that we in the know should call Stag's Leap "Bucks Jump." This set the tone for the whole crew, with the exception of Mrs. Grange, who maintained her air of grande dame of a once-opulent establishment—which had become, along with its mistress, musty-fusty with age.

Van wrote his family, further describing our time together:

How I wish I could continue to live like this instead of going back to sea, which I find is harder to do each time. When I was unattached and before I learned of the delights of being a family man it was all right trotting off, but now it is most disagreeable . . .

. . . Betts, you know, is a marvelous cook so every meal I have at home is wonderful and tasty and I thrive with her. We have so much fun together. We have been driving about the country side after I get home from work looking the land over and picking out a spot we would like to own. It is lots of fun and we have found a couple of lovely places.

. . . Betts brought out six rolls of movies of Pam and the rest of the family, which I've shown . . . when I had the duty and Betts was aboard for dinner. . . . I was crazy about them and think our little Pam is the best thing ever. I do wish I could see her.

We are supposed to be all finished here between Feb. 6-11 and after that there is nothing definite, but I would be very much surprised if we spent much time around here. I certainly don't relish and am not very happy about the idea and prospects of going back out to the South Pacific again.

Well my former boss is now Exec. and I am the 1st Lieut., a situation I hoped would not occur. I don't like working for or with him and wonder how he will act and if he will try to run my job for me and make suggestions which I have to follow, as to how and what I do. He alone is reason enough for me to be very anxious to get off this ship. . . .

. . . All our hull repairs were made at Pearl Harbor in dry dock but they forgot to put in one valve and there was a little extra welding to do so we docked here for four days. The ship will be in excellent shape when it leaves here. . . . We have gotten several new things and several improvements in the guns and fire control.

Surprisingly there have only been about two or three Officers transferred. We all expected a great number would be taken off. Perhaps just before we leave there will be some changes. I guess, unfortunately, all the changes which affect me have been made so I am stuck.

After the second leave section came back, there was a ship's dance. All the ladies wore full-length evening dresses and the men wore their blues. At long last I met some of Van's men as they asked me to dance. Each man I danced with told me of his fondness and respect for my grand husband. One of them, Mr. Swinney, told me Van always stood up for his men and that Van was tutoring him to take extra exams for warrant officer. "I never heard a mean word said against Commander Perkins," he said. "Nor did he ever say a mean thing by word or gesture about our C&R boss, who was not liked by anyone. We were all glad when Commander Perkins became top guy." He added, "We thought he should get an award for getting us home safely, but he didn't." Of course, I agreed with him.

We set out to make a dream for the rest of our lives. The Napa Valley was as beautiful then as any place on earth we had ever seen. Van was fascinated by grapes, and I had loved working at the Rosses' chicken ranch. We knew the two were compatible, so when we heard that forty acres across from Stag's Leap was for sale, we took an option to buy the place after the war. Both of us were now determined to have a dream for the future, to talk about when we were together, and to write about when Van had to go back to war. The war was too horrible to think about. We could not write about it, so we made an ideal life of our own.

Chickens to Feed the Grapes?

Early one morning, we were eating breakfast when a charming field mouse came out of the wall and up to the perpetual puddle on our porch/kitchen floor. Perplexed, he sat up on his haunches. He tried going to the right, no dry land that way, so he tried going to the left. Stymied, he came back to the middle, thought a second, and then took the plunge right through the puddle and up the table leg. He joined us for breakfast. Van chortled as he crumbled his toast for the wee creature. "Obviously his name must be Hellespont. What a brave little fellow. If only we had Pam with us, we'd have everything we need, including a pet."

Hellespont became a regular at our breakfasts and a part of our letter life. In all our association with him he never showed any fear of us. He would sit in Van's hand after he had eaten his breakfast, clean off his whiskers, and spruce up for the day. Then he would scurry off to his own part of the house. What a delight he was.

We spent hours walking our forty acres. We would take a picnic lunch and go up to the top of the hill at the north end of the property where we thought to build our house. We would lay the whole place out in our imagination. Van would get out his pipe and use it to point: "Over there we'll build the winery."

"Oh, Van, I thought that the perfect place for the chicken houses."

"Now Betts, you don't want the hen house on a slope. That's the perfect place for the winery. The chickens should go over there, handy to take the droppings out to the vineyard."

"Where are you going to put the barn if the chicken houses are there?" I got a little feisty and asked, "Are we going to raise chickens to feed the grapes?"

Van laughed and told me we were going to work it all out. "It'll be simple, you'll see. Nothing is too hard for us to figure out." I knew he was right. We had always worked everything out before, and, of course, this was going to be the most livable, charming, and profitable establishment in the valley.

Rain or shine, we spent our days out of doors. If we got wet, we did not care, we would just dry off in front of the fire in our big room. We took advantage of our unlimited gas coupons to poke around side roads. We took one long drive to see the headwaters of the Napa River and talked about the Klamath River property that belonged to my family. Van made contact with a boat-building firm in Napa that offered him a postwar job designing sailboats. Now he had his entire dream put together—a job that kept him in touch with the sea and a farm that would give him his second love, the land. A perfect setup to raise his family—a big one if he had his way. All this within easy reach of San Francisco, the most glamorous city in the world, to our way of thinking. This was the fantasy we desperately needed in order to face the war.

At last our glorious days came to an end. Regretfully, we turned in the car and cleaned the apartment. I checked out the laundry, remembering the day the goat got in the back door and ate my irreplaceable girdle, a pair of my precious rationed nylons, and my best slip, leaving just the straps and a shred of lace pinned to the line. I had liked that funny old-fashioned laundry and always felt particularly wifely doing Van's laundry there. The goat incident had given us a good many chuckles. The goat probably had a splendid tummy ache; I hope he did.

We had a room at the St. Francis Hotel in San Francisco for two nights. The first night Van was due to have the duty but managed to swap with someone. The ship was to sail for the Pacific the next morning, 8 February, and he would have to leave me before first light. We went downstairs for dinner in the dance room. We asked the orchestra to play "Old Black Magic" and "All the Things You Are," our two favorite songs, which I liked to sing to Van as a lullaby, though my singing usually served to wake him up most thoroughly. On this night dancing with him, he held me as close as he decently could and I tried to sing the words but the lump in my throat stopped me. Before I openly cried, I took his hand and led him out of the room. Once alone I clung to him and we talked about his death, remembering the prediction of "the finest fortune-teller in the Orient": "You will be married to each other. You will be sublimely happy but only for a short while. I cannot tell you more." Both of us felt Van's luck was running out. He had been torpedoed twice, and he had been seriously wounded and was overdue for shore duty or his own command.

Finally he told me what he wanted me to do if he was killed: "You must go on, my own darling. I want you to make a life for you and Pam. I want you to make someone else happy as you have made me. I want someone to take care of my girls if I'm not here. You could do a lot worse than to think about Jim; he and I are very close friends and I know from months together on *Atlanta* and in the hospital in New Zealand that we are in accord about everything of importance to us."

We were both overcome by the horror of this parting, and for a bit we just held close to each other. I traced his face with my fingers as though to sculpt every line in my memory forever. When the time came for him to go, he gently took my arms from around his neck and whispered, "Don't cry my darling. Pretend I'll be back this evening. Know I'll love you always and that wherever I am, I'll watch over you."

Somehow I managed to kiss him goodbye, though I could not hold back a sob. I turned my back and told him to go before I made a scene that would be his last memory of me. I heard the door close, and with it my resolve dissolved. Flinging myself on the bed where Van had lain, I sobbed my heart out.

I had hidden two notes in his uniform to cheer him. When I got hold of myself I noticed Van had left a letter on the dresser. He must have written it on the ship, not expecting to get ashore that night. Reading it was both a heartbreak and a comfort:

I think I love you even more now than I ever did before if that could be possible.

We are closer together it seems and have a deeper understanding of what we want together in life. It breaks my heart to be going off again and realize that our beautiful days together have suddenly and rudely been interrupted once more. When I am with you I try not to think about what it is going to be like leaving you again—so today when the shock came I felt very blue. I don't care for anything but you my precious sweetheart. No matter how busy I try to make myself, the thought is always in my mind that Bettsy is right over there, or across an ocean, and I can't be with her. I don't like it. I am lonely and I miss you! I miss everything about you.

This letter will probably make you weep. I feel like doing so myself, because I love you. I love you with all my heart and soul. I want to be with you always.

In the final analysis isn't our job, as man and wife to work for one another, comfort each other and live together to bring up fine sons and daughters. How can I do that at sea? I can't and we are both sad. I think we know what we want most in life, that idea seems crystallized, now remains the method, the means and the occasion to accomplish our aim. We will work that out too, just as we have worked out and attained the other things we have wanted and set our hearts on. Just never forget that I want most of all your love and our happiness together.

I doubt if I have ever been happier or more content than I was this past six weeks. Six weeks of happiness and normal life is a short time, too short and in normal times I won't take that little bit of living for several months of being away from you.

. . . I do hope and pray we will have another baby and that all your symptoms are not false alarms and that nothing untoward happens. Please take it easy these next few weeks and don't tire or strain yourself and do your best not to get upset and unhappy.

I did love every minute of our time in the Napa Valley. Life with you is so full and so enjoyable. We are made for each other and I know we love each other more than average. Ours is something fine and fierce and tender. You are everything to me I want or could dream of having. . . .

I don't know that I have told you all that I meant to or told what I did well. Mainly I miss you terribly. I want to be with you tonight and every night and never want to have to go off and leave you for long again.

I just can't get over how delightful it was at Stag's Leap and the honest joy and contentment that I had living with you. It was better than we ever had before and I want it again.

A Slight Dent in Our Plans

We had always thought it best for me to wait a while after the ship sailed before leaving port. This was no exception. I got hold of Sophie Lou Brocklebank and we kept each other company as we waited. Betty King had already left. We took a ride that evening across the bridge and saw something odd. Instead of anchoring out in San Francisco Bay, the *Birmingham* was heading toward Mare Island! We dashed back to the hotel and waited. Sophie got the first call. She called me to tell me there had been an accident and they had put in to Mare Island for repairs. Brock, being the chaplain, had nothing to do on the ship at this point, but of course Van would be like a one-armed paperhanger, as he was now head of the Damage Control Department. Brock came by to tell me what had happened: the ship had collided with a freighter that had crates of live pigs on deck screaming their heads off. He told me there would be a court of inquiry, which, of course, would take time. He did not know the extent of the damage to the ship but thought it was only slight.

Excitedly, I called down to the desk to ask to keep my room. The clerk said I could only keep it two more days; after that, the hotel was booked solid. Going back to the valley for a short stay would be impossible. I was desperate by the time Van finally got through to me. The exec had immediately contacted the Navy yard authorities and made arrangements for the very few wives who had stayed on to get temporary quarters on the base. The exec had always acted kindly toward me, and thanks to him, Van and I were able to share a Quonset hut, made into two units, with the Brocklebanks.

Van answered a letter from his family dated 10 February 1944, telling them about the accident:

> You must have gotten the telegram Betts sent telling of the slight dent in our plans as she put it.
>
> We had left the Yard and were operating in San Francisco Bay calibrating instruments and so forth. We were going to a pier on the water front and had a collision with a freighter. No one was hurt and there was very little damage done. Mostly a few plates and beams bent but we had to come back to the Yard to get them replaced and so we have a five day reprieve. It was one of those accidents hard to explain but caused by dusk because neither ship saw the other. Luckily we had the right of way and both of us were going slowly.
>
> Betts and I certainly were blue at the prospect of leaving each other again the day before I thought I was departing. She is going to try and change her reservations and leave around the 18th or 20th now. So when our latest plans materialize we will let you know.
>
> About this course at the War College in Newport. It starts sometime late in

the summer and lasts about 5 months. I want to know what sort of duty one is apt to get upon completion of the course. I feel almost certain it would be to a ship right back at sea.

Where I am stumped is that I don't know whether I should try and get some short few months ashore or stay at sea for a while longer and keep plugging for a more permanent shore job. . . .

Perhaps the best I can get is a few months but I am going to try for more before I settle on the short time. Anyway I have already made my wishes for going ashore known to the Captain and he was most reasonable about it but said of course a relief would have to be furnished for me. Anything you hear about which might interest me you will please let me know because I must and want to get the request in as early as possible.

Well my old boss has been busy doing a hundred and one other things and hasn't bothered me, I am glad to say. One ruling about liberty which he recently made has the ship in an uproar but it does not effect me as I am a Dept. Head. However I have talked with him and tried to get a reasonable arrangement for my people. . . .

P.S. Betts will leave a day or so after we leave this time if we don't knock down a bridge or something on the way out!

Van's height became a feature of our Quonset hut living quarters. Quonset huts looked like half a barrel, high side up, both sides curving rapidly down. Van had to be careful not to walk too far to either side of the one big room that served as living room, dining room, and bedroom, with kitchenette and bathroom in the far end. He banged his head once, and after that he ducked when he needed to go to either side.

The officers whose wives had left were wonderfully kind about standing watch for Van. As a result, we had all of our evenings together—and what evenings they were! We were like two people rescued at the last minute from drowning and gulping in air. We could not keep our hands off each other; we simply reveled in each other's company. Van declared, "I won't give this up and that's that! I'm going to ask for shore duty."

We planned what we would do to make that come true. It was obvious that the exec was aware of all the extraordinarily long separations we had had, and his wife was very sympathetic toward us. In fact, most of the men who knew Van and me thought our marriage was something very special. We knew that to be true. I was very hopeful, and Van was exuberant too. It seemed that if the captain forwarded his request now, in mid-February, Van should be home by August.

With some hope restored, saying goodbye the second time, on 12 February, was not nearly the heartrending experience our goodbye at the hotel had been:

> A happy and beautiful Valentine thought to you. . . . Bettsy I go away again with perhaps less apprehension than I've had in the past, but with no less chokey feeling in my throat and aching heart. I hate to leave you and I know it is so hard on us both. How I pray for the time when we can live normally together.
>
> Each time I go it is like tearing something out of me to be parted from you. I love you with all the passion a man can have and I am so devoted and dependent on you.
>
> . . . Take care of yourself for me and take life easy. I feel this time that you are full of health and strength and should be "making a baby."
>
> Dearest one, the next few days will be hard because we will be within sight of one another and yet won't be able to see or be with each other. I'll look up on the hill knowing you are there though, and thinking of me as I am thinking of you.

I had to leave the Quonset hut when the ship left, gratefully accepting an invitation to stay with a friend on Nob Hill. This time I made a grievous mistake. It was an old Navy superstition that one not watch the ship leave. I did. I went out by Coit Tower and watched as the ship went under the Golden Gate Bridge. It shattered me to see the *Birmingham* take my husband away.

Now that the old executive officer had been relieved and Van's boss in Damage Control had been fleeted up, Van was head of the department, a position so complex at all times that he was close to indispensable. This put him in a terrible spot to get a transfer. The captain was obviously loath to let go a man who not only had a great deal of experience but also had demonstrated his capability by bringing the damaged ship home safely. It looked to me like Van would be stuck on the ship indefinitely if he did not put in a formal request for transfer at once.

God Had Good Reason

My trip home from San Francisco was a mix of hope and foreboding. After the ship left, I moved again to be with my friend Helen Hall in Oakland, making sure this time that the *Birmingham* had really left. In addition, I knew I was pregnant and I wanted desperately to carry this baby to term. After the other miscarriages, I wanted to get well past my third month before I traveled.

By the latter part of March 1944, I needed to get home to Pamie, so I took the train because I could not get a reservation on any plane. As cautious as I was and as calm as I tried to be, I could not help but think that every tree we passed, every station where we stopped briefly, was carrying me farther and farther away from Van and he was going in the opposite direction at equal speed. Van and I had felt deep down we were saying goodbye for the last time. On the other hand, he had said he was tired after more than eight years overseas in war-torn countries and had talked about asking for a transfer. So, as I sped along I swung from dejection to wild hope that he would do so and be relieved before he once again was hit.

Going across Chicago, changing trains and stations, with no porters to help, I had to carry my heavy bags. I obviously could not stand on the station platform with a sign on me that read "Please help me with my bags, I'm pregnant." By the time I boarded the New York train I knew I was in trouble, just as I had been with Pam.

Arriving in New York the next morning, I was met by Sophie Lou Brocklebank, who drove me to Greenwich. She took me straight to Dr. Squire, who gave me a shot and ordered me to bed.

I was only able to hold on to the baby a while longer. During that time I rarely turned my eyes from Van's portrait. Every time little Pam came in the room, I would get tearful. That time was a total blur. I am not sure how many days or weeks passed, nor how many prayers I said. All to no avail. One morning I awoke to the certainty that I was losing the baby. I called Doc Squire, who came as fast as he could, but by noon it was all over. We had lost our second little son. I poured out my despair to Van. I felt an utter failure. He had wanted a family of sons and daughters and again I had failed him.

Though Dr. Squire assured me I could have many more children, I was sure that was not so. My courage would have failed me had it not been for the "Day by Day" calendars Van and I had made for each other. I read my March and April ones over and over until I received the answer to my letter about losing the baby:

I received your special delivery with the sad news that there is going to be no bambino this time. I am disappointed too because I had hoped we could start another addition now and really would have been delighted if it had happened.

We both want more babies in the family don't we darling? Don't be sad about it or feel inadequate, as you put it, or that you can't do your part or anything silly like that. I too believe that if it was to have been a baby and you lost it, God had good reason and perhaps you were not ready or He wants us to be together the entire nine months. I know I would rather have it that way and be with you the entire time and watch the wonderful process, be able to see you when you were at your prettiest, with shining eyes and hair and then squire you around and push chairs under you when you get ponderous. It would be more fun for us that way.

Also I know that anybody's first months are extremely touch and go and it doesn't take much to throw the balance one way or another. I know you were a good girl physically and didn't exert yourself, except the train ride is no rest cure, but I know that emotionally you've been upset and unhappy because I have too and it is only natural. Perhaps if you sat down and figured if we had done this or hadn't done that all would be well, but we will only succeed in making ourselves unhappy looking in retrospect. So please darling one, don't think you let me or yourself down. . . . I think we have the ideal marriage, understanding, love and fellowship Bettsy. . . .

The days I sped home in the little green Ford, faster and faster, so I could be with you five minutes earlier and the peaceful hours we spent in our own little world are grand to recall.

Some one of these days when I have some time I will start sketches of our Ranch. . . . I've certainly thought a lot about us and what we want and how badly I want it—you—a farm—freedom—security—a happy home life—seeing the things I love best growing around me. . . .

What a busy and hectic time we have all been having this week or two. Between Officers shifting jobs in my outfit, getting new men and putting some of my methods into effect, we have had a big job re-organizing the C & R department and getting all the personnel of the repair parties straightened out.

I've a little system which I hope works. If I give a person a job to do, to find out why something doesn't work, or to fix something that is busted, and he bungles the job, I do it myself and gradually these men on the ship will learn that the 1st Lieut. can handle tools himself or operate any piece of machinery and make electrical or mechanical adjustments which they as, supposedly, specialists can't do and maybe that will jar their pride or initiative and they will fix something before I get there. Also, they will know that I know what I am talking about.

I get around a lot and chat with people and get a much better idea of what is going on in the ship than The Pooh ever had. He went around infrequently and it was always to inspect and when one "inspects" one generally criticizes. No good! One of the big changes I am trying to make is to get all the Officers to take on the responsibility of seeing their parts of the ship, or equipment they take care of, are in good shape and not wait for me to tell them what to do or how to do it. That is a slow change as most of the Officers came in after the war started. In their early training they didn't know enough to be given any responsibility and they had so much to learn in such a short time they concentrated on their specialty, such as gunnery or radar etc., and never realized their other duties too.

Van wrote his family an even better report of all he had to do now that he was head of the department. For the first time, he told them about his change in attitude about his life—that he was going to leave the Navy.

Jim Shaw and Van had seen very clearly that those in the air arm of the Navy were the officers who were going up the line to flag rank. Jim, who was on an aircraft carrier, confirmed their suspicions. They had missed their chance. He told Van what he wanted now was to write books. Van told Jim in Honolulu that he had found he just wanted to be a family man. He told his parents the same thing:

> I've reached the conclusion that even under the most favorable circumstances it will never be as appealing and attractive to go sailing off as it used to be. I'm getting to be a stuffy old married man now, who likes to relax with his slippers, a pipe and a drink and have a good meal and a quiet evening. During the six weeks or so we were in California I saw the light in a number of things I had not thought of or realized before. . . . I work too damn hard and put myself on a spot where I'm considered indispensable. . . . The only nice thing about arriving out here was that I found Joe and several other friends and had a chance to get off the ship for a bit and be with them. As you know from reading the newspapers, the Navy is pretty busy these days and we may not be around much.

"Old Si," That's Me

Now was the time to get busy. Calling Molly, I said, "Hey old friend, how about reinstating me in the Civil Air Patrol? I know it's been a long time."

"I'll ask Major Crowley," she answered, "and I'll call you back."

Shortly she did just that, with the happy news that I could not only come back but could start teaching navigation. "What's more you'll start as a corporal again, but you will be promoted to sergeant shortly."

Then Dr. Squire called to ask if I could help him out. He had lost his nurse-secretary to the war effort. What I knew about secretarial work you could carry in one side of your cheek. What I knew about nursing I had learned in an eight-week course at Red Cross Hospital on Fourteenth Street in New York when we were living on Christopher Street in Greenwich Village. Undaunted by my lack of training, I went to work mornings for the good doctor. It soon became obvious that I had an aptitude for nursing. Equally, it became obvious that as a medical secretary I was a total flop. Doc Squire made a rubber stamp for me to use on every communiqué I typed: "New Secretary, Please excuse all mistakes, signed Sq." This I faithfully used, despite my chagrin, throughout my checkered career as his secretary, nurse, and aide-de-camp.

As to navigation, Van suggested I read through his sea navigation book. It felt good just to turn and read the pages I knew he had turned and read. I learned a lot that helped as background for the CAP text I had to use when teaching high school seniors in the evenings.

One crewman after another left the *Birmingham*. Many from other ships started to arrive home on shore duty, and my "intelligence ring" became more and more accurate. The *Birmingham* was being used to bombard Japanese positions on the Shortland Islands on 17 and 18 May, where they were at one point straddled by return Japanese fire. Then on 21 May they headed back for Purvis Bay, where they took part in a full dress rehearsal of a landing somewhere up the line.

Van vacillated between apprehension over the ship, wanting to get off, and feeling that he would be letting his fellow officers down if he asked. I was told that if he did not ask, no one would bother to look at his record to know he had been torpedoed twice, wounded once, and overseas now almost nine years—in war-torn areas at that.

I received a letter on 22 May in which he talked about the farm, getting out after the war, and not wanting to die:

> I can see one thing that I still underestimate the necessity for, and your feeling about me not saying anything. It was done mostly from thoughtlessness and because I didn't have my ideas crystallized and ready. Of course you want to know all that I do, what I'm planning and thinking about. Mostly I think about this war, how I don't want to get killed, how long it will be before I can get back to you, how long it will be before the war is over and we will have permanent security. How I can take a vacation from every day strife and struggle for a year or so and then live a simple secure and normally carefree life. At this point any ambition but to relax and enjoy living is gone. Retiring is the word for what I want to do. Retire and putter.
>
> . . . I know I want a period of relaxing and loafing when the war is over in which I can drift or be furiously active in some frivolous thing of no value at all. I'm tired of being separated from you and not having our own things and permanence. I want permanence and security! Enough of being a nomad by myself.
>
> Your news that Bud says I will be a Commander in 6-8 months is a bit startling. I think it must be just talk. The class of 1932 are Commanders so to get down to me they must go through '33, '34, '35 and '36. That seems like a very big order to accomplish in such a short time.
>
> How is my Army wife? What fun. I hope that one of your pictures will be in your uniform. All your drilling and so forth sounds impressive and I must admit I have difficulty in picturing you tramping about doing squads right and left. I am glad you like it though. My little G.I.
>
> I'm glad you like my plans. I will note all your suggestions but had already provided for most of them although the drawings didn't show it. . . .

I planned to have a glassed portion in the roof area between buildings, the glassed roof part could have a sort of sliding door or hatch electrically operated to open or close.

We both tried to keep our chins up with house plans—suggestions for color schemes and furniture from me, floor plans and modern conveniences from Van—but all the while we knew we were playacting. Sometimes I would bubble over with indignation at the Navy for not realizing they had an outstanding officer who was slowly tiring.

With the invasion of Europe, we were given a new term: "brown-out." The black-out at night was partially lifted. We still drove with "dimmer lights" when we had to drive at night. I was a CAP warrant officer now and had been told I would soon make second lieutenant. Every rise in rank made me feel more responsible, so I drove at night with only a small beam of light through the black paper over the headlights, even though it was treacherous going.

We still kept the black curtains drawn toward Long Island Sound, mostly out of habit. In 1944 German subs were no longer the threat they had been to our convoys. We could leave the windows uncovered to the north, and that was a bit less depressing. The huge, ugly curtain that hung across the front hall to keep the cold away from the living room stayed in place. Oil and coal were in short supply, and we did anything to keep the living room warm. That blasted curtain still takes part in my dreams. It swore with the colors in the rug. It swore with the period of the house. It swore with the vacuum cleaner, and it entangled the people trying to go through it. The true end of the war came for me when the damned curtain came down for good.

Few people at home understood that Task Force 58 and Task Force 38 were one and the same group of ships. When it was 58, Admiral Spruance was in command; he was the quiet genius of Midway strategy, and both Van and Jim felt safer with him than with his counterpart, Halsey. When the task force was 38, it was commanded by Adm. "Bull" Halsey (so dubbed by the press, not by the Navy). His grand phrase, "The riders may change, the horses will remain," told the story. Van and Jim were about to find out how true that statement was.

In March, Van sailed from Pearl Harbor headed for trouble. He had looked longingly as they passed Diamond Head, as always his last sight of American territory. It soon became obvious both Jim and Van were heading for the Solomons once again. Though they were in the same task force, they were seldom operating in the same area. Once or twice they had a chance to visit, but it was never long enough to have one of their heart-to-heart talks, just a brief chat sandwiched between incredibly trying battles.

Van worked a great deal on house plans and wrote about many innovations not yet heard of in civilian life: central air conditioning, walk-in freezers for our crops such as they had on board, even an "Automatic Computing Machine for you to do our finances on or I will if I'm home." He added a built-in radio and record-player corner, which included space for "a scope screen on which we could watch the farm." I did not understand that and thought the screen indicated radar. Of course it was some crude sort of television monitoring system. "Frankly I'd rather sit than go to sea," Van wrote. "I certainly wish I could be home with you and that we didn't have anything to worry about but molting chickens and bugs in the grape vines. What a country squire I will be. You have a fitting picture on my calendar for today. It's a farmer with a pitchfork and you call him 'Old Si'—That's me!"

He never missed sending me, six weeks in advance, his silly series of delightful drawings on our Day by Day calendars. We had started this two years earlier. I had all of his calendars, and if his letters were glum or I did not get mail for several weeks, I could read over the jokes and laugh at the drawings of rabbits and mice, which were delightfully naïve and upbeat.

Van received a cheery letter from me and a large envelope to liven up his life. He kept asking for pictures of Pam and me. Finally I asked my CAP boss, Molly, who was a fine photographer, to take some snaps of me. She came with her professional camera and a white bear rug, the latter she spread on the floor. "Betts, get into your black nightgown and sprawl out on that rug. I'm going to send VanO a real pin-up picture of you. Hey, you have a stepladder don't you?"

"Ya, of course we do, what for?"

"Don't be a dope, you're going to lie on the rug. I'll brush your hair up behind you and pull your nightgown off one shoulder and above your knee on one side, then I'll stand on the ladder and take a down shot. Boy will that get your man in a dither."

We staged the whole thing in several poses. Molly picked two of the best shots, enlarged them, and off to the Pacific they went. Van's reaction delighted me:

My Precious darling,

Wow! Wow! and double Woo! Woo! Thank Mol a million times. I love my secret pictures and have them tacked up beside my kiss box where only I can see them when I lie in my bunk at night. . . .

What a treat. The next best thing to having you here in person. Oh, yes, thank her for the pictures of our beautiful daughter, they're great too. I'll try to write her myself.

Your crazy mad in love with you,
Van

I had hoped the pictures would make him a bit more cheerful and it certainly had worked.

Van liked me to stay at Craggy. I loved to stay there and sleep in his big sleigh bed, but it was on a lonesome road and, because the house had been deserted with Mom and Pop Perkins in Washington, the local mice had taken up residence, playing havoc with the house. I trapped mice, removing their poor little carcasses to the stone wall for burial, never without a twinge for Hellespont, our Napa Valley pet. One day when I was going through my usual burial ritual and saying my mouse prayer—"Go to Hellespont Heaven and I'm sorry to have caused your demise"—a rare car came down the road with a bunch of toughs aboard. They stopped and started yelling lewd remarks at me.

I dashed into the house, packed our bags, scooped up Pamie, and we took off for 44 Mayo. I finally had realized that I was too vulnerable staying there with the baby in such isolation. Elderly Miss Reichardt, our loving nurse-housekeeper, was delighted to leave. I looked forward to Mom Perkins coming back for a summer vacation so that I could return to the pond, the rowboat I had made into a play pool for Pam, and the big sleigh bed, where I could dream that once again my Van was holding me close and life was as it should be.

A bed is a sorry substitute for one's dear love, but it was my safe haven, my fantasy world.

Ice Cream and Flies

Van at last gave his captain the request for shore duty at the end of May, after much agonizing over it. Unfortunately, the captain did not send it in right away because the ship suddenly became very busy. Van wrote in early June 1944,

> I was awfully lucky and got your fat Father's Day letter and five cards before losing contact with the mail. . . . I cheated a little and opened three of the Father's Day cards already because I wanted to be able to tell you I had seen them and enjoyed them so very much. I'll save the other two for the proper day.
>
> I always get a lumpy feeling when I read your letters that tell me how much you love me and what a fine Daddy I am to you and Pamela. She is such an adorable child and I am so very, very proud of her and love her dearly. It would be so blissful to be home with you both.
>
> Pamie certainly is a live wire, I get so much enjoyment reading about all your times together. You have such wonderful fun and I am so happy but envious because I wish I could be with you and enjoy all that you do. . . . You both looked very cute and adorable in your mother and daughter dresses. You are such a very clever person to be able to make things like that. I don't think that there are many

other wives or mothers as smart as you. I'm very proud of my Bettsy, she has so many good ideas and can do all sorts of things. . . . Incidentally, you look wonderful in the latest snap shots and I like the way your hair is done, and the ribbons. You know I like my child bride to wear hair ribbons.

Jeepers but I've had my hands full these last few days. . . . The other night we had a small leak in the flushing water system which comes off the fire main. The more the shipfitters fiddled with the leak, the worse it got so they cut off the water pressure and cut the bad part of the pipe out. Then some knuckle head turned on the wrong valve and did we have a flood, until I got down there and shut it off.

My Damage Control people pumped the place out and cleaned it up in a couple of hours and then the shipfitters went back to work and worked all night. In the morning the job was completed, but it still leaked so they fussed about all day with me breathing hot down their necks and finally did a good job that will last.

Then we've been having a sort of epidemic stomach trouble, dysentery. So the doctor tested everything and found flies were causing it. It started when we were in port and is about over now. So I got screening around the galley and have been having a drive on cleanliness of person and of eating utensils and places where food is handled. . . . We even have posted sentries at the doors to the toilets to make sure no one gets out without washing their hands with soap and using an antiseptic solution. I have to run most of that with the doctor's help. I had a touch of it the first few days but wasn't bad off. Am O.K. now.

. . . Why do you have to learn to fly if your job is office or school room work? I don't suppose I object if you want to learn and get a good thorough instruction, but I feel too that we both shouldn't be sticking our necks out at the same time. I am doing enough for both of us unfortunately.

. . . I see the waiting about the invasion in Europe is over and the ball has finally started rolling. I hope and imagine they can make this landing stick. In the Pacific we have a harder time because we have about 2000 miles of supply lines for every 20 in Europe. The world is about to see the entire might of the U. S. unleashed I believe. And it is hard for anyone to visualize just what terrific power we have. If used wisely and well I doubt if anything can stop it now.

Like Joe, I have a very clear picture of what is going on and going to happen. I am not greatly perturbed, perhaps because I realize it is Kismet and there is no way to turn back even if you wanted to. It is risky yes, but others are taking the same risks. There is no safe place to be, you just have to take a chance that where you are is safer than some other place on the ship.

I feel that there isn't much more to say and then at the same time there is a world of thought left unsaid. I love you my darling and Pam too with all my heart and soul and I know there is no one who can take better care of our baby than you. Also I know that if something should happen to me, you will try to give yourself and her all the fullness of life that we would have had together. You are my wife and I love you desperately and completely.

. . . Whenever anything takes place there is always a chance of my plans going wrong. . . . However if one has any remorse about having left things unsaid or undone, I don't want to feel, or do I feel, that I have.

You know what I mean to you and so do I. Also I know what you mean to me and so do you.

On 4 June 1944 they left Cape Esperance, and that evening the captain told the crew that they would take part in the invasion of the Mariana Islands, primarily Saipan and Tinian.

The map of the entire Pacific Ocean and the Orient that Van had given me was so big I had to spread it out on the floor and crawl over it to read it. It was very detailed. The clusters of atolls were clearly marked, so when a news report would come in, I would search the map for the location and circle it. Honolulu and Midway had long since been circled. Then, below the equator, the battles of Guadalcanal. In November 1943 we took the Marshall Islands, Tarawa, and Makin above the equator. We were raiding atolls in a tightening circle north toward Japan and west toward the Philippine Sea. It became clear what the strategy was: push the Japanese Navy back toward its own shores, cut its supply lines to its occupied territories, and starve out as many of its troops and sink as much of its Navy and supply ships as possible. The faster the better.

Now the long, hot summer began. Task force 58/38 was on the move once more. The *Birmingham* and the *Bunker Hill* logs read like Baedeker guidebooks of the far Pacific islands from mid-June on. The ships were there together— their overall purpose the same, their missions different—and, therefore, they were usually in different sectors of the same battle. The *Birmingham*'s objective, most of the time, was to go in close to a proposed landing area, firing to harass and bombarding the shore while the troops established a beachhead. The *Bunker Hill*'s mission was to provide air cover. At Saipan, the *Birmingham* was firing constantly and so close to the beach that they were straddled by gunfire from the Japanese, who in desperation even fired their small arms. Shrapnel peppered the ship, first on the port side, and then, as the captain swung the ship about, on the starboard side. Below deck, people were flung back and forth as the ship swung and fired. The men ducked for cover when their side claimed the Japs' attention and came up for air when the other side claimed the fire. The acrid smell of gunsmoke from their bombardment constantly assailing their nostrils and the impact of returned enemy fire explosions beating their senses were exhausting almost beyond endurance.

One marine, who had gone in with a landing party, came out to the ship later and told the lads, "Those in my boat thought you'd been hit. The entire starboard side was a wall of heat, flame and smoke." At times, the guns were so hot that hoses were played on the barrels to quell flames and cool them down. Van was one busy fellow that day, as were all the damage control crew, for they had both sides of the ship to tend to. After a while the procedure became almost routine, the racket so constant as to be meaningless and the smell hardly noticeable. When the firing stopped, the quiet was almost deafening. No rest for the C&R Department, however, as the decks had to be cleared of debris, shell casings disposed of, decks washed down, everything made ready to start the process once again. When all was secured, the men of the USS *Birmingham* hunkered down to regain their composure for the next onslaught, which they knew would not be long in coming.

Clearing the beaches of the enemy for our troops to land had been tense, terrible, and, finally, sickening, causing some to actively throw up. This had not been an impersonal duel between ships. Hundreds of human beings had been mowed down, and at such close range that our own men could see individual Japanese soldiers hit and killed—many so frustrated that they fired their side arms at the ships before they died, littering the beach with their bodies. A certain admiration for the enemy came into being, an admiration for the incredible tenacity displayed against overwhelming odds.

Right in the middle of the Saipan-Tinian invasion, word came that a large Japanese fleet carrying reinforcements for their beleaguered troops was bearing down on the Marianas. Immediately, the fast carrier Task Groups 58.1, 58.2, 58.3, and 58.4 took off to engage the enemy. The aircraft carrier *Princeton* with her screen, including the *Birmingham,* was Task Group 58.3. The *Bunker Hill* with her screen was 58.2. They took up positions about twelve miles apart, which, in this vast ocean, was like being side-by-side. They were to take on not just the enemy fleet but also the land-based planes from Guam, which we had not yet liberated from the Japanese. The distance between task groups ensured that our ships would not fire on each other but could easily control the intervening waters.

On 19 June the stage was set. Admiral Spruance was in command, and his clearly thought-out strategy paid off. The carrier planes surged into the air, and before long they had splashed almost four hundred planes, many land-based, many from the Jap carriers. Some of the planes got through to the carrier groups and were quickly dispatched by the ships' gunners, while many others were downed by our fighter planes. That was the biggest single bag of planes in one day. The tactical commander gleefully said it was a real turkey shoot; hence, forever after, the battle was known as the "Marianas Turkey Shoot."

When our planes were back on board, our ships again headed for the Japanese fleet. The next day, 21 June, the enemy was within striking range. Once more our planes took off from the carriers. The reports that came back to the ships and were soon published in our papers at home called this a rout, the "greatest naval air battle ever fought!" The World War II equivalent of World War I's Battle of Jutland. Officially, it became the First Battle of the Philippine Sea.

On 3 July 1944, Van finished a letter to me with one of his silly rabbits sprawled out under a palm tree. The legend read, "A droopy bunny, worn down who'd like to be a lazy one." That, plus the news reports, made certain I got the picture.

On one of the days at Tinian, the ship was assigned a given sector to bombard on the northern tip of the island. The battleship *Colorado*, with her attendant support group, was damaged while bombarding a different sector. Van's captain, seeing the ship in trouble, and with "Don't give up the ship" buzzing in his head, turned the *Birmingham* around and headed for the battleship of his own volition. An error in judgment at least; proceeding without orders was a serious breach of regulations. They did not get far before the annoyed bombardment commander ordered the captain back to his designated sector. This odd, independent foray probably influenced the captain's later actions. Perhaps he was uneasy about the collision with the freighter. It is not a happy thing for a skipper to have a collision on his record, right of way or not.

Not until 5 August was the *Birmingham* detached. Two grueling, tedious months had passed. It was at Saipan that Van wrote on 18 July of seeing Joe and how he took him ice cream, despite the heat, still frozen. Nane later heard Joe had the great distinction of getting the first haircut on Saipan. I thought that was mighty brave. Even if my hair had grown down to my knees, I would not have been able to sit still long enough to get a haircut with the Japanese lurking about:

> The biggest news of the moment is that I saw Joe the day before yesterday. Pat and I went ashore and I thought I would just take a chance and drop in at his headquarters and see if he was around. . . . Joe was there. He hadn't had any mail from Nane so I told him the news from your July first letters and we chatted a

bit. Then Joe, Pat and myself and some full Col. climbed into Joe's jeep and drove around for an hour or so until it was time for us to get our boat.

Joe said I looked well and fit to him and that the war seemed to be going all right with me. I thought he looked fine and he certainly hasn't lost any weight. It was grand to see him again. It's nice to pop in on a member of the family every now and then.

. . . I sent Joe over a gallon of ice cream. I packed it in burlap and put it in a wooden box, then I discharged one of my CO2 fire extinguishers into the box and the CO2 solidified into dry ice which I hope kept the ice cream hard until it reached Joe.

. . . I've been busy these last few days drawing another set of plans which embody some changes and improvements. It may be some time before I get a chance to finish them up and make copies for you, but I will send them on eventually. The basic idea remains the same however. There is a re-arrangement of some of the rooms, and the things you suggest were lacking in the other plans, are worked into this one.

One of the officers told me Van kept the wardroom spirits up by starting interesting discussions about subjects far removed from the war. Even in the midst of a battle, Van amused not just himself but the other officers with some of his tomfoolery. He described one of his splendid efforts while the ship was bombarding Saipan:

I am starting this letter at, of all times, seven o'clock in the morning. I've already been up a couple of hours which isn't unusual and am down in Central and the guns are whanging away shooting at the beach. Thank goodness it is generally one sided for our side and once in a while some annoyed Jap will shoot a machine gun futilely at us at this stage of the game.

You might not think ships could take part in land fighting but I've seen them use their own heavy machine guns and shoot their bigger guns right into the mouths of caves that the Japs always seem to like. . . .

You certainly seem to be having your hands full with your C.A.P. work. I hope you don't work too frantically at it or get too furious with your C.O. My wife is a violent woman and it certainly is evident that she doesn't take kindly towards authority or autocracy. Sometimes your problems are humorous and sometimes I think you are taking it too seriously. Don't forget to remain an old fashioned girl for me.

My finger I hurt last week is all right now so you see it wasn't much. I am all right otherwise too, not particularly tired but fed up mostly with almost constant shooting which is noisy more than anything else, and more or less repetitious days. Some days we do anchor and do nothing, others we shoot, and some nights we shoot but more often steam quietly. . . . I have what I call my daily "crisis" like water in the gasoline, or no flushing water for the Captain's toilet or something that displeased the Poo, or a boat that won't run or something. Today it was no flushing water for some mysterious reason because by the time the plumbers got there it was going O.K. . . .

I had a little fun a few days ago when for some reason or another the ship was plagued with flies. Great big lazy fellows. Everyone was swatting them and killing millions but for some reason or another they wouldn't land on a piece of fly paper and get stuck. So, whimsically I decided that what the flies needed because of their size and nationality, was a landing field. In an hour or so I manufactured one with match box hangers, a wind sock, Jap flag, a radar and revetments made with cigarettes. The landing strips I cut out of fly paper. I camouflaged things a bit and set it up in the wardroom. I didn't land many flies but everyone admired my effort. You can see that I can't be too overworked when I have time for that sort of thing.

He had written to his family earlier about seeing Wood and getting ice cream to him also. Getting ice cream to the two members of his family he was fortunate enough to see during that terribly busy summer was a big satisfaction for Van.

On 11 August 1944, the ship had pulled in to Eniwetok for much-needed repairs. This was the end of more than two months of constant battle. If the ship needed repairs urgently, the men needed rest from the constant tension even more.

What Will This October Bring?

Anytime the ship was in port, Van's other job took over. He continued to be mighty busy, not only with repairs but also with loading ammunition and supplies of all sorts and checking the captain's "head," as usual. Notwithstanding, he went ashore to the officers' club to quaff a few and try to forget for a brief time what he now knew was to be their next mission: the Philippines.

Admiral Spruance was still in command, and he saw to it his men got mail quickly, only ten days from home. That was a morale-booster. Admiral Spruance with his quiet and brilliant ways was a leader the men trusted to act in their best interests as well as the interests of the country.

On 30 August, the fleet came under Admiral Halsey, once again leaving Eniwetok, obviously for another all-out attack. First the whole force pounded Palau. Then the *Birmingham* joined the task group that consisted of carriers *Essex, Lexington, Langly,* and *Princeton,* battleships *Iowa, Washington, Massachusetts, Alabama,* and *Indiana,* five cruisers, and twenty-three screening destroyers.

On 9 September 1944, the task group launched their first air strike on Mindanao. The *Birmingham* claimed the distinction of being the first ship to fire on the Philippines since early in 1942.

When Van had word from me that he and Jim were commanders now, he simply didn't believe it! It was true all right, but he didn't get official word until early October. As soon as Pop Perkins told me of Van's promotion, I dashed out and bought him a pair of silver leaf insignia with three stripe shoulder boards to match. I even got him a new cap, with gold "scrambled eggs" on the visor; I didn't send it, for he would have no use for it unless he got home, in which case it would accompany me to meet Van and it would be a pleasure to personally put it on his head.

Just before he left Eniwetok in September of 1944, he wrote me a letter I treasure:

> Probably the first thing you will notice in this letter is the nice crisp ten dollar bill. Well I got paid today and my first thought when the paymaster gave me the nice new money was to give you ten dollars. Just as if I was home and gave you something so you could run down town and buy a steak. I just like to give you little surprises. . . .
>
> Darling as you may have gathered, I've been busy lately and soon will be much more so. I expect I'll be out of touch with you for some time so letters may straggle at best. Don't worry too much if there is a great gap between letters. A wait probably longer than last summer's is in store. Bettsy there is so much I could write to you to explain but at this point I can't. . . .
>
> Today was quite a day. I had one job rigging some gear on the forecastle and a great quantity of stores coming aboard to be stored in the hangar all at the same time. This afternoon after lunch I went back to see how the stowing was going on and didn't like what had been done so spent a couple of hours pushing boxes and sacks around and showing the working party just where to put them.
>
> Boy, Sam Shaw just came in with a cheerful earful which is strictly confidential!
>
> The Poo [the exec] is writing a Captain friend of his in the Bureau a personal letter which mentions among other things that I have a request in for Shore Duty and that it has been forwarded recommending approval in view of everything and the letter adds something to the effect that this Captain should keep his eyes open for a likely successor for me. Most encouraging, eh what? Sam knows this because he handles all the Poo's mail and runs his office. [By the time I got this, I knew Van's relief was on his way.]
>
> . . . You are a good Mother to Pamie, and a good wife to me, and you give our daughter all the love and affection she wants which delights me no end. I

know that you are the right person for both of us. Bettsy, take good care of yourself and of our baby.

I will be as cautious as I personally can but know, if anything happens to me, it won't be in vain. Our love and my soul will be with you always and I'd like you to give Pamie all that we would have given her together.

My darling wife I love you desperately and with everything I possess.

With the invasion of Europe and the success of our troops, we were all agog. People started calling me up.

"Betts, isn't it wonderful! You must be so excited."

"Betts, this means Van will soon be home. Isn't it great?"

They did not even understand how hard it would be to liberate Europe, no wonder so few understood the vastness of the Pacific or knew that our strategy was first to clean out the Japanese island fortresses before mounting an assault on China and then a frontal attack from China on Japan's homeland. We still had a formidable Japanese Navy to vanquish—a Navy that included one-man suicide torpedoes fired from submarines—and a murderous Japanese Air Force gearing up to give their lives in kamikaze attacks on our carriers and any other ship they could hit. Because the Japanese were slowly being beaten back, their national resolve was daily strengthening. There would be millions killed on both sides, for, as was no secret to those in the Pacific, the Japanese were sworn to fight to the last person.

By early October, Van was excited enough to write that he was near Avenida Mabini, the avenue our apartment was on in Manila. He was plainly telling me where he was.

Going down to Washington for a quick visit, I heard a good bit of scuttlebutt. The Navy wanted to cut off the Philippines and head for Formosa and mainland China, thereby encircling Japan. MacArthur wanted to go back to Manila first. Who was going to win this battle of wills, Admiral Nimitz and Admiral King or General MacArthur? No one knew, and, if anyone did, they were not telling me. My guess was we were going back to the Philippine Islands as MacArthur had promised, or Van would not be near our first home.

Van's request for transfer was now in, along with an endorsement from the captain (unfortunately requesting a qualified replacement, which was very hard to come by). A senior officer of his aptitude and training for a job that was so multifaceted and dangerous was not readily available. Neither of his assistants, Alan Reed or Pat O'Day, had enough seniority for the job.

Calls between Pop Perkins and me became more frequent. So many of Van's classmates were being sent ashore that I became hopeful he would be home soon. I even began to plan a bit for the move to "wherever." From experience I knew it meant a preliminary trip to some mythical posting to find a house for all three of us. Wherever there was a service installation, housing was scarce or nonexistent, as we had discovered in Norfolk and San Francisco.

My plans mostly consisted of lists of items to be sent to me in different categories: the box of objets d'art that meant home; my linens and silver and my cooking utensils, to be sent should we have to take a furnished place; another list of our furniture, Van's portrait, lamps, and rugs, in case we were lucky enough to get an unfurnished house. The last were as scarce as hens' teeth, but we both longed to live with our own things. We had only had the pleasure of their use for a brief four months in our apartment in New York.

Of course, the Ming vase in its velvet-lined box and the silver picture frame with our wedding picture in it would go with me in my suitcase to make even the meanest hotel room seem less impersonal. That was the normal procedure and needed no list. They had traveled with me wherever I went. I doubt many Ming Dynasty vases have seen as much of the world as mine has.

Yet all the while there was a nagging thought at the back of my mind—Van's fighting one battle after another. An occasional letter from Jim let me know that Van and he were in the same area, and the newspapers were reporting a lot more about the carrier actions. As the *Birmingham* was frequently serving as screening for carriers, I could see what danger both men were in and how the Pacific war was heating up to overboiling. While I planned for Van's safe return, I shuddered inwardly for his well-being, and I prayed constantly that he would be spared.

Those days, though not the halcyon days of being together, were better than anything since mid-February, but of course it could not last, and by September the ship was back in the thick of it and I was back to figuratively chewing my nails.

Pop called from Washington to say, "Keep this absolutely quiet. Who we want has been found and by mid-October should be on his way. I'll pass the word; it's safer that way."

Joyously I almost shouted, "Where do we go?"

"Probably Philadelphia, but not certain yet. Could be Newport and there are people asking for him, so hold your hat on tight."

What a funny reaction I had. I did not allow myself to believe what I had heard. In fact, it came over me that I should hear the news from Van before I believed it, for being relieved with battles raging was an iffy proposition.

It seemed too good to be true, and so it was best for me to get involved in a foolish play for raising money for the USO. I was to tap dance and sing a silly song: "Hot doggy with a D and an O and a G," and so on. Corny beyond belief, but I practiced on my nights off from CAP as though this was my big Broadway chance. Every night I took Pamie up and hugged her and told her, "Daddy might come home for your birthday. At least he should be home for Christmas."

But not to tempt fate, I sent him anniversary presents. October was a big month for us. Pam's birthday was 11 October, our anniversary, 26 October, and it was October 1938 when Van had come to call on Mother and I had first become attracted to him. I therefore wrote him an October letter discussing all this and ended it with, "I wonder what October will bring this year?"

Van had written telling me he was proud of my accomplishments in the CAP but not to lose my femininity, causing me to think about that. I wrote telling him that as the war was changing the material world radically, so it was changing women's roles and we would never be the same again. Too many of us had to cope with what was supposed to be a man's domain. We had found we could take care of ourselves, and it probably would be hard to give up our independence. But I was far too much in love with him not to be his "child bride" when he wanted me to be, nor as yet was I so far gone into a man's world as to start wearing pajamas instead of his adored black nightgown.

Our life together had consisted of ten months in bits and snatches out of four years of marriage (six including the two years before we were married). We had built a good union, and it had made a woman out of me. Hopefully I would not be a disappointment to Van if we ever got to really live together. He assured me we would work it out as we always had in the past. All I wanted was a chance to live normally, as we had in New York for a few short weeks. I held my breath in hopes that would come true.

I received an anniversary letter written on 7 October 1944 that delighted me, it arrived so quickly. It was like old times, fresh off the press by wartime standards:

A couple of days ago I got all the necessary signatures to make me a Commander officially. So now I am sporting a pair of home made Silver oak leaves and have passed out the cigars.

Obtaining collar marks was impossible because no ship had a supply. I did manage to get one pair but I needed an extra one for my hat, so I took a set of my Lt. Comdr. gold ones and experimented in making them silver. Finally I got one of the lads on the ship to do a fair electro-plating job which will be satisfactory temporarily.

Bettsy darling, this is a combination thank you for Pam's birthday and anniversary letter. The two are really very much the same because you are so very wonderful and such a good wife to me. Darling, I am so proud and happy with you. You are making my life complete and full of meaning because it is for you I want to do things and make something great out of our marriage. You are all to me darling that I have ever dreamed of or wanted. I think you are perfect, my wife. I wouldn't have you any different than you are. I don't know of any two people who have more fun, more companionship, more understanding, or love or passion than we have together. You have that happy quality of having the answer to my every wish and desire. I love you darling more than words can say.

Our four years have been too short and passed too quickly. My only greatest regret is that I haven't been with you more, and been more of a husband to you, giving you all the things I know you want, all the things I want my wife to have.

However, we have had a full time when we were together, a time chock full of beauty and love. As these next years come and go I sincerely hope to be able to devote more, if not all, of my time to being the kind of a husband to you I want to be. . . .

Happy anniversary darling wife. I send you a thousand kisses and wish more than anything that we could be together.

Van must have known his relief was on his way but was not going to say anything to me until he was off the ship. That would be like him, and it would be logical too, since so many things could happen—his relief held up for lack of transportation to the battle area, the ship engaged in a battle and therefore incommunicado, Van's own transportation home of uncertain duration. And he knew me well. I would take off for the West Coast if I had any inkling he was coming in, and he wanted me at home for fear I would be alone if something happened to him. Lastly, he did not want to tempt fate.

7

The Beginning of the End

SEPTEMBER 1944–MAY 1945

Both the *Birmingham* and the *Bunker Hill* had been in one campaign after the other. They were ordered to strike objectives in the central Philippines. By 19 September, both ships were heading to Manila. There was a ding-dong battle of land-based planes against the ships, but by 21 September the Japanese had lost more than two hundred planes and about fifteen ships. On the twenty-third our ships headed for San Bernardino Straits for more strikes in and about the central islands. Finally, on the twenty-seventh the force split up, the *Bunker Hill* to Ulithi and the *Birmingham* anchoring in Kossol Passage, Peleliu. So ended *Birmingham*'s longest continuous period at sea, twenty-two days without a break. She had covered 12,272 miles.

On 8 October, the ship rendezvoused with Task Force 38, now under Admiral Halsey and heading for the sweep against Okinawa, Formosa, and the Ryukyu Islands right in Japan's front yard. On the tenth they successfully struck Okinawa. At Formosa, they were subjected to air attacks that lasted through the seventeenth.

Van had been in that area many times before in peacetime but this was anything but peaceable. The ship was ordered to leave the area and to escort and screen the Australian cruiser *Canberra,* which had been torpedoed and was being towed southeast at about two knots. Task Force 38 was nowhere in sight, and the *Birmingham* opened fire six times at Jap planes before that night was over.

On 15 October 1944, they met up with the crippled USS *Houston* and her tow, the USS *Boston,* including them in the limping formation. Around four that afternoon a report was received that the Japanese fleet had come out of hiding, and Task Force 38 was nowhere near. Van had started a letter to me, but he stopped writing when that word was passed. The captain summed up the situation for the crew and, attempting to allay their fears, ended his message by saying, "God Bless you all." That hit in the pit of everyone's stomach and morale plummeted.

A terrifying night ensued. Not until the next morning did the men find out that they were bait to lure the Japanese fleet out and that Task Force 38 was in the general vicinity hoping to provoke a fight. When the Japanese spotted the main force they fled back to port.

The sixteenth of October was another day of being attacked by planes, the *Houston* taking a second torpedo, but the group kept on. One plane crashed just before it hit the *Birmingham* off her starboard bow. They proceeded east at four and a half knots. The night of the seventeenth, the *Birmingham*'s cruiser division 13 was ordered to rejoin their Task group 38.3, with its aircraft carrier *Princeton,* heading for Luzon, once again in support of the Leyte landings. It would be a prelude to the battle of Leyte Gulf.

Van's relief had left San Francisco, but it seemed he still did not wish me to know (Lord, he must have forgotten Pop would have told me immediately):

> I received the letter you wanted me to get yesterday on Pamie's birthday and was so pleased because it was a lovely long letter and in addition I had another one from you too. . . .
>
> There is so much that you and I feel the same about that I shouldn't be surprised, maybe I'm not surprised at all but just pleased that again we feel alike.
>
> You mentioned in your letter that "It seems more appropriate to me (you, ERP) to tell you (me, VOP) happy birthday than Pam." This is just the way I feel. I think I should make a fuss over you because you did so much to bring our Pamie to live with us.

There followed a long dissertation on how Van would raise his daughter, even how she should be educated and what courses she should take in college. I supposed it would be very useful in years to come, but right then I thought we were a bit ahead of ourselves. He continued:

> I just looked at the date I started this and see it was the 12th. Today is the 17th. Only 5 days by the clock but it seems like a life time. This is and has been a week I am not likely to forget.
>
> There is so much I should like to write about that the trivial every day are chased out of my mind at this point.

My how wonderful that you are going to be an Officer. Probably by the time this reaches you, you will already be one. My very hearty congratulations Bettsy darling, you are certainly being rewarded for all your hard work and you deserve it. I am very proud of you.

· I am very much in love with you too sweetheart. I think that you are the most wonderful person in all the world and I long to hold you in my arms. . . . I adore you my lovely.

Apparently Van had received the pictures of me in my second lieutenant's uniform with my CO in front of the plane I flew, though he had not mentioned it.

The task force had been fighting since 10 October without a let-up. All the men were very tired, near to exhaustion. Van was not far from Manila on the night of 23 October and early morning of 24 October. Surely by now he knew his relief had left San Francisco. Pop Perkins had told me we were going to Philadelphia. Knowing that Van's request was to do with the new damage control school, I presumed that was what he was getting. He expected to get home by, at the latest, the end of the year. So it was with hope in his heart that once again Van geared up for battle.

On 20 October General MacArthur had landed his troops in Leyte, on Philippine soil. That was a glorious day in the annals of World War II. The radio blared announcements and played patriotic music. In 1939, as I was leaving the Philippines, I had written to Van, "I shall return, if you will let me." When General MacArthur was forced to leave the Philippines, his last message to the Filipinos was "I shall return," so the press had stated. Certainly it sounded MacArthuresque.

My Day to Day calendar from Van read on 23 October, "Bout this time, four years ago in Manila, I was in a dither." On the twenty-fourth my calendar read, "Darling I love you with everything I possess."

With battles raging, on 22 October Van found an escape in writing about our dream farm:

In the mail a few days ago I received a letter from you and a little package marked "Don't open until Oct. 26th" [his three-stripe shoulder boards]. So I am saving it until next Thursday which is our big happy anniversary day. Mail and what not being as it is I would not have been disappointed if I had nothing from you but I'm doubly happy to have an anniversary present. I wish I could have given a more personal touch to something for you.

It is bad enough not being with you to celebrate our special days but it is even harder for me because I want to give you something or do something for you myself and I can't.

I'm so glad you are having fun and enjoying it at Craggy. I'm certainly envious and wish we could be together because I know how wonderful these fall days must be. The snap and sparkle in the air just makes life so exhilarating. I love the early fall.

You know that is one thing I question about California. Do you think we would like the climate? It will be more or less even, no well-defined seasons like in New England. Of course I imagine it is only an hour or so drive to the mountains where we could find snow if we wanted winter sports.

I have an idea about the fireplace in the living room but I can't decide just how it would go. Instead of the conventional fireplace, set in the wall so that the full effect of the fire is only felt from one side and you can't really sit "around" the fire, I have dreamed up a fireplace which projects on three sides into the room. In other words, the fire is right out in the room and you can get around three sides of it and the effect is that of an out door camp fire. Catching the smoke and getting it up the chimney presents more of a problem of appearance than anything else. You know how a forge in a blacksmiths shop is set out in the middle of the floor. Over the forge six or seven feet from the floor, is a sort of inverted funnel shaped gadget that catches the smoke and draws it into the chimney. Well, I'd use the same principle probably making the shield out of red brass and it might look something like this.

I've enclosed a better sketch. The door seen in the picture leads to the bar and den. (My newest plan which you haven't seen.) The box on the left is a radio victrola and other gadgets I told you about.

I also have been trying to figure in general how I wanted the exterior of the house to look and what materials to make it out of. I rather imagine a wood frame with a wood painted exterior. And I've got lots of ideas for gadgets on the inside.

I'll bet that you are all delighted with the news of the invasion of the Philippines. It is a great thing indeed and to me it signals the beginning of the end because once we secure large enough land areas, we will have places to put troops, planes and supplies and can get down to the job of defeating large Jap armies either in China or in Japan itself.

I am dying to get the letter telling me about Pam's birthday party and then to get the pictures I know you probably took. What fun it is to have a little daughter two years old, and such a charmer as she is. Golly how badly I want to get back home to you both and to lead a life that is half way decent and normal. I yearn for all the things we like and like to do.

With you dearest life is so full and so delightful. Every minute of our time together is heaven and every moment we are together we have fun. The most wonderful thing about us is that we are so definitely and passionately in love. What could be sweeter Pigeon than to hold you tightly in my arms and to tell you that I love you. I can feel your sweet lips on mine, your caresses and your wonderful softness close to me. My darling with all my heart and soul I love you. Everything I have, all of me is yours. I want only the happiness of being with you and loving you.

Sweet one you are the most adorable person in all the world.

P.S. Did I tell you the Silver Commander leaves arrived. Thank you for them, Bep, they are lovely and I needed them and am wearing them.

In the early morning of 24 October during the operations off Luzon in the Leyte Gulf area a fierce air battle was being waged by land-based Jap planes against our carrier planes and ships. A Japanese plane dropped out of a cloud undetected and placed a bomb strategically on the *Princeton*. On fire, she quickly dropped out of the formation. The *Birmingham* was detached and sent to her aid.

Van stationed himself right in the most hazardous spot, the better to direct fire-fighting and rescue operations. Thank heavens he had received and was wearing the silver commander leaves I had sent him.

Most Precious Gem

Early on I had learned to keep a notebook in which I jotted summaries of my letters. I had written of my distress as I heard about the loss of so many of my dear friends who had given their lives to this war that none of us had asked for. How tragic that they would not live to contribute their talents to their country and see their children grow up. What grim force stalked the land. I was consumed with horror over the utter senselessness that ruined our young lives. I wondered why it was we could never learn there are only losers in war. No one ever ultimately gains. This was the summary of the long letter I had written Van on the morning of 23 October. I could not sit still and paced about, so that afternoon I wrote him a quick note. This was my way of letting him know I was scared:

I just finished writing you a long letter but I've felt squeamish about you all day so I'm just dashing you off another note to tell you to come on and hurry home.

Your sweet anniversary letter arrived today and I was much touched by it. Only one thing in it puzzled me. You said, "I want to take care of (or be with) you more, if not all the time." Does that mean what I think it does—which is O.K. by me. I just wondered.

You know me, I'm always wondering which way the wind is blowing now. I imagine the thrill of going back to the Philippines has changed the wind again.

You're a lamb, I adore you and the nicest thing in the world you could have said to me was, "You are always there with what I need," and I feel greatly touched that you feel that way about me for I don't have that confidence in myself. You are the one that is always ready with what I need to an unbounded degree.

Dearest I love you so much, so very much. You are my life and my world.

I felt more and more uneasy until, in the middle of practice for the "Hot Doggey" show, I knew I needed to get to Craggy right away. I flew up to my safe haven and sat alone in utter despair.

Finally I wrote Van:

Oct. 23rd. Eleven PM
I note the time. [Van's time zone was 13 hrs. ahead]
Oh my very dearest,

What is happening to you—in my heart I know you are gone from me and I sit here holding you close to me and praying that what I think, is not true.

Tonight I was so uneasy I couldn't practice anymore and told Mrs. Ethridge I must go home early despite her annoyance that I was breaking up her little theatrical effort.

When you were wounded I knew in my bones you were in trouble.

Tonight my dearest, husband, I am consumed with pain in my heart and in my mind and in my very soul.

You who are my very life, whom I have loved for so very long and whom I have had in my heart but not in my arms for all these weary six years of separation with snatches of bliss when you've come home for a bit of time and off to the wars again.

You who fathered our beautiful baby, now just two years old. You who are everything I ever thought you were when I was a little girl and who indeed became my all consuming passion. How can it be that God is taking you away and yet I know with surety that that is what has happened tonight.

Know my darling that I will love you always thru' death until our souls are once again as one. I will feel your arms about me and your love protecting me all my life.

I will do as you told me when you left. I will go on living for little Pamie and I'll marry again for her sake and I'll give her all you asked me to give her of your ethics and your love, but I will always love you with all the passion and tenderness we've had, for all my life.

I will not short change a man I might marry, but like getting our daughter made me capable of more love in my heart so it would be for someone else, another spot in my heart that would expand.

My love for you will stay always as my dearest, most precious gem.

Sleep peacefully my love until I come to you one day when my job here is done.

Always in all ways your own. Betts

Oh I shall miss you so my Van, my husband, my love.

On the back of the folded page I wrote, "If you get this tear it up. I will have been wrong. Pray God you get it!" Then after putting it in its envelope and sealing it, I called sister Nane at two in the morning and she came right over. She found me pacing up and down the living room, brushing my hand over everything I knew Van had touched. She made me a drink and we talked. At last, calm came over me.

In the morning I mailed my letter, though I had almost torn it up for I could not stand to believe the message he was sending me. Nane persuaded me to return to Mother's, where I tried to shake the feeling that was still with me. I clung to our baby for comfort.

On Friday, 3 November, I got the letter Van had written on 22 October. It sounded so much like his own loving self. He was back making plans for the house, glad to get his collar insignia for commander, so pleased that at long last we had invaded the Philippines, that wonderful place that was so much a part of our romance. It was such a loving and hopeful letter. I relaxed a bit and I thought I must be crazy to have been so sure something awful had happened.

The phone rang at luncheon on Saturday, 4 November. Iraneo came in and spoke to Nane, saying, "A Mrs. Betty King wants to talk to you Mrs. Anderson."

"Oh that's for me, Nane," I said. "Betty King thinks I'm at Craggy and can't get through to me. I'll take the call."

I dashed to the phone. "Hi Betty, what's up?" I said.

Her voice quavered as she answered, "Have you heard from Van?"

"Oh yes, I had a long letter from him yesterday."

"Oh Lord, dear, what I meant was . . ." I began to shake. "Have you heard about Van?"

"No—oh, no—Oh, no, oh, God no, Oooooooo!"

I remember only that I shook so hard even my teeth shook and then I blanked out. The next thing I remember was sitting on the third floor stairs rocking Pamie back and forth. She, poor little baby, kept patting my cheek. I did not cry, I just moaned and rocked.

Finally I squared my shoulders and, handing my baby to Miss Reichardt to care for, marched down the stairs to make the hardest phone call of my life to my darling father-in-law. I knew he must be told first so he could get to Mom and we could tell her together. His low moan was all he ever let me hear of his heartbreak, but he needed to say nothing more eloquent. He spent the intervening time until I arrived checking at the Navy Department to ascertain that my report was true.

Pop Perkins was unable to get any full picture of what had happened. He did get confirmation of Van's death, caused by the explosion of an aircraft carrier when the *Birmingham* was alongside, but as yet no details were available.

It took a lot of probing to find out what happened to the ship that morning in October. Much later I was able to get a fuller picture of the *Princeton's* bombing, which caused the *Birmingham* to go to her aid. What I found was that the two destroyers that were trying to help the *Princeton,* by taking on board the men who had obeyed the command to abandon ship, were unable to be effective with their fire hose for they were too low in the water. At 10:46 A.M., the *Birmingham* went alongside and, with a heavy sea running, took considerable punishment from the overhang of the carrier. At 11:26 a spring line was put over to keep the ships together. The official report read in part: "By 11:52 a forward spring line had been put over from *Birmingham* to *Princeton.* The bow line parted under strain but by 11:58 a new bow line had been sent across. About this time at least 14 streams of water were being played on *Princeton* from *Birmingham* and excellent progress was being made getting fires in forward portion of *Princeton* under control."

All of this was under Van's supervision, both the setting of spring lines and the fourteen streams of water. He was incredibly busy and throughout the entire period was in personal danger of being crushed by the *Princeton's* overhang, as the two ships tossed up and down in a heavy sea.

At 1:00 Van sent a volunteer party of thirty-eight of his damage control gang, under Lt. Alan Reed, his assistant, to aid the skeleton crew of the *Princeton,* who lacked power and therefore water. Van had to get the ship's hose over to the *Princeton* and pump water there as well as direct spray from the *Birmingham's* deck into the burning hull. The volunteer party on board the *Princeton* found the decks so hot they had to spray their feet to keep from burning them.

After about one and a half to two hours, the *Birmingham* was ordered to pull away from the *Princeton* because enemy aircraft had been picked up on radar and there were reports of possible submarine attacks. The order for the *Birmingham* crewmen to return to the ship came so quickly that many of the volunteers had to leap over open water to the ship's deck as she pulled away, leaving two men behind on the *Princeton.*

At 2:55 all was clear and the submarine contact had been evaluated as false. The captain again headed the *Birmingham* toward the *Princeton* from the leeward side to take her under tow. After two unsuccessful tries, a spring line was attached at 3:20 P.M., with a mere fifty feet of water separating the two ships. Her men could see the fires raging below decks through the opening of the damaged hangar deck, where extra bombs were stored. Van had once again taken his position right in the forefront, along with his assistant Alan Reed.

Three minutes later, the fires below decks touched off the magazines and fuel storage tanks of the *Princeton*. A mighty explosion ensued, killing 233 men on the *Birmingham*, including the dentist, who, had he not been up on deck sightseeing, would have lived to help the wounded. The senior doctor had been sent to another ship to do an appendectomy and had not returned, leaving the *Birmingham* with only the newly arrived junior doctor to care for more than 400 wounded men.

Many became casualties because they were on deck sightseeing rather than at their battle stations. The excuse given by the captain for not sounding general quarters was that the men should have been at lunch and that he had freed the crew so they could help with the operation. The ensuing carnage was heartrending. The dead lay everywhere, and the horribly wounded were cared for by those not so grievously hurt. Two of my informants, themselves seriously wounded, told me that they resented the lack of warning from the bridge. One was a young officer just sightseeing, the other was a chief in the Damage Control Department, who said that the sightseers on the portside of the deck were a hindrance to the working parties. Allowing people with no mission to wander at will proved fatal to hundreds and seriously wounded many more fine young men. Perhaps general quarters had not been appropriate, but at the very least a warning to stay below decks if not assigned a specific duty would have saved many lives. The young officer, Ens. John Reed, who had been aboard only two months, wrote me later that he had been in the wardroom when Van had come down for a cup of coffee while the ship pulled away from the *Princeton* during the plane and submarine alert. John had asked Van what he thought about being ordered back alongside.

"I am really worried," Van said. "I don't like the way this is being handled, John." No wonder Van was worried. As for young John Reed, he was one of the desperately wounded sightseers—he crept to his room and was not found until four days later.

Hunks of steel and shrapnel littered the topside. The wounded writhed on the bloody decks, which were so slippery that getting help to them was nearly impossible until sand was laid. Perhaps more men could have been saved had both doctors, as well as the dentist who had been killed, been on the ship. Utter confusion reigned until the executive officer took over, directing the pathetic few who were left of the Damage Control Department to bring some semblance of order out of the chaos.

Tragically, the *Birmingham* suffered vastly more casualties than the *Princeton*. More than half the ship's company was killed or grievously wounded.

Or Should I Say Betsy

It was Saturday when Betty King called me with the terrible news of Van's death. The banks were closed. Mother and Dad were visiting family down south. Airline tickets were impossible to get, stores and gas stations were closed. We did not have gas enough in the car to get to La Guardia Airport.

Somehow I had managed the call to Pop Perkins, but now that I needed help badly, sister Nane took over. She called Doc Squire, my boss and friend— thank God he was not delivering a baby—and he went into action. He called the president of American Airlines (or maybe it was Pan Am), who lived in Greenwich. We had tickets within the hour. He called the police, who opened a gas station for us so we could fill the car. Somehow he produced two hundred dollars; I do not, to this day, know how. I do not know who packed my bag, maybe I did. I was in a strange suspended state—cold—oh, so very cold, and I had only one thought in my mind: Van is with you, make him proud of you. It was very real to me that he was right there.

I must have been dazed, for when the flight attendant brought around the in-flight progress report for Nane and me to look at, I whipped out my pen and signed it "Lt. Eliz R. Perkins—O.K." The flight attendant was startled, and sister Nane explained to her that I had just lost my husband and was in shock, that I was a second lieutenant, CAP, and thought I was signing a flight report. The stewardess shook her head. For a minute she sat on the arm of the seat. Reaching over, she squeezed my hand to let me know she understood. She took us off the plane ahead of the other passengers, having radioed ahead for a taxi to await us at Washington Airport.

We went directly to the apartment building, where Pop was waiting for us in the lobby. We went up to tell Van's mother. As we came in, she stood up, and no one needed to say a word. She knew. Putting her fist to her mouth, she went to her room in her tweed skirt and blouse and shortly she came back wearing her red dress. "This dress Van liked," she said. "I wore it the last time

I ever saw him, and he said, 'Mother I like your dress, you should wear red more often.'"

The awful cold stayed with me, and soon I saw that my dear mother-in-law was shaking also. I think Pop got a blanket to put about her shoulders. We tried to talk about Van. I wanted to shout my love for him. I could not. We were all stunned into silence.

Finally, I blurted, "Oh Mom, I love him so—I can't live without him."

"I know my dear, I know. You and I will have to somehow be strong and help Pop take this." Bless her dear heart, she was trying to help me find a purpose that she herself needed.

Pop spoke for himself. "My firstborn was a fine boy. He grew to be a splendid man. He came to manhood with his dream of a happy marriage come true. He knew the joy of fatherhood and he knew he was the best at his chosen profession. I am well satisfied with my son—our son—God bless him and keep him."

For him it was a long speech, and it was torn from his heart. He could say no more, and so he excused himself and went to his room.

Mom and Nane and I sat on. Then Nane said goodnight, knowing Mom and I needed to talk. When we were alone I went to Mom and, sitting on the floor, put my head in her lap. She stroked my hair as she started comforting me. "My poor dear girl. You two who were so perfectly matched. Our Van would want you to be happy. 'There's a time to mourn' is a saying, and one should do so of course, but dear little Betts, no one could have made life sweeter for Van than you—hold on to that."

"Oh I will Mom, but I shall miss him so terribly always. I'm so cold. It's like I died with him, and yet I know he's here with me."

"And he'll stay with you until you find peace, and then he too can rest. You know, my dear, it is woman's lot to lose the man she loves and to have to go on alone. For you that has come far too soon, but you have Van's child to live for and in time you'll love again. Dear heart, you'll always be our beloved daughter, as surely as though you were born to us. You are part of Van, hence part of us."

I sobbed one deep, grief-laden sob and I shook once more as though I would come apart, but neither Mom nor I could cry. We just clung to each other. Finally I said to Mom, "No matter what, I will love Van in my deepest heart for the rest of my life. I will think of him every day, and every night I will tell him good night. If by chance I find a happy life as he wanted me to, it will never change the fact that Van was and is my great, my breathless love, and I love you, Mom, for giving him to me. Oh God why? Why take away my love? Why take the best?"

"Hush now—hush. We have much to do, you and I. Pop needs us both to be strong, so now I will get a glass of milk and then I think I need to go to Pop. Not before I tell you I love you, Betts, and I'm proud of you."

That was our private women's grieving. I never tried again to voice my total devastation to anyone. But my mother-in-law knew, and I knew what was in her heart. I never did forget, and I wrote her a special letter every year, on our anniversary, of my love for Van, until she died not too long ago.

The next few days were tense as we tried to find out what had happened and thought about a memorial service for Van. Nane followed me around, attempting to get me to swallow some eggnog, for I could not eat. A wild thought struck me. Two years earlier at this time Van had been wounded and I was making the curtains in the guest room Nane and I were now occupying. For some silly reason that was comforting, and fitfully I dozed the night away.

Mom Perkins, Nane, and I went back to Greenwich. Pop followed as soon as he could get leave. Mother and Dad had returned home on hearing of Van's death.

Flowers poured into the house, and I had a time with my Victorian father, who thought I was acting in a frivolous way when, after a particularly large box with a dozen long-stemmed football mums arrived, I laughed and cracked a football joke. He thought I should keep the shades drawn, wear somber colors, preferably black, and not laugh. I knew Van wanted me to be as near my own self as I could be. I could not eat and weighed only ninety-eight pounds once again. Surely everyone must know I was screaming inside. I know my sister did, and she understood that my laughing was a way of keeping up my courage.

I chose to wear navy blue to the memorial service; Dad thought it improper, but I did what I knew Van would like, and I wore my silver fox jacket he had given me our first Christmas together in New York. I held it close around me as he had done when he put it on me that morning three years earlier. I held my head high as I walked down the aisle at Christ Church, and I heard in my mind over and over Van's words to me in his letter: *Know our love and my soul will be with you forever.* I knew that he was with me as surely as though he had my arm tucked through his and we were walking together.

When the organ began to play "Eternal Father Strong to Save," the Navy hymn, my heart beat so hard I thought I would suffocate. Then I heard the marching, I turned, and—oh, Lord—there was something about the size of a log on wheels, draped with the American flag, rolled to the steps of the chancel. I only looked at it once and bit my lip to keep from crying. Pamie, standing on the seat beside me, said, "Look Mummy, there comes Daddy." Poor little darling, she did not know what she was saying. That was not my Van. I did not know why it was there and I thought it was horrible, but I guess the minister thought he needed something to speak to. I heard the prayers for Van, and the minister said the poem I had specifically asked him to include in the service. The last two lines were my inspiration for the future, and I held them close to my heart: "Complete those dear unfinished tasks of mine / And I perchance therein may comfort you."

All of a sudden I realized this was November thirteenth. Two years to the day the *Atlanta* had gone down. How devastating that thought was to me! Did all beauty and joy die on November thirteenth? For a brief moment I felt a scream start deep down. The moment passed, and again holding my head high, I walked up the aisle carrying Pamie. As I left the church clutching my baby in my arms, I was handed the American flag, folded in a triangle. Now I walked to the car with all my little family held close, all I would ever have to hold of my dear love.

For a short while, I wore a black armband on the left arm of my coat to save unsuspecting friends the embarrassment of asking questions like "What do you hear from Van?" or "When's Van coming home?" Then I heard that little gold stars were available through The Gold Star Wives of America. They were a brave group, newly formed, who had banded together to try to lighten the burden of the bereaved. Though they had no military standing and no political clout, they were mighty successful with their little gold stars, one of which I wore with pride.

Somehow we stumbled through Christmas. Of course we had the baby to think of, and we tried to make a it good day for her.

It was so hard to deal with Van's death. Not a single one of his good friends was with him when he died. He had been buried at sea as fast as was possible during that first evening after the explosion, along with 233 others. Seven more died later of their wounds. A hasty, generalized prayer, a splash, that was all. Not even a longitude and latitude reading to mark their graves, somewhere in the Philippine Sea.

The seriously wounded were transferred to a hospital ship, and a memorial service for those killed was held aboard some time later. Although not badly hurt—suffering from shock, a fractured arm, and a bit of shrapnel—the captain retired to his cabin, unable to carry on his command, turning it over to the senior officer on the bridge. He was, however, able to participate in the memorial service held by the chaplain. He walked ashore, leaving his ship for the last time when the *Birmingham* finally reached San Francisco. The executive officer, himself wounded, had taken over until the ship reached port, when a relief captain came aboard.

We started all the tedious paperwork attendant to a serviceman's death. My time with Tek when Ted was lost had given me a foretaste of what widowhood was to be, so it was no surprise to find I could not collect even one trip's worth of transportation expense to travel to the ship's new home port on the West Coast, nor was it a surprise that either months passed before I received answers to my letters or they were ignored altogether.

A pathetic few of Van's personal effects were sent to me: the desk lamp I bought him in Norfolk, some of his pictures of Pam and me, house plans on paper, some underwear. That was about all. Very few of my letters to Van written after February 1944 were returned; fortunately, I kept briefs of the letters so I could tell what Van was answering. The two letters returned to me, one marked "Addressee Unknown" and the other marked "Deceased," were returned from Fleet Post Office. Not my Day by Day calendars for him, not the collection of rabbits, not the beautiful Chinese rug on the floor, nor the pictures we had picked out to make his quarters homelike, none of his uniforms or his new shoulder boards still unopened, not even his new silver leaves. None of the things that meant so much to both of us.

When I received the inventory of items supposedly sent me, there was one laughable but infuriating inclusion at the bottom of the page: "2 pictures inappropriate to forward." They were the two pictures Molly had taken of me in my black nightgown that had caused Van's "Woo Woo and Wow!" and that Van kept over his bunk for his eyes only. Obviously they thought Van had a couple of "pin-up girl" pictures that were not nice to send his widow. Well, he did, but they were of me, and anyone who knew us would have known Van did not go in for that sort of thing; in fact, he would have been chagrined that they could think such a thing of him.

It made me indignant that strangers had so mishandled Van's effects and heartbroken that so few things to remember him by came back. I fought to get his things without success. All they sent were letters saying no one knew where or how they disappeared.

It was a surprise that nothing was said about Van's Navy Cross. Two of the officers from the ship had come to see me and both had told me a citation for that award had been written by the officers of the ship who were not hurt but had been witness to his bravery in the face of personal danger.

Pam and I moved down to Washington in January to be near Mom and Pop

Perkins. Later, when I heard the *Birmingham*'s captain was right there in Washington at the Bethesda Naval Hospital, I went to see him. He was reclining on his hospital bed fully clothed and reading a book, which he laid aside. Uneasily he said, "Good afternoon, Mrs. Perkins, or should I say Betsy?"

"You've always called me Betsy, sir," I answered, thinking to myself that he was acting a little more than distraught. He seemed tense, and his eyes were darting around, looking anywhere except at me. Best I get this over quickly, so I said, "Captain, I've been told that Alan Reed is getting the Navy Cross and that Van will, of course, get it also. Is this true?"

He looked straight at me and said harshly, "Certainly not. I am getting the Navy Cross. Who told you that?"

It felt as though I had been slapped. There was nothing for me to say or do but to back away from him toward the door. The expression on his face was one of naked distaste if not out-and-out hate. Why? What was this all about? I was mortified by his reaction. Walking, not running, to the elevator took all the dignity I could muster.

My father-in-law was shocked when I told him of the incident. He wrote a letter to the Awards Division asking what medals Van was entitled to. The answer was a Bronze Star, no citation forthcoming. We never heard further about it from the Navy. We did hear that besides Alan Reed, a young ensign, a boatswain, and the captain received the Navy Cross. The first three richly deserved it. So did my Van, God knows he did, and I knew so too. But it was heartrending to have Van's valor summarily dismissed by the Navy we both had loved.

After I heard the details of the tragedy, I figured out what was wrong with the captain. He was still in shock. My mere presence was a reproach to him, and my question about Van's award had unnerved him. His reaction was not callousness as I had thought. It was, after all, his own ambitious decision to go alongside the *Princeton* a second time that had caused the loss of so many lives unnecessarily. Perhaps he hoped such action would wipe out past errors—and it did. He got the Navy Cross (and somehow denied it to Van, which I guess he thought shifted a bit of the blame to Van; I never really understood). The cross he would have to bear in his heart for the rest of his days was the terrible loss of lives of his crew. I came to pity him, though I never was able to overcome my resentment completely.

It was written in some history book that the *Birmingham* was the most tragic ship of World War II. I do not know that to be true. The *Juneau* and *Indianapolis* certainly were even worse tragedies in a single blow. But the *Birmingham* had been hit three times, and later, under a new captain, she was hit again. So perhaps my early feeling that she was star-crossed was on the mark and she was the most tragic ship.

Fearless Disregard

Though Van never got his Navy Cross, forty-five years later I received the commendation that obviously had been written for that honor. It was knocked down to a Bronze Star by the review board, and it took my senator to pry the commendation loose. The citation described Van's final service to his country, but it was not signed by the secretary of the Navy or anyone else, and it was not forwarded to me with the medal I received more than a year later:

COMMANDER VANOSTRAND PERKINS,

UNITED STATES NAVY CITATION

For heroic achievement while serving as First Lieutenant and Damage Control Officer of the U.S.S. BIRMINGHAM when a hostile bomb struck the U.S.S. PRINCETON during an enemy Japanese aerial attack in the Second Battle of the Philippine Sea on October 24, 1944. When his ship went alongside the stricken PRINCETON to assist in fighting raging fires after she had withdrawn from the formation and her crew had been ordered to abandon ship, Commander Perkins skillfully organized and supervised a volunteer fire control party, effectively bringing all possible fire-fighting apparatus to bear on the flaming vessel despite the constant danger of further imminent detonations and enemy aerial attack. Steadfastly maintaining his position on the main deck of his ship, he persistently braved the danger of being crushed by the overhang of the carrier in order to direct operations more efficiently and succeeded in bringing the fires partially under control before his ship was recalled to the screen when a strong force of Japanese aircraft approached the task force. When his ship subsequently returned alongside the PRINCETON in a further effort to save her, he was mortally wounded during a sudden violent explosion of the magazine section of the crippled vessel. By his brilliant leadership and fearless disregard for his own safety throughout this hazardous period, Commander Perkins upheld the highest traditions of the United States Naval Service. He gallantly gave his life for his country.

I was unable to pry Van's fitness reports from the Navy, though I knew I was entitled to them also, and so it is to this day.

I later heard that the Navy, at about that time, had quietly ordered a limit of only four Navy Crosses per ship. They felt that too many Navy Crosses were being awarded, potentially demeaning the honor. Why Van was not one of those four we never understood until years later. Ironically, of the hundreds of men killed on the *Birmingham*, Van was the only senior officer killed and the one who best knew what was wrong with the maneuver that caused such a terrible loss.

A typewritten letter received earlier from the captain said that Van was killed outright without suffering and that at the time he was carrying out his duties bravely and in the best tradition, etc. I knew when I received it that it was not true. We transferred thoughts so constantly. I knew Van had told me he was dying the night I wrote him. Years later, one of his damage control gang, whom Van had tutored in preparation for taking his warrant officer exams, told me he was there with Van when he was horribly wounded. Bill, not as badly wounded, had crawled over to Van, who said, "Bill, go help that man, you might save his life."

When Bill crawled back he thought Van was dead. But Van was carried below and lived another hour or so. Bill said he never knew a finer or braver man, nor in all his years in the Navy a finer officer, than my Van.

Van knew his chances of living through this action were practically nil. Ens. John Reed, who had told me he had spoken to Van when they pulled away from the damaged *Princeton,* said Van was of course correct in his assessment of the situation. John also told me that he himself was furious that the captain had not ordered general quarters to be sounded and that the two excuses given by the captain—the men should have been at lunch and he wanted to free everyone to help fight the fires—were puerile.

The *Birmingham* had already taken a pounding from the *Princeton*'s overhang, but Van's department could have repaired that at sea and kept on fighting. He was thoroughly aware that the *Princeton*'s fires were not under control when they had pulled away, and he was being told to take the ship under tow without being consulted about the advisability of so doing. Van had not been consulted despite the fact that he had both the knowledge and sole responsibility for all phases of the damage control efforts. Van had organized all of the available ship's company and trained them for just such an effort. Allowing the crew to remain on deck had made it possible for many nonessential personnel to watch the operation and, from Van's point of view, to be in danger as well as in the way of the working parties.

There was an outpouring of love for Van and sorrow over his death from all of his former shipmates. Admiral Wilkes, the first captain of the *Birmingham,* wrote, "He was one of only a few Officers on my ship that I could count on to do what I wanted and to do it well." Capt. Sam Jenkins of the *Atlanta* and his executive commander, Dallas Emory, both said he was a great loss to the Navy and to his country, as well as to me. Captain Jenkins had told me he had recommended Van for the Navy Cross for bravery on the *Atlanta* but the review board had reduced it to a Silver Star. This time he wrote that Van surely would get the Navy Cross, but in any event, he, Sam, wanted me to know that he deemed Van's death a great loss to the country and it hurt him personally. He wrote that he had been unable to get Van off the ship, something that distressed him also. Van's peers wrote letters that were outspoken in their praise of him as an officer and as a friend, and civilians who knew him wrote about his charm and his loyalty. I received more than 450 letters. I tried to answer them but could not keep up with so many.

In Our Hearts and Minds

In the summer and fall of 1944 Jim Shaw saw precious little rest and relaxation. Jim's job on the *Bunker Hill* was both arduous and boring. It was arduous because his battle station was seven flights up from his quarters. Every time general quarters was sounded he would run up the seven ladders to his battle station above the bridge, high up on the ship's island, where he stood long hours with his binoculars hung around his neck, directing the scores of antiaircraft batteries and larger gun mounts when the ship was under attack. Just waiting for such action to happen was boring, but there was also constant tension. Should he not maintain his alertness and that of his men, it would spell disaster to the ship.

Flyers came aboard, flew missions for a period, then were relieved, a new air wing taking their place. At first Jim tried to make friends with the aviators. He soon gave that up as it was heartbreaking to watch a friend fly off the carrier never to return. A full squadron would come aboard; when they were relieved, their numbers would be sadly depleted. Then a new squadron would arrive full of verve. Jim knew many of them were doomed.

To relieve his tension, Jim dreamed up stories about the flyers and the crew that supported the flyers and their planes. He also created a character named Tubby, a sailor out on the prewar China Station. When they secured from general quarters, he would hurry to his room and bang away on his typewriter, starting his first book as a series of short stories in the ship's newspaper. He signed them with a nom de plume, "O. C. Hand," which stood for Old China Hand.

Often he was aware that he and Van were fighting the same battles, but communications of a personal nature between the ships of this vast armada did not exist. The ship was a little world unto itself, carrying out orders from on high.

The Navy never reported damage to ships for fear of aiding the enemy. The invasion of the Philippines was no exception. Jim was to the west of Luzon, while the planes were pounding Manila, Cavite, and Subic Bay, all places that were more than familiar to him. He had married his Jane in Manila, sailed out of Manila harbor every time they went to sea, spent countless hours in the Navy yard at Cavite or Olongapo. It was exciting to be back at long last.

In October he wrote me a card: "No time to write a letter, just thought you'd like to know St. Mary and St. John are in my thoughts, and Van's too, I should imagine." Cryptic, but the message was loud and clear, as well as being thoughtful. We were, all four, married in the Cathedral of St. Mary and St. John in Manila in 1940. Here it was late fall of 1944 and Jim's and Van's ships, so far as Jim knew, were heading back.

Briefly, the *Bunker Hill* left the area heading for Okinawa and then Formosa, pounding the islands in Japan's front yard. Now the mission was to destroy the supply lines from Japan to the Philippines, and it was carried out in force quickly—and devastatingly to the Japanese. Twenty-five thousand tons of their shipping was destroyed in just one day; shore installations were wiped out, and the enemy ships were out-classed. Our own losses were heavy, but the mission was accomplished.

The crew and flyers were close to exhaustion as they headed back toward the Philippines invasion. The flyers had demolished more Japanese planes than they could count. The ship's gunners had shot down wave after wave of enemy planes swarming around the *Bunker Hill*. Jim Shaw, now gun boss, was weary to the bone.

On 22 October, the *Bunker Hill* was pulled out of action, for replacement of their air group, refueling, and resupplying. Jim never saw Van again.

As Jim had witnessed Van's will, my lawyer sent a verification document to him, along with a note from me. It was the first firm word of Van's death that Jim received. His reply to me was typically succinct:

> It is difficult to express feelings in words on an occasion like this. You must understand that you have my most heartfelt sympathy.
>
> Van and I went through a lot together, good times and bad—we knew each other well. He was a fine Officer and a loyal friend. It hurts sorely to have him gone.
>
> I'm certain you'll feel free to call on me for any aid or information I might be able to give.

At the same time the lawyer sent a letter to Jack Broughton, the other witness, who wrote me in his more expansive manner:

> I received Mr. Brush's letter and enclosures this morning, along with your sweet note. And right now it is airmailed in the mail box and should be back to him in a week or so. I hope it is all satisfactory.

I feel like such a bum for not writing you before, and yet now in some ways I'm just as glad I didn't. Too much all at once doesn't help.

Betts dear, how can I tell you how heartsick I was when I learned of Van's death. I was sitting at my desk writing Ellie when Dave came back from the "B" and told me. I had worried about him terribly but somehow I was actually unprepared for the ghastly reality of it. I can't explain how it made me feel, but it was the same hellish dead feeling that overwhelmed me after the Atlanta. I never could explain it, even to Ellie, and made her unhappy because I said it made us all feel that we almost didn't want to go back, as if there wasn't anything left.

All that I know of what happened is what Dave told me. Van was out doing his job, more than that, trying to save another ship. There was a terrific explosion and everything topside was riddled. It all happened so quickly and I believe he didn't suffer. As far as I can see he should receive the Navy Cross, maybe has already.

I still can't believe it. Only a month or so before we had such fun together. In all my time out here till then, I'd made very little effort to actually see any of our old friends, but for some reason I did, to see Van. We were ashore together and back on the ship for dinner. And then were tied close together and he came over again. We had such a good time, laughed, looked at pictures of you gals, our girls, and I just thank God for it now.

He seemed so happy, was so proud of his ship and his job, little things and big things. And always his sense of humor, his appreciation, his laugh. . . . I can see him the morning after our battle, directing all kinds of things, walking around, limping with a cane. I can see him that day in the Fairmont, when Ellie and I met him and he had the flowers for you, the time he came home from N. Z.

You two had so much and will never lose any of it. Nothing can ever take away what you have. He will always be with you. I know that, loving you, helping you in every way he can, and nothing now that may happen on earth will change you, the two of you. God takes care of things like that, somehow, I know it.

I won't waste time saying I'm sorry for you. You have my deepest whateveritis from the bottom of my heart. Ellie wrote me how perfectly marvelous you have been. But you know and I know, that he's right there with you and that you are just being the kind of person he would want you, does want you, to be. Oh, I'm proud of you lassie, mighty proud.

God bless you dear girl and your wee daughter, who has in her the life that you and Van gave to her. Don't ever hesitate to call on me nor on us (Ellie and me) for anything, in any shape or manner.

Brother-in-law Joe had seen Van last when the ice cream was such a welcome treat on Saipan. Now, back in Hawaii with his general, he saw the badly damaged *Birmingham* come in briefly and leave again before he could get to her.

He combed the hospitals trying to find someone who could tell him about Van. Most of the wounded there were too badly injured to know much beyond their own selves. Joe wrote me what little he could find out. His informant, like so many others, was wrong about Van, but he, like the others, was dazed and badly wounded. I think they all thought it was a kindness to say Van died instantly. I knew the truth in my heart. Joe wrote,

> All that is in my heart longs to pour out on this paper, and only the numbing ache that grips me now prevents it.
>
> Van was my dear, close friend. I think very few brothers-in-law were ever so closely drawn together by mutual understanding, friendship and respect as we were. . . . My own sense of loss is deep and abiding. . . . When your little girl is older, I want her to understand what a fine man, what a brave, a gallant Officer her Daddy was.
>
> In a letter to Dad, I told him the essential outline of what happened. For days I knew that something had happened but could not find out what, or whether or not Van was involved. But I started combing through the hospitals and yesterday I found a seaman named Smith who was alongside Van. The seaman told me Van was killed instantly. He had been with Van for two years, and was very broken up about it. I was too, and as a consequence couldn't question him much. Today I'm going up again, and I shall get the whole story.
>
> Betts, my dear brave sister, you know that my heart is with you and that you are in my mind and thoughts. Know also that I'm goddam proud of our Van.

Only Pat O'Day, Van's assistant on the *Birmingham,* understood my need to know what really took place. I had the true story in his letter, received much later:

> Van was killed on the afternoon of October 24, 1944. And was buried at sea that same day. There was no question of identification.
>
> I realize there is no way for me to soften the blow—that he is missed aboard ship so badly is just an indication of how you, his wife, must feel.
>
> His personal effects are being sent home, including the plans for your vineyard Ranch House.
>
> I rounded up Van's things but did not actually pack them Bettsy. A small detail of Officers took care of all the deceased Officers. I remember going over his letters and files with them and saying to send them home, so you should get the letters you spoke of.
>
> I don't remember what happened to the models frankly. His room was considerably inhabited by wounded for some days and I never heard them mentioned by the "packing Officers." But trust you'd receive them also.

Van lived for approximately 30 minutes after the explosion. He was standing on the starboard side of the focsle right next to Alan Reed, Adey, Bos'n etc. After he was hit he was carried down to the wardroom stateroom and Doc MacArt managed to get in to see him. (Even the Capt. didn't get a Drs. attention). Mac told me that he knew Van didn't have a chance—would die in a few minutes and nothing he could do to save him.

No one I spoke to since who saw Van remembered his saying anything although he was tossing around a bit and, I gathered, not unconscious. He was buried at sea that same afternoon. I did not see him for I had to remain in Central, but what I have just related is a composite from those who actually were with him and I think, fairly accurate. In those first few minutes, of course, nothing was very clear to any of us. But I questioned all those who saw him before he died.

The ship is certainly not the same anymore—the new 1st Lt does not fill Van's shoes and there are a lot of other new people with small feet. . . .

That is all I can think of for now Bettsy, if anything else is on your mind please write. I promise you better answering service next time.

Of the more than 450 letters I received, a few showed Van in a different light. J. A. McGrane, one of the C&R gang whom Van had spoken highly of, answered my thank you note for his original sympathy letter:

I received your most kind letter today, it was forwarded by Lt. O'Day. I wish to thank you for the compliments which I know I do not half deserve.

I assure you that I deemed it one of the high points of my Naval career to have served with such a fine officer as Commander Perkins. His high sense of duty and his ever ready humor smoothed out many a rough path. His loss was not only a great blow to the ship but to the entire service. . . .

In closing, let me say that any thing I did for Commander Perkins was only in the hope that his last cruise might be a little easier.

Martha Pierce Rafferty wrote a young woman's reaction to Van. She was a great beauty whose opinion I prized:

About Van, I want to tell you that the first time I saw him I wanted him for my very own and immediately Walt said, "Van was no dope, had picked you and I would just have to put up with him." I liked his smile and his face and he was tall and perfect. I can only figure, the way I would, if it was Walt. I think you had that kind of marriage, the kind that is rare, but really good.

Some jokes, some fun and NO ONE else. Nothing can take that away because it is all yours. You had it and no one else even figured. Best sort of love and I hope I can see you soon. . . . I bet Van's damned proud of you.

Ed Ryan wrote, "He had personally directed the work of his men with the utmost skill and courage, as he has always done. The loss of Van was a terrible blow to all of us, individually and as a ship's company. The memory of his brave example will be with this ship as long as it floats and in the hearts of us all forever."

Brock Brocklebank had finally been detached shortly before the *Princeton*'s explosion. In answer to my thank-you note for his earlier letter, he let me know how much Van was thinking about his possible death and how he hoped I would take it:

> Your note of the 22nd did much to hearten me. It is so gallant, so much the sort of spirit Van hoped for. I've never known, until the testing comes, just what another person is made of. We loved you for your loveliness and kindness, now we also honor you. You have adorned yourself with "garments of the brave."
>
> You have been very much in our thoughts, we have been eager for some word but knew that we should be patient. The letter is finer than we dared hope for. A fitting tribute to one who longed for the years ahead with you, but was ready at all times for the sacrifice that was made. Those last few months together brought me closer to him, perhaps because our wives were close. There were many moments of danger and anxiety which caused us to talk of our hopes for the years ahead. You had given him much and his love for you was great . . . leaving love and happy memories, making possible a joyous life which shall be his tribute. . . . At present there is a first sense of sorrow and personal loss.

Tucked in the letter was a little card on which Brock had written:

> *And ye now therefore have sorrow.*
> *but I will see you again.*
> *And your heart shall rejoice.*
> *And your joy no man taketh from you.*

I read it over and over, for it comforted me at the times hopelessness engulfed me.

Woodie, Van's brother, had seen him for a brief two hours two weeks previous to Van's death. In the midst of the battle, inexplicably, he received orders to a base hospital in the Admiralties. Because his PT boat was not in contact with the squadron commander's boat and Wood could not get his orders signed, his skipper signed them. As transportation out of the area, Wood chose a badly damaged destroyer with a 10-degree list over a submarine. When he could, he transferred to a supply ship and bummed his way across the Pacific on any available vessel heading east to his new assignment. It was not until weeks later, when his mail caught up with him, that he had word Van was killed—and he had been ordered out just when he was so badly needed.

When at last Wood came home, he was physically and emotionally wrung out. It was wonderful to have one of the boys home safe, but the night after he arrived, I rocked myself to sleep repeating over and over, "Oh, God, why Van? Why Van?"

The War as Perkins Sees It

As soon as Van was killed, I had to leave the civilian air patrol, as it was thought improper to chance making Pam an orphan. I had our baby to support, to plan for and to nurture. My widow's pension, plus Van's personal and government insurance, came to $105.50 a month. Though my family was more than willing to help, I wanted to be Van's and my own independent family as nearly as possible. A job was going to be an absolute necessity. I could manage that, as Miss Reichardt insisted on continuing to take care of Pam with no more than a little pocket money instead of pay.

It had been a year since last I had seen Van. We had known then that it was our last meeting—we had made a fantasy to make life bearable. With Van's death the unbearable had happened, and despite my practicing in my mind how to cope without him, it was proving much harder in reality. Getting busy would be an essential part of pushing down the hurt in my heart and mind. Getting a paying job was now a must, and it was important to go where I thought it most likely jobs were available.

We moved to Washington, where Mom and Pop Perkins got me a starkly furnished one-room apartment down the hall from their own establishment. Pam and Miss Reichardt stayed with them in their guest room. The building was grandiose on the outside, crummy on the inside. Once it had been fumigated to get rid of the cockroaches and the walls and woodwork had been given a good scrubbing, the room was livable. Furnishing the room with some of my own things, including my Ming vase and jade grapes from China, which Van had given me in Manila, and hanging Van's portrait over the couch where I could look at it gave me a sense of living in my own establishment.

Young ladies of my generation and circumstances did not have the skills and credentials for getting a job that paid much. Our skills were homemaking, entertaining, and, in my case, sculpting. None of them very useful in Washington. I needed a good paying position.

My first job was working as a volunteer soda jerk at Bethesda Naval Hospital, where I was told that if I proved reliable I could apply for a job as a quasi-physical therapist using sculpting to restore finger dexterity. Two weeks into soda jerking I was let go when I was mixing a strawberry milkshake. The machine, which had a short in it, gave me a shock that caused me to jerk my arm, thereby throwing the gooey contents of the container all over the poor marine who had ordered the concoction. I worsened the situation by attempting to wipe off the strawberries and milk now decorating his dress uniform, smearing the entire front of his blouse, and he on his way to his first dance since being wounded on Guadalcanal. I went home despondent.

My father-in-law, feeling, as did others, that the time had come for me to begin having a normal social life, started introducing me to young naval and marine officers from his office. My popularity increased immeasurably, and it soon became apparent that a twenty-five-year-old widow was fair game in the eyes of young bachelors. Within days I learned never to be alone with a man if I did not want to have a wrestling match. I had thought surely my wedding rings and little gold star would be some sort of protection, but just the opposite appeared to be the case. One young man dared to say, "You're a widow and you need it, and I'm prepared to give it to you."

My reply to that was a well-aimed kick, the lesson harshly put. "You jackass, what makes you think you or anyone could take Van's place. Your conceit is even more obnoxious than you are."

Needless to say I did not see him again. Van's friends in the area came to be the only people I trusted. Captain and Mrs. Jenkins were wonderfully kind to me, and when the *Birmingham*'s captain told me he, not Van, was getting the Navy Cross, it was Captain Jenkins who comforted me, saying, "Van was the real hero of that day, and those of us who knew him and who know the story of the whole episode know that. You know that, and no mere medal can enhance his heroic actions."

Still, that Van would not receive the Navy Cross hurt me deeply, and it hurt others as well, as I found out when people started writing me letters of amazement that no recognition of Van's bravery was forthcoming. It was comforting to know how many people were outraged and that it was not just me.

Answering Jim's sympathy letter, I told him I would like to write him more often as I could no longer write Van. His ship had returned to Bremerton, Washington, to pick up a new air group, effect modifications to the ship, and give the crew some much deserved R&R. On 5 February 1945, Jim answered my letter after the *Bunker Hill* returned to sea:

Your letter was most welcome, waiting for me as it was, when I returned from leave. Here's hoping there will be many more like it though there's no guarantee that my letters will be any scintillating gems. Hemmed in by censorship as they are. How wonderful that day is going to be when we can all settle down and say whatever we please whenever we please.

My leave has already acquired the dream like quality of a pleasant memory. Two weeks were granted to me to do as I pleased and I pleased to go to San Francisco. It was the first time in America in a year and a half so there was a lot of lost time to be recovered. Our country seemed like fairyland. Everything was just right. My sister had found an apartment for me atop Nob Hill about a block from the Mark Hopkins, the apartment being completely equipped for bachelor occupancy with a fireplace, a borrowed Welsh Terrier, and a case of Teachers' Scotch while out in front was parked my car with a full gas tank.

It was just too bad that time had to be taken out for sleep. Every day Betty Lou would trot out another gal for me and I left a trail in all the night clubs in town—well, hardly all, but the ones I liked at least. . . . Good Lord, I'd forgotten what fun dancing could be! Round and round I went.

Did you know that my sister married a boy in the class of 1938? Ken Robinson is his name; hails from Newburgh, New York. He being a widower, Betty Lou acquired a two year old stepdaughter whose slave I am completely. Now she's expecting one of her own this spring so I'm really excited. As for Robby's whereabouts, he's skipper of a destroyer out in the Pacific and his brother-in-law is terribly jealous of his job.

It seemed that people at home were much more aware of the war, much more concerned about those of us who fight it, than they were when we came back in early 1943. Perhaps it was my own feeling that resulted in that impression. I came back with none of the bitterness I once harbored. So I found no bitterness at home. Word has it that this condition is only true on the West Coast, that the Mid-West and the East are still on a business-as-usual basis. What do you think?

The return to the wars after such a short time away was a horrible hang-over. Depression and gloom are mild words to describe the emotions. It had been my fond hope to acquire a command of my own but it didn't happen that way. It's taken a little while to readjust to the old way of thinking and living but everything's all right now. The only way to get this mess over with is to get on with it and I dare say I am quite well qualified to help with that getting on. Nonetheless, your cheerful letter was certainly a help, coming when it did.

Where are you living, Bettsy? Do you have your baby with you? What prompted you to move to Washington? Is the city still the giddy madhouse? What's the latest scuttlebutt as to war's end in Europe? Is Rock Creek Park as lovely as ever? Do you ever see any of our mutual acquaintances? I'd better stop the questions now though I have many more—equally unrelated in subject matter. . . .

The only hobbies I now have are reading and writing (plus perhaps sleeping—sleep being rare enough to be classed as a hobby). Christmas brought me huge stacks of lovely books and the moment I can take the time, I'm going to be in the midst of them. As for the writing, we have a little ship's paper for which I wrote a series of short stories based on the fantastic escapades of a couple of pre-war destroyer sailors on the China Station. While in San Francisco, I took the stories to a publisher and discovered they will be published in book form. Amazing.

Also on leave, I took a try at two of my old hobbies, golf and photography, and couldn't work up the slightest enthusiasm for either. Did Van ever tell you about the crazy game of golf he and I played one day in New Zealand? That would make a story too.

Thanks again for writing. I'll be looking forward to your next letter.

I was writing two letters to Jim's one but expected that to be the case, as he was far busier than I was:

What fun it was to get your letter. I am wasting no time in answering it as is obvious when I tell you it arrived less than three hours ago. Somehow the gruesome cliché "pen pal" came to mind and I have been chuckling over it ever since. So from now on I am your old "pen pal Perkins." Really that is the most horrible thing I have ever said but it's so trite I love it.

About coming to Washington, Van's family is living down here and I am with them. They are wonderful people and it is the perfect solution for me as Greenwich is one of the towns where the war simply does not exist. The people at home commute to New York on the club car and wrangle over whose son is the best football player as usual. It's not that most of them don't have boys in the service, but they haven't been put out in any way. Van was the first boy from Greenwich to be killed and I was absolutely swamped with sympathy and pitying looks which didn't help me to get back on my feet at all, so I just packed up and moved down here where I am just another person which is what I wanted, and also I can get a job down here directly connected with the war, which in Greenwich is impossible as it is a purely residential town.

What is the name of your book? I want to get it right away. I think that's about as exciting a thing as could happen to anyone. Do you now refer to "my publisher," no I don't suppose you do. I suppose you go around pretending you've never written a book. I am more than anxious to read it for I know it will be good and thoroughly interesting to me.

Writing you seems to be the most natural thing in the world to be doing. I am rambling on with a thousand ideas of things I want to tell you for no particular reason, So far I haven't started philosophizing which is my favorite indoor sport, but I suspect I'll be doing so in another few minutes.

You asked about the Washington slant on the wars and the end in Europe. Everyone I've heard talk about it says it will end late this summer which I'm personally inclined to agree with. The more startling and less credible prediction is that your war will end almost simultaneously. The idea seems to be that the Japs will collapse when the Jap Islands themselves are attacked continuously. I am not so sure myself being suspicious of any optimistic predictions and also thinking that face saving is a factor that most people, who haven't been out there, can't grasp.

This evening's news that you are attacking Tokyo with a giant carrier operation has all of the commentators and prognosticators in a high state of elation as well it might. Every time this happens we have a wave of optimism that sets production back considerably. . . . The war in Europe is going to be a grueling show from here on in. The Russians have been fighting on the Oder interminably. We have gained a mile here and there in the last few weeks but we haven't hit the last ditch battle yet and that is going to be a wild one in my opinion. That is the war as Perkins sees it.

As to the attitude on this Coast about the war. It is just as it is on the West Coast except that here the European war is uppermost. Emplacement of troops seems to be sectional, consequently the majority of families here have boys in Europe. Also we are closer to Europe. Having my family in the Pacific has made me most ignorant of the European war. . . .

Places like Greenwich, segregated little towns, still don't know what it's all about by your standards and mine. They can't get butter and they have one maid instead of the four and five they used to have etc. It sounds very petty I know but if you think of it for a minute you realize that everything is relative and if people have never had to face any kind of crisis, the smallest one reaches gigantic proportions.

I am of the opinion that the country over is all the same, for we hear that the West Coast goes on strike at the drop of a hat while we of the East Coast are patriotic and work no matter how bad the conditions (implying the conditions are rotten), people love to gripe and they love to be better than someone else. . . .

Rock Creek Park is a delight by day and a horror by night as it has been the scene of the three latest and most sensational murders. Pam and I go there by day to play. Pam has made two fast friends there. One the patrolman, a wonderful Irishman whose name is Mr. Ned and who brings Pam candy and lets her climb trees which is strictly prohibited. Pam saw him one day and walked right up to him and said, "I like you very much." He said, "Thank you miss, I like you too." Pam then said, "Your hands are very dirty, I have a dog, my name is Pamie Vans Perkins, I am two, I like to climb trees, I am so-o-o big." The policeman said, "Sure my hands are dirty and if you'll come back tomorrow I'll boost you up in a tree with a clean pair of hands." And we've been going to the park to climb trees ever since.

The war in Europe was eclipsed in my mind as I became intrigued with what I was hearing about China, which I thought would interest Jim as much as it did me. Perhaps just as important was that Pam was asking about her father and I was uncertain how to handle this. As Jim was so close to Van, I asked his advice:

Pamie and I went to the park yesterday and there we discovered the first touches of Spring. Green shoots on the bushes and trees and an early robin industriously building a nest. The sun was warm and we took off our coats and found a large flat rock to stretch on. No one was around to bother us and I thought it was a good time to tell Pam about Van. Poor little thing, a rotten child here in the building teased her unmercifully one day with a sing song chant about "Nyan, nyan, nyan, you haven't got any Daddy" and Pamie kept saying, "I have so too, I have so too" and started to cry. This in the elevator where I could do nothing about it. So we talked in the park, lying in the sun, about Van. I told her that Daddy was never very far away but that we couldn't see him anymore and she said this of her own accord, "My Daddy is gone away like my flowers had to go away, my Daddy is like my red roses." That I thought was pretty wonderful, as I brought her red roses a couple of weeks ago and we'd had quite a discussion about why the roses had to be gotten rid of. Then she said, "They will take him to a forest way up north and plant him so he can grow big and strong." I said, "Who will?" and she said, "Santa Claus and his lit-tel teeny helpers." That came from her Christmas tree having to leave abruptly. Of course she doesn't really understand and I don't really know what I can do about it. I want her to be terribly proud of Van. I know it would wreck Van to think he caused her any grief but I don't know how to protect her from things like this and I am really up in the air about what to do about all of this.

Children hate to be different from other children in any way and all I can hope to do is give Pam a feeling that she has one up on other children until she and her contemporaries are old enough to understand. If you have any thought on the subject I wish you'd tell me. This is one of those things I'd run to Van about because between us, we'd come up with the solution and I can tell you think as Van did. Do you think I'm crazy to start explaining right now to Pam about Van? My two reasons are to let her grow up with the thought naturally and not have it as a shock later, and to keep her from being hurt the way she was in the elevator. She's smart as a steel trap but the whole subject is so tremendous that I have trouble understanding it let alone reducing it to a level that a two and a half year old baby can comprehend. Have a bright thought Jim and let me know what it is.

I could gladly strangle anyone for bringing any kind of unhappiness to my sweet baby who is naturally the happiest child I have ever known. Really you'd love her. She's one of those rare babies who have a sense of humor. Typical of her humor was a car ride we were taking when I got fatuous about some ungainly cows and said, "Oh Pamie look at the lovely cows."

She looked at me quizzically for a minute and then said, "Mummy is a big fat cow," much uproarious laughter. She thought better of herself and said, "But I love you Mummy" and when I laughed at that she threw her arms around my neck and heaved a great sigh. Now what can you do with such a one as that.

Thanks for listening.

I'm Looking Forward

It was to Jim I wrote my problems. He became my confidant. Hearing his advice was the same as hearing from Van, for they had talked together so much that Jim understood and agreed with Van's point of view; this made our friendship invaluable. Jim wrote:

Can you feature it—the Navy relaxing on the censorship rules? It's true we are going to be able to relate portions of our personal experiences and even tell about where we've been. It isn't all free and easy by any means but it's such a vast improvement that I feel as though a heavy weight has been lifted from my mind. Reminds me of recently when the ship fitters came into my room and unsealed the welds on the port hole and let the daylight in after a year and a half of gloom. Wonderful, wonderful daylight and fresh salt air!

The log of the *Bunker Hill* up until the first of this year reads like a history of the Pacific War; Rabaul, Tarawa, Nauru, Kavieng, the Marshals, Truk, the Marianas, Palau, New Guinea, the Bonins, Philippines, Formosa, Nasei Shoto—the ship was always on hand. Not a single calendar month went by in a whole year and a half that we weren't mixed up in some kind of a scrap. As for the holidays, the press correspondents began to call the ship the Holiday Express. Armistice Day, Christmas, New Year's, Washington's Birthday, Fourth of July and other days found us in action. Rather surprisingly, few people outside the Fleet know much about our ship. Maybe what we need is a good press agent.

I am rounding out nine years at sea now and feel that it won't be long until I move on to another job. Most of all, would I like a command of my own. Trouble is that everybody else in the Navy wants one too. It would also be nice to have a few months in America so that I can really feel like a native of my own country.

Thanks for the picture of Pamela. She's a very attractive young miss. Like you, I prefer baby girls to baby boys but am very strange around any child or infant. In Bremerton I went to call on an ex-shipmate's wife. She promptly left me with her year and a half child while she went on an errand. I don't know who was more frightened, yours truly or the child. Each of us backed off into far corners of the room and looked suspiciously at one another. That was my only experience with the rising generation while on leave since Betty Lou's stepdaughter had not yet been brought out from the East Coast.

The other day a rather startling thing occurred. Somebody offered me a job on a big staff. What sleepless nights followed! The job would have meant being shore based on one of the Pacific islands. Well, the outcome was refusal on my part. If one must sit behind a desk, it would be preferable to have the desk anchored somewhere in America. Now, I'm hoping to be assigned to the War College in Newport for a few months and then land that command job.

The war is certainly becoming big business what with the gigantic fleet now available for anti-Jap activities. In the old Guadalcanal days it was all very simple—find the Japs and slug it out with them, the while being slugged in return. Now it's a precision operation. The reams of professional literature that pours over my desk have increased a hundred fold in the past two years; indicative of the change. . . .

Thanks so much, Bettsy for your pleasant letters. I'm looking forward to the next one.

My life in Washington became intolerable. The silly jobs I got were either temporary or part time. Miss Reichardt was homesick, financially it was a disaster, and my baby was suffering from being cooped up in the apartment and from city life in general. I took Pam and Miss Reichardt to Greenwich and returned to Washington to wind up my affairs. I wrote to Jim on 16 April 1945:

During the two weeks that I haven't written, the state of the nation has changed from calm to chaos and back to calm again. The death of the President [Roosevelt] was as great a shock to those of us who were not in utter sympathy with him as it was to his ardent supporters. I don't believe it had anything at all to do with his policies but merely the fact that we were without a President even for a short while. I have never been one of the dogmatic despisers of the Govt. nor have I ever wholeheartedly been in favor of Pres. R's policies but he did have great influence not only in the country but in the world and I think that it is sad for him to have to go before Germany's fall.

This is very confused thinking but it is about typical of the thinking of the average person as well as I can see it. I arrived down here in Washington the day after the President died. It was quite an impressive thing to see. All the flags at half mast, black bunting in store windows, the newspapers without any advertisements, the radio playing quiet music and nothing else, and the population openly crying on the streets. We went down Saturday morning to watch the procession. We were struck with the numbers of people crying, it was very solemn and impressive and we came home in low frames of mind.

Truman has taken over in a big way. He has persuaded Molitoff to come to the San Francisco conference. He has ousted or neutralized the radical members of the cabinet. He has recalled Jimmy Burns and it looks to me like he is going to take an honest stand and stick by it. I hope so anyway. Washington is full of ideas about Truman. He is honest, he is smart, he is a man of the soil and likened to Lincoln. He is in every way a good man, so the pundits say.

Westbrook Pegler [the conservative columnist for the *Herald Tribune* newspaper] is away on vacation and until I read what he has to say I'm not making any predictions as to Truman, but it would seem that he has held the people together. That he has been pretty clever with Russia and that he has conducted himself with dignity which I would think indicates that we have a fair chance to find he is a good President.

Greenwich was all that I expected it to be. Perhaps even better than I had anticipated, for the entire visit was spent in sunshine and I loved every minute of it. Now I am brown as a berry and feeling healthy once again, and in fact am getting back to a proper perspective on life. There was a point where all I wanted to do was tear out to parties and more parties and the average bachelor, on being introduced to a young "wider lady," that's having fun, seems to have just one idea in mind. They are amazed when they find that idea isn't mine. So going to Greenwich gave me a well needed rest and a chance to look at my life of the past six months in retrospect and come to a few conclusions. Mainly that this is not what I want for a permanent mode of life and that it is about time I decided what I do want.

Washington is not my permanent home and I don't want it to be. So I am going to go up to New York and learn to write and I am then going to get a job writing for something. My idea is to go to Columbia and see how much of a course I can take this summer as a starter and then commence in the fall with the regular English Lit. class.

I think maybe it's about time to look to the future. You know Jim, Van and I were so happily married that I can't imagine staying un-married the rest of my life and I have taken a long time to realize that whether I can or cannot imagine such a thing, the chances are equal that I won't get married again and that I better darn well plan for Miss Pam and me to have a future. So do you think I'm shirking if I get into something that is not connected with the war? Something that will be a sustaining interest for the rest of my life, if need be. . . .

My young sister-in-law-to-be works at Scribners. I have had her on the lookout for any or all books by Cdr. J. C. Shaw. Not knowing the name of the book or the publisher has been quite a handicap to her but undaunted she has proceeded with my mission. On my arrival home I found a package of books, four of them to be exact, all written by men named Shaw (though none of Bernard's). One is "How Dark a Moon," another is "Aunt Siwash Comes Home," another is "Breeding and Raising Hogs" and the last is "Your Hand Next" (bridge). I am confused by her sense of humor. At any rate, I will get your book when it comes out if she is still on the job.

Jim did not answer my question with regard to telling Pam about Van until April, presumably as he wanted to ponder the matter, as was typical of him when dealing with something he felt strongly about:

Life has been the usual hectic go-round that features the sea going war time Navy in general and carriers in particular. Last February we steamed up to Tokyo, apprehensively I'll admit, and gave the Nips the long promised working over of their capital. We had a repeat performance on that too and the Nip reaction was surprisingly mild. We also did some support work around Iwo Jima and lashed out at the Ryukyus. All in all it was a busy profitable but nerve racking time. We had one mild scrape with the air-borne Japs and I was rather glad of it since it gave some seasoning to the many new men now under me. The Japs are definitely on the defensive now but Lord how they do fight! Well, you know how tough the little so-and-sos can be. I just wonder if many Americans do realize what a scrap is ahead out here before we finally whittle Japan down to size. . . .

Bettsy, you rather pose a problem in whether or no, if and how, to tell your daughter about her father. Unfortunately I've not been around children, much as I like them, in many a long year and find that my understanding of their mental processes is so scant that when I am around a child, I'm as shy as a five year old myself. However, it would seem that you're starting off on the right tack in letting her understand that her father has gone away and treating it as something natural and not frightening or morbid. It really should be easier now than at any other time since so many children have fathers overseas in the services. The mere fact that her father is not in and around the house every day can easily be compared to the homes of other children whose fathers are away. Instill in her a pride in what her father stands for. Talk of him to her in such a manner that she will obtain a living flesh and blood mental image of him. And don't let her take fright at the word "dead." We all tend to shy away from the implications of the word but the thing to do I would say is to eliminate its ugliness as a word with sometimes grim associations. The red roses simile seems to be an effective presentation.

Our generation has rather had rough going which is all the more reason to see that Pamela's generation doesn't have a repetition. It's so easy to become all twisted up inside. I admire the well balanced manner in which you've reacted to all that's happened.

Spring again. A fellow Minnesotan and I were talking about spring in our home state the other day until both of us practically had tears in our eyes imagining the smell of the lilacs, the feel of the lush grass under barefoot, the rustling of the tree leaves stirred by a lakeside breeze, the sight of a rolling verdant fairway, and the clean satisfying sound of a wood shot well hit. Oh, me! Oh, me!

Fate took a hand. My dear Doc Squire once again lost his nurse-secretary to the Army and he offered me my job back. My pay would be more than adequate. I moved back to Greenwich, this time to Mother's house, where my sister and her two children were living out the war along with my sister-in-law, who had one baby and was presently expecting twins.

What I knew about being a medical secretary you could still summarize in one word—"nothing"—but with the help of a medical dictionary and Raymond Squire's infinite patience, I began to master that part of my job, though I never was able to leave off that rubber stamp: "New Secretary, Please excuse all mistakes. SQ."

I loved the nurse part of my job. I was good at it, and I knew I was helping the morale of the men involved. So many of Doc Squire's patients were ladies whose husbands were overseas and were, as I had been, facing childbirth alone. He would dispatch me to quell their fears and dry their tears. In fact, when asked what my job was, my reply was, "Fears and Tears Department."

I assisted in the examining room when the trained nurse was busy. I typed up reports, filed records, and accompanied the doctor on house calls to lone patients so he could not be accused of wrongdoing. But I was always home to give Pam time each day and tuck her in bed every night.

A year and a half had passed since I had last seen Van; it seemed like a lifetime ago. Time dragged endlessly by. I was a veritable scarecrow, made even worse by my nurse's white uniform and cap—one skinny white stick. Even so, there were men who asked me to marry them, and, at one point, I even contemplated Raymond Squire's proposal, knowing it would amply provide for Pam. But I thought only briefly about it. I knew myself well enough to know I could not accept any proposal halfheartedly.

I remembered Van's admonition to me before he left the last time. I would have to be able to love, unconditionally, someone who could understand that Van would always be in my heart, someone who would love Pamie as his own, someone who had known another love and knew you could love as much but differently—a tall order! I knew that Van and I had had a rare, intense love for each other that would stay with me all my life and that such a love would not ever occur again for me. Equally I knew that I had a need to cherish another man, to use all that caring energy that I had once showered on Van.

A Heavenly Hash

The war was progressing at a furious pace. Island after island fell to us or was bypassed. Admiral Mitscher, his flag on *Bunker Hill,* had masterminded a brilliant plan that kept the Japanese fleet so baffled that they were in complete disarray. Their great desire was to get the *Bunker Hill.* Time after time the ship was attacked and Japanese planes were splashed by Jim's gunners or fought off by the fighter planes.

I wrote Jim a letter about all I had heard, hoping this would give him a smile:

Unofficially, Washington continues to be pessimistic, though the past few days they have started talk on reducing fighting in Europe to Guerrilla warfare by June and a complete mop-up by October. That would release some few troops for the Pacific and I think it might force the Russians into a decision, which would be a victory of sorts anyway you look at it. Even if they decide not to fight in China, it would be a help to know just where we stand. Everyone around Washington seems to feel fairly confident that the Russians will fight in China though why they are optimistic I fail to understand. I personally feel no such confidence in the Russians on any score at all.

One of my friends is in the Jap section of communications and the other night I made a remark about the Bunker Hill and how many exploits it has had and he said, "Oh, yes indeed, the Japs would love to get hold of the B. H., they refer to it as the "Boon Ka Hirue" and talk of sinking it in glowing terms about once a week." By now I have you all lined up in all various departments. I've found a friend in each one who tells me all I want to know. . . . Oh yes, I forgot about telling you that this lad who is in the Jap section is a Jap language student and often tells me something ridiculous the Japs have said, one of which was, "Our bombers successfully laid a chicken on a plane carrier this morning making a heavenly hash out of it," that was in reference to you. All this in Japanese but obviously for our monitors to pick up. I think it must be often amusing to listen to them. Gil says they try to imitate our slang in Japanese with the idea that it annoys us, instead of which, it gives everyone a great laugh. Another thing that tickled me was that Gil said the Japs have an awful time talking to each other by radio as they often cannot detect the inflection of a word over short wave and that inflection can diametrically oppose the meaning of the word. . . .

Mrs. Perkins said for me to tell you even though she hasn't met you, hello for her and that she hopes you'll come home soon and come and see us, which motion I, heartfelt, second.

Mom Perkins had returned from Washington. I was splitting my time between my two families, and Pamie was well taken care of by her grandmothers while I worked.

On 7 May 1945, Germany surrendered to the Allies. On 9 May, Jim wrote,

> So at last the war in Europe has come to a close. It's a relief but the effects of war's end over there will not be felt out here for some months, I'm afraid. The pace of Pacific offensives has been increased many fold in the past year but there's still a long hard struggle ahead. Celebrating seems a bit premature and almost sacrilegious.
>
> . . . Your story of the books by gents named Shaw was highly amusing, particularly the receipt of the book on hog culture. My experience with hogs has been entirely on the consuming end so I'm glad to hear that at least one member of the Shaw clan is taking avidly to animal husbandry.
>
> Van's experience with the Bureau in trying to obtain the type of duty he desired is not, I regret to admit, unusual from other cases. The ordinary . . . line officer has a devil of a time in lodging himself in a desirable berth. After three and one half years of the same type of duty, I'm fed to the ears but there appears little prospect of a change. Patience is one quality that must be acquired in the service. We're always waiting for something: boats, meals, bedtime, action, leave, promotion, orders and mail.

Then came the news on the radio that the *Bunker Hill* had been hit on 11 May off Okinawa, so "heavenly hash" was true, even though premature by a month. Within days there were front-page pictures of the ship on fire, which sent chills down my spine. From the pictures, I could not imagine how Jim could possibly have escaped being injured so I steeled myself for more sadness. Hardly a full month went by that I did not hear that I had lost another friend, and now the *Bunker Hill,* with Jim very liable to be seriously involved. To my superstitious mind Jim had one advantage. This was not his third life threat, as Van's had been, but his second, so maybe he had made it. I fervently hoped so. I did not even have Betty Lou's address, so there was no way I could find out about Jim but to wait for word from him. What arrived three weeks later was an exuberant note:

> America is a wonderful place, and as usual finds me goggle eyed over everything. Such food! Such weather! Such people!
>
> I'll write at length later. Right now I'm busily involved in flying to Carmel to have a peep at my nephew.

Work went on as usual until one day, while I was sitting at my desk, the phone rang. "Dr. Squire's office," I said, in my best telephone voice.

"May I speak to Mrs. Perkins?"

"Speaking," I answered.

There was a pause, and then, "This is Jim Shaw. I'm in New Rochelle and

wondered if you'd have lunch with me. I could be there in half an hour."

"Wait a minute," I replied. "I'll ask the doctor if I can have an hour off."

I ran to the office. Doc's answer was "I guess so, if you can finish my last letter in time to get it in the 2 o'clock mail."

Dashing back to the phone, I gave Jim directions, quickly bummed some unbecoming orange lipstick from the trained nurse, put my Dictaphone earpiece back on, and began typing furiously. Spelling be damned, just get the letter finished.

I was so absorbed in my work that I jumped when Jim tapped me on the shoulder and said, "May I speak to Mrs. Perkins please?"

"Me—I—well, I'm Bettsy," I stumbled, and, jumping up, I kissed him. He opened his big brown eyes even wider with surprise and said, "Lord, I didn't recognize you. What have you done to yourself, you're so thin. I'm awfully glad to see what's left of you." We both laughed the first really hearty laugh we had in many a moon.

"Where are you going to be stationed, Jim?" I asked.

"At long last my prayers have been answered—I'm to go to the Naval War College in Newport."

"Oh yes, Van put in for that when he heard Sam Jenkins had recommended him for his own command. His captain put the kibosh on that saying he had to have a qualified relief. That's what your prayers were for, eh?"

"Exactly, first I have five months of study and then presumably I'll get a destroyer or maybe even a light cruiser. I'm pretty ranky for a destroyer, but you know I'm really a destroyer sailor and that's what I want."

At lunch we talked about Jane and Van and Lord knows what else. My hour stretched into two hours, and still we were not finished talking. Jim drove me back to the office and we sat in the lobby and talked some more, this time about how the *Bunker Hill* took the kamikaze right down the island of the ship, setting fire to the planes on the flight deck. It had not damaged anything below deck and they were able to travel under their own steam once the fires were out, making the trip to Bremerton in jig time.

Finally Jim left, and I almost lost my job. I doubted I would see Jim again, for I knew I looked like hell and thought I had acted a bit crazy too, jabbering away like a schoolgirl one minute, the next dumping all my woes on his shoulders when he had plenty of his own. But then, he was my good friend.

Jim said he would call me, so I did what any red-blooded American girl would do. I went to the hairdresser and had my long hair cut off, bought myself a pretty dress, one that did not hang on me like a sack, and settled down to await developments.

It was not much of a wait, for Jim called two days later. He wanted to come down from Newport for the weekend but thought he would have to take the train as he had used all his gas ration and needed new tires, which were not to be had. No problem—my car was in working order and I could meet him in Stamford, if he would let me know what time.

Funny how such a meeting can crystallize vague thoughts and memories. I knew clearly the next day the only person I could even contemplate marrying was Jim. For he would understand as no one else could that my love for Van would always be with me. Not only had he lost his own beloved wife, but he was exceedingly fond of Van and knew that our marriage had been very happy—he had heard that from Van and I had told him that in a letter. Lord, what a quandary. How to handle this situation consumed me to such an extent that I flubbed a whole day's office work and was bawled out again.

Doc Squire said, "You've found him, haven't you? Which one is it?"

I hotly denied I had found anyone, but he replied, "If that was your problem today I was willing to forgive your goofs, but if that isn't the case you can just stay late and rewrite the fantastically lousy letters you typed for me to sign."

I did what I was told and missed Jim's call, but Mother took the message that he could not come that weekend and would drive down the following one, as he had located some retread tires.

As Mom Perkins was home, I thought I had better go back up to Craggy, where I had Van all around me and could see Jim in a background that meant everything to me.

Eight days later Jim arrived in his beloved red convertible. Pam dashed out to see him, planted her feet squarely in front of him, and, looking up and down at his uniform and cap, asked, "Are you my Daddy?"

"Well that's a mighty nice idea," he replied. "We'll have to talk it over, you and I."

"Would you like to see my cat who is named Black Raspberry but of course we call her Raz, don't you know?" said Pam.

Jim answered, "No, I didn't know you called her Raz, and yes, I'd like to see her."

So before I could even greet Jim, Pam dragged him off behind the house to see her cat, holding his hand in a vise-like grip and pulling with all her strength. Jim, grinning from ear to ear, allowed me a brief sentence by way of a greeting, over his shoulder, "At long last I meet the first lady of the *Atlanta*."

Once inside the house, I introduced Mom and Pop Perkins to Jim. Pam, much to Jim's delight, started crawling all over him. I hesitated to stop her, for she had never taken to any of the other men who had come to see me with such exuberance.

Mom and Pop Perkins welcomed Jim as though they had known him a long time. He seemed at ease with them, so it was a happy dinner we had. I wanted to talk to Jim alone, but my daughter and my parents-in-law had thus far completely monopolized him. When nobody made a move to go to bed, I said, clear out of the sky, "Well Jim, if we're going to go to Lucette and Dave's party, we better get a move on."

Jim looked startled. Mom and Pop Perkins looked even more so. I had started a lie which had to be finished. "Oh goodness, I forgot to tell you my pal Lucette, called this morning to ask if I'd come over this evening. I told her I would if I could include Jim."

We got in the red convertible and drove up the road to the bridge over the Merritt Parkway. "This is Lucette and Dave's, stop the car," I said. "Besides it's a full moon tonight and this is a good place to see it."

So far Jim had not spoken a word, but he stopped the car. He gave me a cigarette, took one for himself, lit both, and finally asked, "What is this all about anyway?"

I swallowed hard. It was now or never, so I simply said, "I think maybe I love you."

Jim stamped out first mine then his cigarette, turned, and kissed me. Then he said in a low voice, "Oh, Lord, it's too soon. I thought yes and then no and now I don't know."

"I understand, Jim. It is too soon, but I had to tell you because that's the way I am. I can't play coy games, but I do know that if this is as right as I think it is, you'll know in good time and so will I." Then I lit a new cigarette. I gave myself a brief space to think. "To go further, Jim, I said 'think,' not 'know.' You know as well as I do that I will always love Van as you will love Jane. This is something different that we need to think clearly about. Compassion for each other isn't enough. With time we'll find out if we have something good here or not."

Jim's reply was to turn and kiss me tentatively, but seconds later his kiss was no longer tentative.

8

A Predatory Female

JUNE 1945–DECEMBER 1946

Jim spent the following weekend at Wesleyan College with a young WAVE officer who was teaching ROTC students. He said she was a very nice, "intelligent" girl he had met in Boston, who had been writing reams of letters to him ever since Jane's death. Sunday evening Jim called to tell me he had had a nice time. "I got myself in a jam when my ensign friend said she'd like to come to Newport next weekend," he said. "I said that would be nice, but before I could finish my sentence, she broke in with, 'O.K. that's settled, I'll see you Friday.' Now what do I do?"

"Jim, why don't you bring her down here for the weekend; there's a dance Saturday night. I'll get a date so all four of us can go. That would be fun, eh?"

Boy, it worked! He agreed.

Jim's emphasis on the word "intelligent" made me think I had better spike this in a hurry. The first order of business was to get myself a date who would help me play my little game, showing me to have as many smarts as Ensign Ruth.

I called my old sailing friend, Tim, and asked him, "Do you think you could help me dispose of a young lady who is doing her best to oust me from my friend Jim's affections?"

"What do you want me to do, Betts? Give her the old heave ho?"

"Just go to the Beach Club dance, supposedly as my date. In fact, you should tell Ruth that I taught navigation to CAP youth, that I crewed for you on your Star boat, anything you think of that will let Jim know I'm not a cream puff.

Don't tell him any of that, just tell Ruth when you're sure Jim is listening."

Next Saturday I took Jim and Ensign Ruth to a restaurant for lunch, sat briefly with them, and then excused myself, saying, "I must be going, I have some urgent business. I'll be back in a couple of hours to pick you up."

Jim shot me a look of sheer desperation, which his lady friend, engrossed in reading the menu, did not see.

"Bon appétit, my dears," I said, hoping that sounded a touch worldly. And off I went. Two hours later I returned to find a glum Jim and a silent young lady who was gazing out the window.

That evening Ruth made a splendid mistake all on her own. She chose to wear an evening dress with a "sweet sixteen, never been kissed" effect that belied her thirty years. It made her look kittenish. Tim played his part to perfection. "You two ladies have a lot in common, I gather," he said. "You teach ROTC students and she teaches CAP students. Is that right?"

Ruth replied, "Well I would hardly call that anything in common! After all, I teach at the college level."

"I should think it harder to teach an advanced course to seventeen year olds than to college level," Tim answered.

Ruth turned to Jim, but he was looking at me in amazement as he said, "Van told me a lot about you, and the Civil Air Patrol was part of it, but he didn't mention your teaching that I remember."

When we finished dinner Jim continued to talk to me. Ruth directed a few inconsequential remarks to him, but he answered her as briefly as politeness would allow. Obviously my ruse had worked, and by the time we left for the dance, we had switched dates. I heard no more about brilliant Ruth for quite some time.

Once again Jim came for the weekend in July. We walked in the woods with Pam, who not only climbed several trees but also persuaded Jim to climb one also. He told her, "I used to climb seven ladders to my battle station at the top of the ship's island which was a pretty scary place to be, but not near as scary as it is up here in this tree. I think you'll have to help me down." Miss Pamie instructed Jim: "Put your foot on that limb below your foot. Now the other foot down there, see, it's easy. I knew you could do it because Navy men can do anything, Mummy says."

Pam was entranced with the man she had "saved from the tree," and I was entranced with the way Jim had captivated her. Jim was entranced with Pam's earnest endeavor. We were just plain entranced, all three together.

We had had a pleasant time dancing at the club Saturday night. Though Jim was not the fine dancer Van had been, it was easier to dance with him, for he was not as tall as Van so I did not have to stand on my toes or stretch my head quite so far. The next morning we went swimming up at the dam. Once again I compared Jim to Van. They were equally graceful swimmers, something that pleased me tremendously. I lazed atop the dam, and the sculptor in me looked with pleasure as he swam.

We returned to Craggy and joined Mom Perkins reading the Sunday papers. Jim found the funnies to read to Pam. Wood arrived in time for lunch, and the two men talked a bit about the war. It was obvious they liked each other, which also pleased me.

After lunch we walked around the pond while Pam was napping, Jim holding my hand. We talked about Van and Jane and what they meant to us as easily as though we four were together. It was a shimmering time. There was a mossy spot in the pine grove where we sat down. "Bettsy darling," Jim said. "I love you. I don't know what I want, I don't know where I'm going. I just know that when I'm with you I'm content. When we're apart I have nightmares, I'm all tense and I miss you. I love you girl, how much I don't know, I want to stay right here always."

"Jim, I want to stay here too, and shut the war and the world out. We've a long way to go before we know what we're doing, but for now, to feel like this is enough. It's so wonderful just to feel needed once again, isn't it?"

I drove Jim up to the train that evening and sang all the way home.

Jim had no phone, so I wrote:

Here is another letter written by the light of the "midnight oil." I seem to have so much to tell you and I would so much rather speak it to you than write it to you. What's more, I miss you unbelievably tonight and wish I could tell you.

Sunday night when I got home Mom was acting a bit strange as she always does when she has something on her mind. Sensing it might be about us I started talking about Woodie and his girl and kept that up 'til bedtime which was early as I was exhausted.

But tonight when I got home from work Mom was fidgeting again so after dinner I said, "What is it Mom, you upset about Jim and me?" She said, "No, I was just afraid you wouldn't tell me about it and I want to know because I want you to be happy."

Now darn it, isn't it wonderful for her to feel that way? Well, I didn't tell her very much but I did tell her how I felt when I was with you and that I wanted to see a lot of you. She said that she hoped you'd come down often. That she'd think of some way for me to stay in Newport and if we knew what we were doing, she was all for it. I told her we didn't know what we were doing yet and that was why we wanted to see a lot of each other. I feel so much better about having her know and approve because Jim, I am devoted to both Mom and Pop Perkins and I wouldn't hurt them for anything in the world.

Also today, at lunch, Mummy said, "Bettsy you're in love with Jim aren't you?" and I said, "Sweetie it's none of your business yet but what makes you think so." She said "Because I know you and you don't act delighted with everyone and you were obviously delighted with Jim." So I said, "We will now drop the subject until I feel like talking about it please," and that was that. All of this amazed me because I thought we were as casual as could possibly be, didn't you?

Jim, last night I went off to sleep in a pink mist. I was just floating around in happy thoughts, but today, more particularly tonight, I am scared. Scared that I imagined the whole thing and that what you said you didn't mean. That you arrived in Newport and said to yourself "ho hum tomorrow's another day." And went happily on your way. The only thing I'm sure of is that we had a wonderful, wonderful time and that it was too short. Much too short.

The following weekend Jim said he was going to stay home and study. Instead, he hitched a ride with Dick, one of the War College aviators who needed to get in some flight time.

At Quonset Point, where they climbed into an SNJ two-seater plane, Jim was surprised to be greeted by a plane mechanic from the *Bunker Hill*. "Hello, Sir," he said. "I haven't seen you since that day! Here, let me buckle your shoulder straps."

Off they flew heading for the Westchester Airport, just outside of Greenwich. Coming in over Greenwich, the motor spluttered and then conked out. The heavy plane rapidly lost altitude.

"I didn't do that!" Dick said. "I'm going to head for that golf course, it's the only open space I see. I'm going to ride her down. You can jump if you want to."

"If you're sticking, so am I. Watch out for the golfers!" Jim shouted over the headphone.

Dick, picking the only unoccupied fairway and thinking to save the plane, lowered the wheels.

They careened along until they plowed into a sand trap, stopping so abruptly the plane nosed over and Jim, in the rear cockpit, felt his head smash into the ground; a searing pain shot down his arm. The plane rebounded, suspending Jim upside down, hanging by the shoulder straps his *Bunker Hill* shipmate had buckled for him.

Golfers from all over the course converged on the crashed plane. One fellow dashed at Jim to unstrap him. Jim shouted, "Don't touch me! I've broken something. You'll have to have help to get me out."

Leaning over Jim, still hanging upside down, the brilliant fellow asked, "Who's your doctor?"

"Where the hell am I?" Jim snapped.

"Greenwich, Connecticut, of course," the puffed up fellow replied.

"Dr. Perkins, Guinea Road," Jim said between clenched teeth.

Meanwhile, unaware that Jim was coming to see me, I had taken Pamie to the Beach Club to go swimming. I was paged. When I answered the phone, Mom Perkins said, "Bettsy dear, I've just had a call from the Greenwich Hospital for Woodie. They say they have a Commander Shaw there with a broken neck. Could that be Jim?"

I flew into my ratty old dungarees, tossed Pamie to Nane, and took off for the hospital, arriving just in time to hop into the Red Cross ambulance in which they had already loaded Jim. A Navy doctor who had come down from Noroton Navy Communications Installation insisted that Jim, according to naval regulations, be taken to St. Albans Naval Hospital on Long Island. The Greenwich doctor in attendance vigorously protested, to no avail. Nevertheless, the Navy doctor allowed me to ride with Jim.

Dick, the pilot, who had suffered only a minor cut, drove my car, following us. We proceeded at a sedate thirty miles an hour until the parkway ended, at which point the lady ambulance driver sped up, hitting every pothole she could find until the doctor finally ordered her to slow down. Poor Jim, he only said in objection, "Judas Priest!" every time he was bounced about.

I stayed with Jim as long as the doctor would allow me, then Dick and I proceeded to Greenwich. After one drink, Dick insisted we go to a dance at the club as he did not want to jitter the evening away. I was beside myself with anxiety, but with no official status, I knew there was nothing to do but wait for tomorrow.

So started my daily treks to St. Albans. Once again the family chipped in gas rations and Mom and Pop Perkins took care of my daughter. Doc Squire let me leave work at three instead of four. Everyone conspired to help me visit Jim.

Jim's old skipper, Deke Evans, came to see him, and we sat out in the corridor together while a corpsman was attending to Jim. We talked for about half an hour most enjoyably. "You know I never had a finer officer than Jim Shaw," he said. "He is not only brilliant, he's a leader and he has an hilarious sense of humor."

"Oh Deke," I answered, "Van used to tell me that before I knew Jim well and I didn't believe him for Jim was always shy around me."

Deke laughed. "Rest assured, Jim Shaw is not shy and he is funny. He must like you a lot if he's quiet around you." And off he went to see Jim, leaving me to puzzle over that last remark.

Shortly Deke returned, announcing, "I just told Jim Shaw he was nuts if he didn't marry you, and you're nuts if you don't marry Jim. In addition, I knew and loved both Jane and Van also and now I think you and Jim would make a great pair."

When I went into Jim's room, he laughed and handed me a letter from his sister Betty Lou. "Take a look at that and maybe you'll get some idea about my little sister's erroneous ideas about you," he said. Betty Lou wrote, "You have to realize that you are both vulnerable, and a most eligible bachelor. You should be on your guard, Big Brother, I don't want you to make a mistake. . . . If you ask me, yes I know you haven't, I'd say she's a predatory female. You know it takes one to know one. Watch out."

Ouch, I said to myself. I'll have to get to know Betty Lou better and mend some fences.

Jim's eyes were twinkling. "On the other side of the ledger," he said, "here's old Deke telling me I'm crazy if I don't marry you. Who do you think I should listen to?"

"Commander Shaw, you're a big boy," I told him. "I think you shouldn't listen to either of them. You make up your own mind and I'll make up my own mind. If we are of like mind, the answer will be obvious. Your sister has every right to be leery of me. I was awful to her in San Francisco. I was a star-struck kid at the time. Maybe I'll get a chance to see her again and I hope I can change her mind."

The next day, 11 August 1945, Jim was given three hours' liberty. Not long enough to go to Greenwich and too long to sit on a bench out of doors or in some two-bit restaurant without air conditioning. Heat really bothered Jim's neck. He was fitted with a cast of plaster of Paris over felt. The pressure had already rubbed his skin raw, and it made his eyes bulge. What he needed was an air-conditioned room with some sort of lounge chair so he could rest his top-heavy head. We opted for a room at the Howard Hyatt Motel, and there Jim suggested that Deke was right. We had better find a justice of the peace.

"No siree-bob, Jim Shaw," I answered to this suggestion. "If we decide to get married, we'll do it properly, in a church, with a proper minister and our families there to show they approve."

My Lord, I was acting like my own father, talking about being proper and acting most conventional, while lounging about in a motel room in a most improper fashion and flying in the face of prewar conventions. Odd about-face it may have seemed, but I was simply recognizing that Jim and I were not ready to get married.

Jim was released from the hospital the next afternoon. I drove him back to Greenwich for a week of sick leave complete with the "Queen Anne Collar," as the cast on his neck was dubbed. He looked very strange in his uniform, which would not button over the cast, his eyes as big as saucers. We stopped in Greenwich to pick up some beer.

By chance, my good CAP friend was coming down the sidewalk. I stopped her. "Hey Molly," I said. "Come over to the car a sec, I want you to meet the man I think I might marry."

Molly went home to her husband that night and told him, "Bettsy Perkins introduced me to the guy she says she thinks she's going to marry. You should see him, he looks like a G.D. frog! He doesn't have any neck and he is popeyed. Whatever has got into her I'm sure I don't know."

One week later Jim's cast was replaced by a light metal brace, and he was on his way back to the War College by train. Molly was on the station platform as I was saying goodbye to Jim. She came up to me as the train pulled out.

"Who was that good-looking man you just kissed goodbye? I thought you said you were going to marry the Frog Man. You're fickle, old girl."

"That, my dear friend Mol, was the very same Frog Man and I still think I may marry him. You'll have to wait and see what we do decide."

Molly pestered me all fall about Jim, and I just let her guess. I did not have the answer myself.

A Penny a Pull

During Jim's stay on the paraplegic ward at St. Albans, on 9 August 1945, the second atomic bomb was dropped, this time on Nagasaki. The radio on the ward blared the news and declared it meant the end of the war. That day a great shout rose up, then silence profound. Suddenly the triple paraplegic lad I had befriended cried, "What will become of us now! Oh, my God, we'll be forgotten and lie here to rot!" My attempt to stop his hysterical crying and to comfort him came to naught. I had to call a corpsman, who gave him a shot to quiet him down.

The Navy stayed on a wartime footing while negotiations took place. Finally, the true end of the war came on 2 September, and with it many odd emotions.

Writing to Jim, I described my day. I did not tell him of the empty feeling I had, nor how Mom and I cried together for Van. It was the only time we ever cried. When the bells started ringing, I put aside my sorrow once again:

> The true end of the war is incredible. I am celebrating in bed with a mild sunstroke brought on by a series of events culminating with a day in the hazy sun which burned me and my brain to a crisp. Neither body nor brain big enough to take much burning at this point. At least it has immobilized me and I am listening to the entire country go wild instead of going wild myself.
>
> . . . Down Stanwich Rd., the little church bell has been pealing constantly for two hours. I think every kid in the neighborhood must be paying the Parson a nickel for a pull on the rope, or perhaps it should be "pay the Parson a penny a pull." Pam has tooted her tin horn out in the road 'til she is dizzy, over she knows not what, except that everyone else in the road is making noise. I wish I weren't so dizzy, I'd go add to the clamor.
>
> Mother, Nane and Dad have just left. They came bearing a bottle of champagne which celebrated the occasion by exploding in the car, but enough was salvaged for me to drink a long one to "Peace and plenty of it."
>
> Happy, Happy end of war sweet one.

I did write another note that night. Here we had just won a world conflagration and already we had no idea how to handle peace. It had come so suddenly and in such a violent way!

> I wonder if at this moment they, the Japanese, are despairingly turning their heads to the wall?
>
> Do you realize that we have no conception of the emotion of National disgrace let alone degradation. I can't conjure a picture of peace in our land let alone one of defeat, and I think that right this minute Japan must be in the throes of all the painful emotions possible. I can't help feeling a moment's pang for them for not all of them are bad. I am a sentimental fool when people are in trouble.
>
> Have just talked to you and am sorry you are so tired. Perhaps you have followed San Francisco's mood? Sleep heartily for two days, my pet. Perhaps you will feel better. I love you more than you know.

Alone in Newport, it struck Jim for the first time how lucky he was to be alive and in one piece. On a roller coaster of emotions, he became unsure of himself, depressed about the war and its aftermath and shaken by his plane accident. He worried a lot about his next assignment, about the lads on the ward who would spend their lives in devastation, about Jane's parents' reaction to me when he introduced me to them, and finally about Betty Lou, whose opinion, above all, he cherished.

About this time Jane's family, Colonel and Mrs. Holt, arrived to take up their new post, finding an apartment in Brooklyn Heights. We went down to see them. Jim was so nervous he took a wrong turn in lower Manhattan and we headed the wrong way on a one-way street. Halfway down the block the car horn got stuck, and in seconds a police car pulled us over.

"What do you think you're doing?" the cop said. "Stop that racket and turn around."

"The horn's stuck; I'm lost. I'm trying to get to the Brooklyn Bridge and I'm from Minnesota," Jim explained.

"Well, I'll be!" the cop replied. "So am I. Come on, we'll pull the horn wires and I'll lead you to the bridge."

What luck! Jim relaxed a bit. By the time we got to the Holts' apartment he was laughing. He told them about our experience, then he said, "Elizabeth and Rufus, you are my family, and it is important to me to know how you'd feel if Betts and I decided to get married."

An awkward pause ensued until Rufus walked over to Jim and clapped him on the shoulder. "Congratulations," he said. "We want you to be happy."

Elizabeth joined in with a hug for me, saying, "Jim is like a son to us and though we'd hoped he'd marry a girl with no parents whom we could adopt, we want mostly his happiness, and with your mutual backgrounds, I'm sure you'll make our Jim happy."

That meant that three of the four sides of our family approved of our marrying. Only Betty Lou left to go. Jim went to the phone and called her in Carmel. Her letter, which came several days later, laid to rest my fears:

> You sounded so happy last night. I'm glad for you. We will just let bygones be bygones and start all over again as though I'd never met her.
>
> Robby is going to be stationed on the East Coast and I'm coming East with the baby. I'm not sure where we'll be but I'll let you know as soon as possible. New York, I think.
>
> Congratulations, Big Brother, I'm glad you're happy.

Jim gave me a beautiful engagement ring, which I wore when we were together, for there was still some hesitancy between us when we were apart. The end of the war had something to do with it. For so many years, ever since Manila days, we had lived in fear, under pressure. Now the pressure was gone—like a dentist, after endlessly drilling an aching tooth, stopping abruptly. You can't believe the ache has gone for good, and you hold your cheek waiting for the pain to return. So it was with us.

When we were together everything was fine. We even went so far as to plan to get married in February or March and to announce our engagement the second of December. That would be after graduation from the War College, where Jim had been asked to stay on as an instructor. This would give him time to settle into his new job and, important to me, it would be two years since last I had seen Van, almost three years since Jane had died.

Betty Lou arrived with her baby to stay briefly in Newport, to see Jim and pick up her stepdaughter, who had spent the summer with her grandparents also stationed there. I went to Newport, ostensibly to visit Deke and Peg but actually to see Betty Lou and, I hoped, to make amends. Our lunch together was a grand success, and by the time it was over we had become good friends. We had much in common other than Jim: Manila, China, the Navy, and Dale, her stepdaughter, whose mother had died giving birth. Boo had married a widower. My daughter and Betty Lou's stepdaughter were both blue-eyed, blonde, almost–four year olds. We could have talked on and on.

Betty Lou stayed with us as we had house-hunted for her without success. Purely by chance I got wind that a friend of mine was closing her house and going south to join her husband, not due to be released from the Army for another eight months. What a break for Bou and Robby. It was a secluded and charming house with a beautiful guest cottage attached by a long walkway. Robby would have quite a commute to the Navy Yard, but the train service from Greenwich was more than adequate. Jim was well pleased with the arrangement, for he could visit his sister on the weekends I did not go to Newport.

On one of the Greenwich weekends I decided to get our vague plans finalized and made a mistake on the subject by pushing Jim into a corner and asking him to make a decision.

A Decision and a Deadline

I called Jim on the apartment house phone Sunday night. He told me it was definite that he was being ordered to the War College as an instructor, to which I said, "Wonderful, we can go ahead as planned and announce our engagement on December second. Then get married anytime after that when you're used to your new job. You set the date, OK?"

Jim's reply was that he wanted to think about it and would write. The hesitancy in his voice set me back on my heels enough to warrant writing him the next evening. That same night he wrote me. Our letters crossed. His letter first:

> Your phone call yesterday set in motion a long train of thought which had been bogged down inside my head for some time. You told me you'd like some information, some definite word on plans. Well, my dear, that's what this letter is about.

Previously any attempt to elicit dates from me has always been countered. Whether I gave any reasons or not, the reasons in the forefront of my mind were two. Namely, I did not know what my orders would be, and I wanted to see my sister before taking any definite steps. Neither of those reasons holds good any longer. So a new analysis of my hesitancy must be undertaken.

For definitely there is hesitancy. I do not want to commit myself. I'm afraid to make any crucial decisions. Now, you will admit that from both our viewpoints that is not good. Marriage must be welcomed completely by both individuals. It is a contract for which there can be no reservations. Yet the fact remains that I do not feel myself ready for marriage.

It is not difficult to realize your position Bettsy. You want to know what the score is and you deserve to know it. Yet neither of us would ever be happy if we embarked upon a life together wherein there was not complete understanding.

You will now ask why I didn't say something about this previously. The answer to that is that I wasn't aware of it. My mind would automatically leap to a logical reason as to why we should delay. There are no logical reasons of that type left to confuse myself with.

Is it that I'm not in love with you? Is it that I don't want to assume the responsibilities inherent with marriage? What is it? I don't know at this moment. There have been times, as you well know, when I would have hurried you off to a J.P. if you'd have gone. There have also been other times when inexplicable doubts have assailed me. You've known of some of those occasions. These doubts are present now.

All of this has me more than a little perturbed. I'd have preferred to talk directly with you about it since it doesn't appear that I'll be able to get away this weekend, I want you to know my thoughts even if they must come in this written fashion.

Now what of the future? Bettsy, my dear, if you wish me to continue seeing you in the hopes that all this uncertainty is transitory, all right, we'll do it that way. But if you feel that the whole thing is hopeless, then say that too. It's unfair for you to be tied to me when I don't know my own mind.

We've both had our share of emotional ordeals and I hate to precipitate another one. Honestly though Bettsy, I must be honest with you and myself. I am not going to marry until I am certain sure it is the right thing for me to do. With the war over, the urgency of life has ceased to be. There is no necessity for taking any steps which will be a subsequent cause for regret.

What your reaction to this letter will be, bewilderment, sorrow, anger, or relief, I can't say. It hurts like the devil writing it and it will cost me much courage and loss of sleep to post it.

To more pleasant subjects than my confused mind.

I have ordered two tickets for the Army-Navy game. If I can get away and if you will consent to go with me, we'll go together.

This coming weekend is Command on Saturday with Navy Day [28 October 1945]. There will be official goings on which I cannot skip so I've foregone plans for a trip south. . . .

There are a million and one things left unsaid in this letter. I'm at a loss for further words.

My letter to Jim had the right effect on him, counteracting his letter:

My sweet, tonight I think I am thinking clearly. Probably more clearly than I have done in the past five or six weeks. Perhaps because I don't feel any urgent reason to make decisions. Which point of view I reached last night while tossing around in my bed.

I pushed at you this past weekend, a decision and a deadline. Now I feel strongly that I was entirely unjust in so doing. I don't want you to make up your mind before I see you next. I want you to make up your mind either way at such time as the situation becomes intolerable to you. I don't mean to say I'm going to sit around and wait for two or three years for you to make up your mind. I'm not. Because if you don't know in the next six months or so what you want you never will and because I am so constructed that I'd tear myself to pieces inside. I can take what I know about.

You are in a state of mind that I have been in, and I know how utterly impossible it is to make decisions. You honestly don't know what you want. It is a pleasure to be together and that is enough for right now.

Also you put your finger on a point that it took me a while to apply to your present status.

You said, "out there we lived for what the next eighteen or twenty four hours would bring us."

Quite true, you have had no time to re-adjust to the way of life that demands that you plan in the future. You schooled yourself in looking only as far as tomorrow when the war started. It took time to get yourself to that point of view. Now it is going to take time to realize that life is normal again.

There is no violent incentive to do anything except relax. That my darling, is the most urgent problem you should have at the moment and I don't want it any other way. So I beg you not to even try to make up your mind. It will come to you without your struggling over it. Either you do or you don't want to marry me. It will become clear later on.

Each day I see you, you have relaxed a little more. You no longer tell me that there is a car about to hit us when the car is a hundred yards off to the right. Nor do you tense up as obviously when someone makes a stupid remark about the war or your part in it, and in many little ways, you are relaxing a bit at a time.

What I want is for you to feel completely at ease and still want me to be around always, and if you feel that way later on it will be a mighty and glorious thing as far as I am concerned.

Jim was involved with Navy Day the following Saturday, but he had not said he was busy Saturday night or Sunday. He called me Thursday. I told him a bald-faced lie I had rehearsed several times to try to make it ring true. "Darling," I said. "I've decided it would be good for both of us if I try going out with other men. So I've accepted an invitation to go up to Boston tomorrow and go to a party Friday night with an old beau of mine."

"Er-r-r," was his answer. And after a pause, "What are you doing Saturday night?"

"Coming back to Greenwich as things stand now." So far, not bad.

"Well, what would you think if I hopped the Boston bus after the Navy Day ceremony is over. Could you stay over?"

"I guess I could if Adelaide, my brother-in-law Joe's twin sister, can have me an extra night. I'm not sure, I'll have to call her."

"Do that and call me back. I'll wait right here."

Quickly I called a surprised Adelaide. "I need your help in a scheme, Adelaide. Can you put me up Friday and Saturday night and maybe have Jim Shaw for Saturday night also? I'll explain later. It's very important and I'm in a hurry."

"Certainly Betts. Fortunately my girls' rooms are free this weekend. What are you up to?"

When I talked to Jim he said he would get to Adelaide's by seven and we could go to the Ritz Carlton for dinner by eight. "I'll not have time to change out of my uniform to make it," he added. This was a smart ploy on his part. He knew from many parties in 1943 that in uniform he would get the best service at the Ritz. He also knew I thought him handsome so dressed.

Saturday night in Boston was total perfection. We did not need to talk about anything to do with indecision, for the minute Jim walked in the door at Adelaide's I could see he now knew what he wanted.

At dinner Jim said, "Would you have me, Betts? I know the only person for me is you. Will you marry me, beloved?"

"Oh yes, oh yes, you know I will. I knew we were right when you called me Thursday. You knew I was lying, didn't you?"

"Yes, darling, I did. You're a rotten liar. Your letter turning me loose convinced me I didn't want to be without you ever. I thought it would be good to play your game out. Oh you tickle me, my girl."

"You know Jim, I knew something good would happen tonight. Important things happen to me in October. Pam was born October 11, Van found me in October eight years ago, married me in October six years ago, and today you ask me to marry you, in October! Of course, Van was killed in October—that was tragic. Odd, isn't it, that if Jane and Van hadn't died we'd not be sitting here holding hands. I think that says something. I think they are smiling down at us. Let's thank them for leading us to each other."

"Bettsy girl, I've felt that way too but didn't know how to say it. Now for the first time I tell you, unconditionally, I love you. I love all four of us."

When Jim returned to Newport he wrote me the only love letter I had from him before we were married:

This has been a lonely week away from you yet it's hard to express my feeling in words. My mind and heart fill up to overflowing with emotions you should have described to you. Then I see you or start writing and they don't come out.

I love you. It's as simple as all that. Ah, but it isn't. The statement is simple but the sentiment is oh so complex. It's a feeling of sharing things, experiences, hours, material objects. It's a feeling of unselfishness—wanting to make you happy. It's a feeling of pride—pride at being with you, pride at looking upon you. It's a feeling of repose—contentment in your company. These are just a few of the most elemental of my thoughts. . . .

Bettsy, beloved, you looked more beautiful in Boston than you ever have. You were positively radiant and I basked happily in the glow of that radiance. It was wonderful.

I wish you were here to be clasped in my arms at this moment. I love you, I love you. X-X-X for Pamela.

When I got home from Boston, I told Mother and Mom to go ahead and make plans to have a party to announce our engagement on 2 December, which would be the Sunday night after the Army-Navy game. We made a small list of my friends, another of Mother and Mom's friends. Jim would call the Holts, and of course all the family would be included. As my wardrobe was woefully depleted and because the really pretty winter dresses would all be sold by Christmas time, I set about getting a few clothes to round out my meager wardrobe, including something appropriate for a second wedding. Mother wanted to know when we intended to get married. I said that was still undecided, probably February or March. No great hurry, for Jim would be at the War College for a couple of years, where he was to be an instructor on the staff.

The Naval War College was the Navy's graduate school. Jim already stood at the top of his class but needed to write his final paper. There was enough for him to do to finish his thesis without me to bother him, so I stayed home for a bit to see brother-in-law Joe, who had come home from the war. He and Nane were going to the Homestead in Virginia for a postwar honeymoon. Also, Pop Perkins was out of the Navy, working in Hartford and home for the weekend at Craggy. I took Pamie up to visit with him.

It was so pleasing to have Pop put his arm around me, kiss me, and say, "Betts, you couldn't have chosen a finer man. Mom and I are so delighted about you and Jim, though I'd think it's hard on you to marry in the Navy again."

"Pop, I don't feel comfortable in civilian life. Despite all, I love Navy life. I guess I'd have married Jim if he had been a civilian. I won't ever know that, however, for there's no doubt Jim is definitely in the Navy. I'm glad you like him so much."

A letter from Jim written on 20 November said he still suffered from his years in the tropics:

> I think you better come up here for my graduation, a number of reasons being in view. We can start lining up this house business for one thing. We'll discuss it at the Army-Navy game.
>
> (Incidentally, tell your father that I will bet him a scotch and soda on the game offering him Army and seven points.)
>
> This weekend promises to be hectic. Tomorrow night is the War College party. Then dinner on Thanksgiving at the Farrions. Saturday, two cocktail parties and a dinner party. Friday, for some unknown reason, I've been invited to lunch with the Admiral and some Major General. . . .
>
> I love you completely, beloved, always and always. —It's 75 degrees below zero and I miss you.

Damn, I thought, I am going up this weekend. I have stayed home long enough and those parties sound like fun. Up I went Saturday morning. We had a grand time all right. The drive home Sunday was exhausting. I flopped into bed without even unpacking.

In a Cocked Hat

Early the next morning, Pamie woke me up by jumping on my stomach. "Mummy, Mummy," she said excitedly, "Uncle Jim Shaw called me yesterday afternoon and asked me to marry him along with you. Did you hear me?"

"Ya, I heard you. What did you tell him?"

"I told him Okey Dokey of course. I wanted to stay up late last night only Gramma wouldn't let me. Now what do I call him?"

"Pamie darling," I said, "What do you want to call him?"

She puzzled on that a minute or so and then said, "Daddy Jimshaw. Is that OK?"

"That's OK, my Pumpkin. Now let me get up, I have to go to work."

"Oh Mummy, I love you," she said and flew off to wake up the rest of the house.

Jim called me at the office, something he never did, or at least he had not done since the day he had arrived from the war. Apprehensively I said, "What is it, darling?"

"Betts, I can't stand what's happened. I just received dispatch orders to Japan."

"Good God! What does that mean? Can they just cancel your present orders like that?"

"It means, Betts, that I have ten days to get transportation to Japan, there to report to commander, Fifth Fleet, Admiral Sherman in command, to be his flag secretary. I barely know the man. He was on the *Bunker Hill* for a time but I hardly had anything to do with him. Why he asked for me I'm sure I don't know, but I do know it shoots our plans in a cocked hat."

"Jim, I'll get home and re-pack and come right up. I'm going to take the train. Can you meet me in Westerly? I'm too tired to drive. I'll just stay there through your graduation."

Telling Doc Squire I was taking a week off because I had an emergency, I tore home to Mother. She was absolutely great. She said, "Bettsy, you and Jim work this out anyway you see fit. You just get up to Newport and call us when you know what you're going to do. Oh my! Would you be going to Japan?"

"No, Mum. No dependents are allowed out there. Oh, Mum, it's happened again!" I bit my lip, horrified. "How much do I have to take? Am I star-crossed and will I star-cross Jim—Lord could I have jinxed my Van?—oh, no, I'm not going to think that way."

"Hold on Bettsy Perkins, you hurry up and get to Jim. We'll do all we can on this end. You get hold of yourself. The last thing Van would want would be for you to think this way. He wanted you to be happy. You and Jim get on with living! Now hurry up!"

Jim met me in Westerly. It did not take us five minutes to decide we would get married right away so that when families were allowed to go to Japan I would be a dependent entitled to join my husband. We went to Jim's apartment and talked about arrangements. We decided to be married Saturday, then go to Washington and see if Jim could get out of going, or at least get thirty days' leave. We called Mother and Dad around 9:30 to tell them our plans.

"No sir!" said Dad. "You will get married on Friday. I have never missed an Army-Navy game since the 1915 game when I came home from the Philippines, and I don't intend to miss this one."

Jim and I collapsed with laughter. When I got hold of myself, I said, "OK, we'll make it four o'clock at Rosemary Chapel."

"Nope," Dad replied. "It will have to be at noon. We're going to the theater in Philadelphia with some of my classmates Friday night."

Jim grabbed the phone. "Anything you say, Colonel. I have to graduate on Thursday afternoon, but anytime Friday suits me! Noon it is!"

I told Mum to get hold of all of the family who were home (my brothers Jim and Bill were still overseas), the Holts, the Perkinses, including Van's brother Woodie, and of course Betty Lou and her husband Robby, my godparents, and a couple of my best friends, and to make a reservation for a hotel in New York Friday night.

The next day I started packing up Jim's apartment, making arrangements to put his books and the handful of furniture, china, and glassware into Navy storage. Wednesday, as soon as the moving men left, I packed Jim's clothes and scrubbed the apartment so that Thursday all we had to do was throw bags in the car and go to graduation. Then by two o'clock we ought to be on our way to Greenwich.

We did not spend much time saying goodbyes after graduation, which had been most impressive, but we took somewhat longer than we had expected. We hustled into the red convertible and made our way in pouring rain to the ferry. By the time we got to the top of the hill on the other side of Narragansett Bay, the rain had turned to snow and it was beginning to get dark. Soon we were in a blizzard, the wind swirling the snow in front of our headlights. We crept along the unplowed road, following the red taillights of a truck ahead of us. By seven o'clock we saw the turnoff for New London and decided to take the train. We headed for the station, where we left the car and all our gear except our overnight bags and Jim's briefcase. We called the family, telling them to meet us in Greenwich at 10:30, and collapsed on the train just as it pulled out of the station.

"I can hardly believe this," I said. "There must be eight or nine inches of snow out there already. The train will make it all right, though."

Wrong! Somewhere between New London and New Haven the train bogged down and the power went out. We sat huddled together in the rapidly cooling, dark car for a good two hours. Then we inched our way along through New Haven. Another long and cold stop in Bridgeport, and finally, at 3:30 in the morning, we arrived in Greenwich. Miraculously, the family were all there to meet us.

Nane and Joe had cut their second honeymoon trip short on hearing our news. Joe and Dad took an exhausted Jim to the pantry for a drink and to regale him with family lore and off-color jokes. It was, they said, Jim's bachelor party. Mother, Nane, and brother Jim's wife, Bobby, whisked me upstairs, where my hair was put up in curlers. Mum outlined what had been done or needed still to be done. "We've invited the people you wanted. We pinned down the Rosemary Chapel, notified the minister, and told the license bureau you'd be there at eight. They said they'd do all the preliminaries. Dad, with Doc Squire's help, got your blood tests waived and he persuaded Judge Hirshberg to waive the three-day waiting period. Iraneo has made you a cake. Marie has cooked a sumptuous feast. Mr. Rocco is coming at ten-thirty to take wedding portraits and will stay to record the proceedings."

My eyes were unwilling to stay open but the list went on.

"Nane and Bobby bought you gloves and a purse to go with your dress. Nane arranged all the flowers in the house and on the altar at the chapel."

My sister-in-law Bobby chimed in. "Nane also ordered you a spray of little yellow orchids for a corsage. The color is just great for your dress."

Rousing myself, I said, "Jim's sword went down with the Atlanta. Did anyone think to get Van's sword from Craggy to cut our cake? That's important!"

"Yes, Mom Perkins brought it down. Pop Perkins gave it a good polishing. They called all the Perkins clan, and Mom bought Pamie an outfit."

Nane continued, "Your sister-in-law-to-be has little Dale all ready with a new outfit as well as one for herself. Robby is taking the day off from his ship to be best man, and Joe is going to stand up with Jim too."

The clock on my bedside table said 5:38. My head was spinning. I wanted nothing so much as to kiss Jim Shaw and go to sleep when all of a sudden it struck me. "Oh Mum," I wailed, "our little red car is sitting in New London with all Jim's clothes and most of his papers! What will we do?"

"Good Lord!" Mum said. "We'll have to think of something. Your father will find someone to go get it. Call your father, Nane, and then everyone go to bed for an hour."

Early that morning Jim and I dashed about Greenwich doing all Mother had outlined. The snow had stopped, but we had to jump over piles three feet high in places. Fifteen inches had fallen during the night.

A weary bride proceeded to the ceremony. The chapel was at Rosemary Hall, my former school, which was in a rather out-of-the-way spot. Twelve o'clock came and went. The guests were all seated, the Holts, the Perkinses, and the Rileys in the front row with the two little girls. Standing at the back of the chapel, I stared at the ceiling for a bit. No Jim. I listened to the creaking chairs and occasional cough. No Jim. At 12:25 the door from the choir room burst open with a bang and a distraught Jim landed in the middle of the guests, snow caked on his trousers up to his knees.

Pulling himself together, Jim addressed our friends. "I'm sorry I'm late. We slid off the road into a snow drift. I'm glad you all waited. Now to the business at hand."

In all respects but one our wedding proceeded traditionally. When the organ stopped playing, my musical daughter piped up with, "Twinkle, twinkle little star," which she sang throughout the service. She certainly had every right to contribute, for she too had been asked to marry Jim. The reception lunch went off without a hitch. Jim unsheathed Van's sword, and for the second time I grasped the handle with my husband. Jim looked down at me, knowing my thoughts. He ran his hand over the place where Van's name was engraved on the blade. He leaned toward me, whispering so that only I could hear, "Thank you, dear friend."

Heroic Achievement

Not too many brides and grooms throw rice at their departing guests, but we were the exception. The family left, heading for Philadelphia, and most of the guests with them. We sped them on their way, with the rice that was meant for us.

Dad had found someone to go to New London for the car, so we unpacked it. Jim fished in his suitcase and pulled out the citations he had received, asking if I thought Dad would put them in a safe deposit box. I put them on Dad's bed with a note of explanation, and we took off for New York.

The rooms we had at the Vanderbilt Hotel were outrageously luxurious and filled with flowers. A note from Mother instructed us to go to Chez Gene, where she had ordered something special. Something special? I should say so. The restaurant was arranged in three tiers. The top one contained a lone table, two chairs, a mammoth bouquet of flowers, and a pair of branched candlesticks. We were escorted to the place of honor. Gene hovered over us while Jim and I attempted to see each other around the flowers and candles. We finally gave it up and sat alone on either side of the table.

Shortly, Eleanor Roosevelt and her party arrived. It was obvious that she was used to sitting where we were. She graciously, but with an inquiring nod of her head in our direction, allowed Gene to escort her to a table on the tier below us. She murmured something to Gene as she took her seat, then, smiling broadly, she stood up facing us and started clapping. A few people joined in, and then the entire restaurant stood clapping. Gene waved his arms and sang "Happy Wedding to You," his customers chorusing along.

Blushing furiously, I stood up and bobbed a curtsy. Jim bowed, saying, "Our deepest thanks and congrat—no—let me start again. Thank you all for so honoring us." We finished our meal, which was indeed superb, and beat a retreat, again amid clapping and congratulations.

We had breakfast in our suite the next morning. Jim pulled out our tickets to the Army-Navy game. "Not much sense to waste these, is there, Betts?" he said.

We flew down to the car and sped toward Philadelphia, wondering where in the world we would park. Unbelievably, at that late hour, we were able to drive the sporty red car right up to our gate and park. We were too late to watch the midshipmen and the cadets march in, but the game had not started. We headed for the class of 1936 section.

The first two people in our row, Dick and Annie Pratt of Manila days, were good friends of Van and me, Jim and Jane. Annie said, "Hi, Bettsy Perkins, I didn't know you knew Jim Shaw well enough to be going out with him."

"Well enough to have married him yesterday," I answered as we continued to our seats.

Annie did a slow double take and, just as we were about to sit down, she shouted, "My God! They're married!!!"

Jim was pounded on the back by his classmates. I was hugged and kissed. We had a wonderful reception right there in the stadium.

Someone piped up, "Hey, you're a double '36 wife, Betts." That pleased me. A friend of Jim whom I did not know clambered up over the seats and asked Jim to introduce me. Jim took my hand, saying, "I'd like you to meet my wife, Mrs. Perkins." Much laughter ensued from Van's and Jim's friends; they were all pleased, and so were we. (On top of that, Navy won the game, so Jim won his bet from Dad.)

We spent the night with Dave and Helen Hall and lazed about the next day talking about all our friends on the *Atlanta*. Then we headed for Greenwich. The road and driveway at Mother and Dad's was full of cars, which was puzzling. Obviously there was a party in full swing.

"Jim, do you know what this is?" I asked. "It's our engagement party! Mum must have forgotten to call it off!"

Sure enough, when Dad spotted us he called for quiet. "You were asked here today so that Gene and I could announce Bettsy's engagement to Commander

James C. Shaw. We are a bit late; we need to amend that. They were married Friday, two days before we got around to the engagement. Never ones to toss over a good party, we saw fit to go ahead with the engagement." More laughter, more congratulations!

Then Dad turned serious. He gave a little speech about Van, he told of Jim's and Van's friendship, he said how proud he was of Joe Anderson, his Army son-in-law. "And now," he said, "I welcome another heroic Navy son-in-law into our family. I want you to hear the citations he received for his achievements during the long years he spent at sea during the war."

Jim was thoroughly embarrassed, but there was no stopping my father when he had an audience's attention. He read Jim's Silver Star citation for the *Atlanta* first, then he read Jim's citations for the *Bunker Hill* actions, which I was hearing for the first time. I was, of course, aware that Jim's chest was full of medals, but he had not talked about the citations.

I listened avidly. Jim fidgeted beside me as Dad read:

Bronze Star Medal: "For heroic achievement while serving successively as Assistant Gunnery Officer and Gunnery Officer of the USS BUNKER HILL, during operations against enemy Japanese forces in the Pacific War Area from November 21, 1943, to May 1, 1945. He assisted in organizing the inexperienced ship's gunnery personnel into an effective fighting team and maintained the fighting efficiency of this department at a high peak, contributing materially to the achievement of an enviable record of destruction of enemy aircraft."

Gold Star in lieu of a Second Bronze Star Medal: "For meritorious achievement as Gunnery Officer of the USS BUNKER HILL during operations against enemy Japanese forces in the vicinity of Okinawa on May 11, 1945. When his ship was struck during determined enemy air attacks, Commander Shaw directed the reorganization of the batteries despite numerous raging fires, and enabled the crippled ship to shoot down a subsequent attacking plane. His professional skill, courage and devotion to duty were in keeping with the highest traditions of the U.S. Naval Service.

Turning lighthearted, Dad quipped, "Let me say that Friday, our son-in-law added one more heroic achievement. He married Betts!"

We headed for Washington on Monday. Three days of Jim's leave were already gone. I sat in the Fairfax Hotel twiddling my thumbs while Jim went to the Naval Bureau of Personnel. He had with him the extraordinary notice of his death, recently sent to his aunt, which he took pleasure in presenting to the personnel officer! This gentleman spluttered that he knew not how such a thing had happened, that never before had such a thing occurred.

"Go on," Jim replied, "I know of at least ten others. I just want to collect my insurance, or assure you, in Twain's words, 'The report of my death is greatly exaggerated.'"

He asked for a thirty-day leave extension and refused to fly to Japan, telling of his recent plane crash and broken neck, and his second marriage of three days' duration. By good fortune, Dick Pratt came into the office as Jim was talking. He said, "I'll do all I can to get you back to shore duty as soon as possible. God knows, you deserve it!" Turning to the detail officer, he said, "Cut new orders giving Commander Shaw thirty days' leave and transportation by sea on 'first available' thereafter from San Francisco to Yokosuka. Does that help, Jim?"

Bless Dick Pratt for giving us such a break! We wasted no time in Washington, catching the first available train back to Greenwich.

Keep Eating

We moved into Bou and Robby's guest cottage, installing Pam in the main house with her new cousin Dale, just in time to be hit again with a blizzard. What fun! We were snowbound in the beautiful guest house with a fire crackling in the fireplace and days ahead to do exactly as we pleased.

We talked a lot about having a baby, for Jim had wanted a child so much, but Jane's death had precluded that. We played with Pam and Dale, making a giant snowman and an igloo of sorts. Jim taught me to target shoot, as he thought all girls should know how to handle a gun. I thought it more likely he just enjoyed training gunners. I never did understand the rationale but was game to try anything he wanted.

The time came to depart for San Francisco. We took Pam to Grandma Perkins. Kissing her goodbye was harder than ever before, for she understood her longed-for new daddy was going away for a long time.

"Don't leave," she cried. "Oh, don't leave me, Mummy, don't leave me, Daddy Jimshaw."

"We'll be back soon, little daughter," he answered her, "and if we're lucky we'll bring you a baby all your own." That cheered her a bit. She waved goodbye, her poor little tear-streaked face giving us a wan smile.

We blew ourselves to the most luxurious accommodations possible on a luxury train, taking stateroom A, where we ordered breakfast in bed, going to the dining car for lunch and dinner, with linen tablecloths and napkins, icewater and butter—all commonplace in trains and restaurants before the war but things we had not seen for a long time. There were real flowers in bud vases and, built into the wall, fish tanks with exotic fish swimming in softly lighted water.

How lovely it was to have our food served by immaculate waiters in white uniforms, even a wine steward sporting a silver chain from which a silver wine tasting bowl was suspended. It was our own private honeymoon fling. During dinner Jim's conversation stumped me.

"Leghorn chickens lay white eggs,' he declared, "and Rhode Island Reds lay brown eggs."

"Hm hum, yup," I mumbled. Fifteen hundred chickens on the Napa ranch had made me chicken savvy.

"Jersey cows produce the most butter."

"Bully for them," was my retort.

"Now about hogs, they too have different characteristics," my brilliant new husband informed me.

"Dear Jim, what's this hogwash about?"

"Bettsy it's about keeping my mind so busy that I won't think about laying my hands on you. Now, about hogs . . ."

We hastily finished our dinner and left the dining car.

When we arrived in San Francisco, my favorite city, Jim dropped me off at the Fairmont Hotel. I settled us in while he went to the Twelfth Naval District to report and find out about his transportation to Japan.

It took me no time at all to unpack, so I went to the window and looked over San Francisco Bay, thinking about how many times Jim and Van had sailed under the Golden Gate Bridge together and separately. I had loved the *Atlanta* for her beauty and the friendships we had all formed. I hated the *Birmingham,* which had carried my darling Van under the Golden Gate Bridge to his death. Now Jim was to go under the same bridge to be stationed on Admiral Sherman's flagship, the USS *Iowa.* He had found me a picture of her that showed another graceful hull and superstructure placed in such a way as to please the sensibilities of my artist's eye. No more deviousness or overweening ambition, Jim's new boss was a man well known for his ability and integrity. Once again, I was filled with a sense of pride. My horror of the *Birmingham* was behind me, my fears of the past were allayed. This would be the Navy I knew and loved.

Jim would be getting back to the hotel shortly, so I decided to use those few minutes to write him a note:

In case you leave before I have time to tell you all that is in my heart for you, I am writing this letter for you to take along and ponder over at your leisure. For some unfathomable reason, I am unable to say with my lips what is brimming over inside me. Yet when I take pen in hand, I can write my love for you as though a dam had burst and my pen puts down a flowing river of words.

How long have we been married? Not just a month, we have been married a space of perfection. Dearest, how very right we are together, how fine it is to love you, fine with the fineness of some rare and delicate object, before which one is awed. How intoxicating it is to love you, to be so frank and passionate with you. And what great fun to love you, so silly with your "I seem to have."

Now if you are down and unhappy, don't be. We are both so lucky "Rollo R." I am full of happy shimmering dreams of the future in which we will go on with our loving and laughing—and soon they'll be real, so there is really nothing to be sad about.

I am about to order you a drink, which you will need when you come in. I am going to wipe off some of my lipstick because I am liable to be kissed and I have too much on for a good one.

. . . Be happy my own, that is the way I love you best of all, tho' I love you no matter what. . . . I will be with you soon and am with you now.

Jim came in the door as I finished my letter, with the happy news that it would be about a week before he would leave for Japan. That gave us a few extra days, which we used to good advantage.

George Mardikian at Omar Khayyam's insisted, once again, on treating us to one of his fabulous meals, saying this was his wedding present. We went to Izzy Gomez's crazy bar. We went to the Top of the Mark, watching the lights come on all over the city as we sipped our drinks. We went to Coit Tower and looked over San Francisco Bay, where we tied a lot of strings together and dusted some cobwebs about the Pacific Ocean out of our minds.

I began to suspect that Jim was to get his heart's desire. Maybe he was going to be a father. He was thrilled and apprehensive at the same time, insisting I see Dr. Norris, who had taken care of me when Van left. Though I protested it was probably too early to tell, Jim badgered me. "I know you've gained a little weight since we've been married, but I want to be assured you're healthy and you're both going to get the right foods. Come on, Betts, go see him like a good girl."

Dr. Norris took me in right away. He had called Dr. Squire to check my health record. "Why, you've gained a mighty four pounds since you've been married," he said. "You weigh 102! Of course, at your height, you should be at least 118 pounds. However, everything else seems fine. I'm pretty sure you'll have your baby in September. We'll be positive when your test comes back, but I think you can safely tell your nice new husband he is going to be a father."

Once again the time had come to stay behind while my husband sailed off to the Pacific. How different this parting was. I had no terrifying premonitions, no fear that this was an ending.

Jim took me in his arms and, kissing me, said, "Goodbye for now darling girl, it won't be long. Six or eight months, not more." As he turned to go, he hesitated, handing me an envelope. He gave me a fleeting smile and was gone. I stood there with my letter a minute or two and then went to the window, the better to read:

Dearest Elizabeth Riley Perkins Shaw,

It is a fact that I am overwhelmingly in love with you, my own. It is a fact that I shall miss you beloved. It is a fact that I am happier than ever before in my life. It is a fact that you are my inspiration and the purpose of my life.

I'm going to try to have as pleasant a time as I can while away from you and I want you to enjoy your days too. The harshness of war has gone. We've a life of happiness ahead for both of us together.

Don't worry. Keep eating!

All my love always,

Jim.

Epilogue

Van was right: other than himself, Jim was the funniest man I ever met. Besides that, he was a strong and steady man who hated killing but was willing to fight to defend his country. His sense of loyalty and integrity was evident when I married him, but I still had much to learn about him.

It was not too long before I found I had married something more than a fine heroic naval officer. I had married a gentle genius. He was incapable of doing a job well—he had to do it superbly or not at all. His writing was outstanding, though much of it for the Navy was anonymous, as in-house naval publications never gave credit. He was an outstanding professor of strategy and tactics at the Navy Line School. He turned out to be a fine historian. Samuel E. Morison named him his chief collaborator for several of the volumes of the history of the Navy in World War II series after Jim had written for four years on that project.

During his career, Jim became head of the Navy's Office of Current History and speechwriter for the Secretary of the Navy and for the Chief of Naval Operations. He was sent to Hollywood to oversee the making of *The Caine Mutiny*. He wrote articles of a historical nature for various publications, and one of his fictionalized pieces was produced on TV's *Ford Theater of the Air*. He also wrote several articles for the Naval Institute *Proceedings,* one of which won him the prize for the best article of the year. Jim was sent to Holland, Belgium, and the Belgian Congo as naval attaché, where he was given the "Order of Orange Nassau, Knight Commander with Swords" for his "immeasurable help" in showing the Dutch Navy how to organize a public relations program, among many other accomplishments.

This is but a brief and incomplete summation of the life of my second remarkable husband, Rear Adm. James C. Shaw, USN (ret.). Among his many friends there were those who called him Admiral Shaw, those who knew him by his work for the Humane Society of the United States and called him Animal Shaw, and many more who called him Gentleman Jim. He always referred to himself simply as Jim. For myself, I called him my best friend Jeems.

About fifteen years ago, for his class reunion, around the time when he and I first talked about and then began compiling this book, Jim wrote the following about Van:

> One certain way to know the worth of a man is to serve in a man-of-war with him in combat. Thus, while I had known Van as a classmate and friend at the Naval Academy and as a fellow China hand in the Asiatic Fleet, it was not until we became shipmates in the anti-aircraft cruiser ATLANTA in Pacific battles that I realized what a truly outstanding person he was.
>
> The qualities which made him outstanding were numerous. He was a leader in a field where leadership is demanded; namely damage control, where every problem is a new problem. Inspirations and innovation are needed. Here too, tenacity and courage go hand in hand. Van not only had the "right stuff," he knew his stuff. The night the ATLANTA was sunk at Guadalcanal, the ship, mortally battered by torpedo hits, battleship shells, cruiser and destroyer shells, was in flames and going down. Yet there was Van working to save her despite his own serious and painful leg wound. Except for the proximity of the enemy, the damage controllers might well have won (on a later occasion Van was instrumental in patching up the BIRMINGHAM so that she could steam to a safe haven).
>
> Van and I, both wounded, were evacuated from Guadalcanal to a New Zealand hospital for three months. While there, we spent much time together and I learned more of this remarkable classmate. I never saw him lose his temper. He was sure of himself without being vain. We went on a fishing trip to the New Zealand lake country (another way to find the worth of a man) and talked a lot about the war, the future and our own philosophies.
>
> All that was over forty years ago. Today Bettsy and I talk frequently about what a joy and a privilege it was to know Van, and we look fondly at his grandchildren, knowing that Van's life will always be an inspiration for them.

As to my life, I was lucky enough to have two husbands who considered and treated me as a partner, involving me in their work both at sea and ashore (entertaining dignitaries all over Europe, wiping away tears of distressed wives, and dealing with tragedies when needed). I found that it was not possible to acquire a reputation as a sculptor while bouncing around the world with four children and attendant cats and dogs. It became evident that teaching applied sculpture and art history could fit our lifestyle. After teaching hither and thither all around the world, I became head of the Art Department at Rosemary Hall (now Choate-Rosemary) in Connecticut.

My poetry was sometimes published (with Jim checking the spelling), and Hollywood was fertile ground for a series of articles dubbed "My Day in Tinsel Town." Building on a teenage dress-shop experience, I opened my own shop after Jim retired from the Navy. Cricket Corner materialized right across from the Goodspeed Opera House, where I had worked during the development of *Man of LaMancha*. When Jim was writing, he called on me to edit his first and second drafts and oversee the finished manuscript. The greatest accolade of my life came when Jim called me "Bettsy, my best editor."

Our life together had its share of tragedies and a sight more of joy, made happier by our children, all of whom we named after our extended family. Pamela VanOstrand Perkins, Christopher Gratton Shaw, Samuel Allan Riley Shaw, and Elizabeth Holt Perkins Shaw.

Yet throughout there was an ache in our hearts for the two we loved and lost. Our closeness to each other was what made our marriage so right. Neither of us was at all jealous of our first loves and talked about them quite frequently. They were very much part of our marriage. Others saw but two of us. We knew we were four entwined for all time.

Shortly before Jim died I wrote the following poem about our four lives:

WE BUILT A CASTLE

We built a castle on the beach.
*   We made a dream we couldn't reach.*
A dream for such a lovely life.
*   But it was washed away by strife.*

Fifty years of dreaming thus
*   Is still a castle meant for us.*
My love lies miles and miles from me.
*   Deep within an Asian sea.*

And yet he walks beside me still,
*   In quiet woods or far-flung hill*
And comforts me when I would flee.
*   I know his soul abides with me.*

There'll be a time not far from now
*   When from this life I'll take my bow.*
Then once again we'll dream our dream
*   Midst stars and moon in heaven's stream.*

But meanwhile there has been one man
Whom I've loved dearly, and his plan
Was plain to see with naught to hide,
To keep me safe and at his side.

For forty years and several more
We've been a team, not two but four.
His Jane, my Van, all four together
We'll be one core and that forever.

Our children, bless them, every one,
Some gone before, some yet to come,
Are symbols of the love we bore
Not just for one but for all four.

So God in heaven look after all,
Make room for us in your great hall,
Where nothing dies and all things live
And bonded all, with love to give.

Elizabeth R. P. Shaw
Alstead, New Hampshire

ABOUT THE AUTHOR

Elizabeth Riley Perkins Shaw was born in 1919 in Washington, D.C., and grew up in Greenwich, Connecticut. Called Bettsy from early childhood, she was schooled at Rosemary Hall and Bennett, where she excelled in art. In later years, Shaw returned to Rosemary Hall to teach sculpting and art history.

While still a young woman, she traveled extensively in the Far East, particularly in French Indochina. On her second trip to the Philippines, she married Lt. VanOstrand Perkins, also a Greenwich native. Following her marriage, Shaw traveled to many different countries as a wife of a naval officer. Three of those years were as the wife of the United States Naval Attaché to Holland and Belgium.

After her four children were grown, she returned to her early love of writing.